Swinscoe, Blore

and the

Bassetts

David and Martine Swinscoe

Photographer Anthony Blore

Published by **CHURNET VALLEY BOOKS**
43 Bath Street, Leek, Staffordshire. 01538 399033

David Swinscoe,
13 Grange Avenue,
Exmouth EX8 3HU
1998

SWINSCOE, BLORE AND THE BASSETTS

1954 was an eventful year for me. I got my first job in computers. I was married. I went to Thorpe and Dovedale on my honeymoon. I visited a place called Swinscoe. I went to church at St Bartholomew's at Blore. I met Tom Allen, the Swinscoe Postmaster and local historian. All this spurred me to start collecting information about Swinscoe, and since it is in the parish of Blore-with-Swinscoe, I extended my search to include Blore. As Blore was a seat of the Bassetts, my research led me back in time through Staffordshire to the Bassetts of Normandy. Many years later, my daughter, Martine, as a school project, wrote a history of Swinscoe and has continued to take an interest and accompany me on my expeditions.

Ten years ago, there was a momentous meeting at the Blore Family Reunion in Blore Church. I met Mr Anthony Blore. Tony is a very keen photographer and, as you will see, a very good one too. He has photographed just about everything in the parish, and it is his photography that has turned my research and words into a proper book.

This book is really a compilation of other people's efforts and memories, although the errors, omissions and interpretations are all mine. I am grateful to all who have contributed in any way, and hope that I have included you all in the acknowledgments. A number of people have made particularly significant contributions to my work. Christine Smith, Peter Bassett and the late Dr H.T. Betteridge have been Bassetteers extraordinaire. Dr Ian Rowney's advice enabled me to turn the Bassetts of Blore story from a collection of references into, hopefully, a more reasoned account. Lindsay Trevarthen and Stuart Worthington have helped in more ways than can be counted. Phil Mottram, and Roy and Eva Tuff researching Ilam across the river, have swapped valuable information. At Blore Hall, I was lucky to be adopted by John and Janet Massey, and then, Ivan and Cherry Cope. The residents, and ex-residents, of the parish have been a fount of knowledge and local lore.

In particular, I would like to thank Sheila Allen, Grace Bailey, Annie and Marian Morris, Joyce Robotham, and George and Mo Mansfield. I am grateful to Kevin White and his father and to John Robotham and his mother for allowing me to examine deeds to their properties. I am the proud possessor of a full set of the Collections for a History of Staffordshire, a copy of the Calendar of the Okeover Papers and a unique copy of The Deanery Magazine for the years 1890 to 1895. All three of these have been very important sources. The William Salt Library and Stafford Record Office have always been my idea of paradise - complete with ministering angels.

Last, but certainly not least, I would like to apologise to Margaret for not doing all my household and gardening jobs, and not being at home when I should have been, and for spending so much time with my computers in my Bassett Room. I would like to thank her for the support and understanding without which I would never have achieved this book.

David and Martine Swinscoe. September 1997

CONTENTS

ACKNOWLEDGMENTS

Margaret Allen: Sheila Allen: Tom Allen (deceased): Margaret Allsopp: Barbara Anderson: Frances Appleby (deceased): Mrs J. Ayres RCMT: Reg and Grace Bailey: Bass Brewing: Audrey Bassett: Peter Bassett: Royston Bassett: Tony Bassett: Ella Beardmore: Eva Beech: Marcus Bennison: Mike Bennett: Philip Beresford: Dr H.T. Betteridge (deceased): Mr Binder: Chris Birch: John Birch: Florence Bishop: Arnold Bloor: Tony Blore (PHOTOGRAPHER): Richard Booth's Bookshop: Charles Bowden: K. Bowden: Margaret Bowyer: Professor C. Brook: Ed Buck: Margaret Bury: Geoffrey Chawner (deceased): Alex Chatwin: Faith Cleverdon: Mr and Mrs Clowes: Charles William Clowes: Pearl Clymer: Des Cooper: Ivan and Cherry Cope: Peter Cowell: Antony Cox: David and Christine Coxon: Bevan Craddock: Maxwell Craven: Valerie Cresswell: Sue Daniels-Knight: Susan Dear: Joan Devitt: Evelyn M Dodd: John Downes: Monica Draper: Colin Dunkerley: Michael Egerton: Frank Ellis: Fletch: G.W. Flint: Alan Foster: Dudley Fowkes: A.V. Freeman (deceased): Jessica Freeman: Christine Frogatt: Joan Gilday: Jim Gould: Ken Griffin: Jane Hampartumian (deceased): Evelyn Handley: Betty D. Harris: Howard Harris: John Harrison: Alice Harvey (deceased): Arthur Hayes: Connie Heath: Richard Heathcote: Adrian Henstock: Mr Hewitt: Rev Tony Hodgson: Peter Hodgkinson: Lynda Hodkinson: Mr and Mrs Holyoak: David Horovitz: Betty Housecroft: D.H. Howson: Eileen Howson: John Howson: Nicholas Hurt: Neil Jackson: D.J. Johnson: F.J. Johnson: A and P Kassam: Dorothy Kilsby: Valerie Kyte: Mr and Mrs Large: Graham Linley (deceased): John Littleton: Joan Lumb: Charles Mansfield: George and Mo Mansfield: Mr R. Marks: Mrs I.Y. Martin: John Massey: Janet Massey: Gloria McLeod: Bob Meeson: Keith and Christine Mellor: G. Meynell: Stella Middleton: Patrick Montague-Smith (deceased): Annie & Marian Morris: Phil Mottram: Sam Mottram: May Mulkern: Jean C. Noble: Rhona Oakes Mildred Oldfield: Mr and Mrs Pain: Ruth Parr: Velma Peake: Eric Pegg: Mr R.J. Phillips: Catherine Pochon: Margaret Poulter: Doreen Pountley (nee Bradbury): Vivienne Powell: Mr and Mrs Poyser: Geoff and George Prime: Mrs K.M. Prince: Brian Rance: Emma Rees: Dr Bruce Richardson: Douglas Rivett-Carnac (deceased): Barry Robbins: Alice and Ken Robertson: John Robotham: Joyce Robotham: Dr Marie Rowlands: Dr Ian Rowney: Adrian Sherwood: John Scherer: Joan Sinar: Christine (Colloby) Smith: Ian Smith: Peter Starnes: Christine Steward, NIMH: Bertha Sutton: John Titterton: Pat Thornton: Graeme Tobyn, NIMH: Lindsay Trevarthen: Roy and Eva Tuff: Mr and Mrs Twemlow: Sir Peter Walker Okeover: Heather Ward: Peter Warrilow: Peggy White: Graham White (ex Swinscoe School): Mr and Mrs B.White (deceased): Kevin & Sheila White: John Winton: Violet Wiseman: Jolyn Wong Chai Ley: Mrs Woodley: Stuart Worthington: Villagers of the Parish of Blore-with-Swinscoe: The British Library: College of Arms: William Salt Library, Stafford: Birmingham Public Library: Burton upon Trent Public Library: Cambridge University Library: Cheadle Public Library: Derby Local studies Library: Guildhall Library: Hallward Library, University of Nottingham: Hanley Public Library: Hull Public Library: Lambeth Palace Library: Manchester Public Library: Marquis of Salisbury Library, Hatfield House: Matlock Public Library: Matlock Local studies: National Institute of Medical Herbalists, Ltd: Nottingham Archives Office: Plymouth Public Library: Poynton Public Library: Royal College of Midwives Trust: Shrewsbury Public Library: Stafford Public Library: Stockport Public Library: Stafford Record Office: Derbyshire Record Office, Matlock: Public Record Office, Chancery Lane: Public Record Office, Portugal street: Nottingham Archives Office: Merseyside County Museum Department: City of Derby Museums&Art Gallery: University of Birmingham School of History: Buckinghamshire County Council Archives Dept: Devonshire Collections, Chatsworth House: Leicestershire Record Office: University of St Andrews Department of Mediaeval History: Historic Manuscripts Commission: Staffordshire Record Society: Ancient Monuments Society: Moated Site Research Group: Monumental Brasses Society: Birmingham and Midland Genealogical and Heraldic Society: Society of Genealogists: Talbot Research Organisation: The Harleian Society: Derbyshire Family History Society: Derbyshire Record Society: Military History Society: The National Trust: Staffordshire Parish Register Society: Cheadle (Staffs) Historical Society: The Iveah Bequest, Kenwood: The National Portrait Gallery: Staffordshire County Council, Ashbourne Telegraph: Tony Swinscoe: And all those other unsung heroes who have helped us along the way.

David Swinscoe
1998

Blore

St Bartholomew's Church

St Bartholomew's church cross

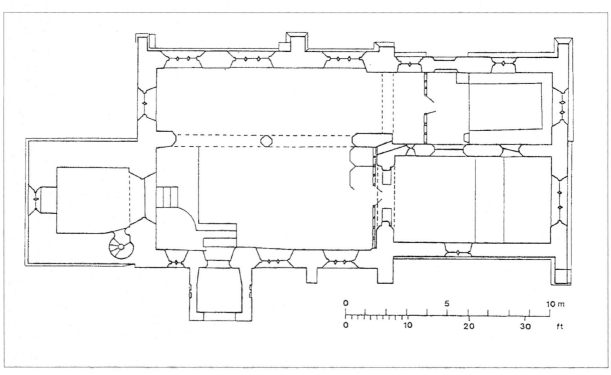

Plan of St Bartholomew's church
Reproduced with the permission of Mr R A Meeson, Senior Archaeological Officer, Staffordshire County Council

The Squint Window

The east window

The North Window in the Bassett Chapel

The north aisle window

The East Window in the Bassett Chapel

The chancel window

Hidden brass, discovered under the
floorboards behind the organ

The organ

Church chests

Architect's plan of the Bassett Tomb
Reproduced with permission of Mr D Fowkes, William Salt Library

The Bassett Tomb

William Bassett, the 5th and last male.

Elizabeth Bassett

Catherine (or Elizabeth), daughter of Elizabeth Bassett
and Henry Howard

Henry Howard

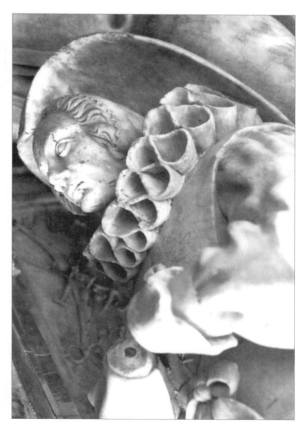

Judith Bassett née Osten

The Font, St Bartholomew's Church

The headstone of James Yates

The blocked up
Norman doorway

BASSETT of BLORE

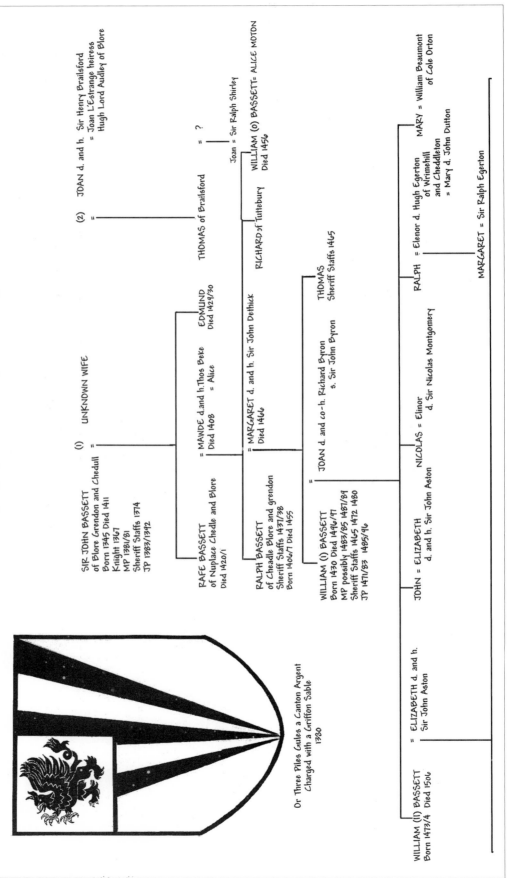

Or Three Piles Gules a Canton Argent
Charged with a Griffon Sable
1380

SIR JOHN BASSETT
of Blore Grendon and Cheadll
Born 1345 Died 1411
Knight 1367
MP 1381/81
Sheriff Staffs 1374
JP 1383/1342

(1) = UNKNOWN WIFE

(2) =

JOAN d. and h. Sir Henry Brailsford
= Joan L'Estrange heiress
Hugh Lord Audley of Blore

RAFE BASSETT
of Nuplace Chedle and Blore
Died 1420/1

= MAWDE d.and h.Thos Beke
Died 1408 = Alice

EDMUND
Died 1424/30

THOMAS of Brailsford

= ?

Joan = Sir Ralph Shirley

WILLIAM (0) BASSETT = ALICE MOTON
Died 1456

RALPH BASSETT
of Cheadle Blore and grendon
Sheriff Staffs 1437/38
Born 1406/7 Died 1455

= MARGARET d. and h. Sir John Dethick
Died 1466

RICHARD of Tuttebury

WILLIAM (I) BASSETT
Born 1430 Died 1496/97
MP possibly 1483/85 1481/89
Sheriff Staffs 1465 1472 1480
JP 1471/83 1485/96

= JOAN d. and co-h. Richard Byron
s. Sir John Byron

THOMAS
Sheriff Staffs 1445

JOHN = ELIZABETH
d. and h. Sir John Aston

NICOLAS = Elinor
d. Sir Nicolas Montgomery

RALPH = Elenor d. Hugh Egerton
of Wrimehill
and Cheddleton
= Mary d. John Dutton

MARY = William Beaumont
of Cole Orton

MARGARET = Sir Ralph Egerton

WILLIAM (II) BASSETT
Born 1473/4 Died 1506

= ELIZABETH d. and h.
Sir John Aston

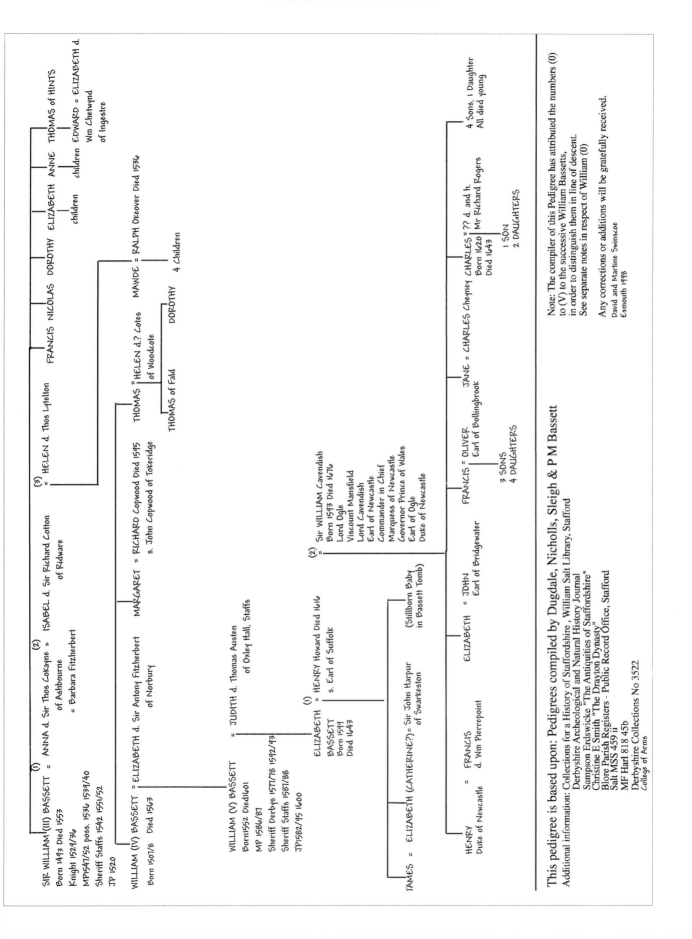

This pedigree is based upon: Pedigrees compiled by Dugdale, Nicholls, Sleigh & P M Bassett

Additional information: Collections for a History of Staffordshire, William Salt Library, Stafford
Derbyshire Archeological and Natural History Journal
Sampson Erdswicke "The Antiquities of Staffordshire"
Christine E Smith "The Drayton Dynasty"
Blore Parish Registers - Public Record Office, Stafford
Salt MSS 459 ii
MF Harl 818 45b
Derbyshire Collections No 3522
College of Arms

Note: The compiler of this Pedigree has attributed the numbers (0)
to (V) to the successive William Bassetts,
in order to distinguish them in line of descent.
See separate notes in respect of William (0)

Any corrections or additions will be gratefully received.
David and Martine Swinscoe
Exmouth 1998

Swinscoe School, 1910

ONE
BLORE-WITH-SWINSCOE

This is the story of the parish of Blore-with-Swinscoe, as told by books, maps, records, residents and others who have been connected with the villages. The village of Swinscoe lies on the main A52 road, and has almost forty houses, bungalows and scattered farms, an old Methodist Chapel, an old Schoolhouse and an Inn. The village of Blore lies about one mile away by footpath over the hill. Blore has a mediaeval church, St Bartholomew's; Blore Hall, the Old Rectory and a small cottage stand close by. There are two farms, the sites of a watermill and a windmill and one or two other buildings

The two villages each stand on high ground, with an even higher hill and deep dale between them. The population of Blore-with-Swinscoe is around one hundred, and has varied from time to time, but has never exceeded three hundred people. This book tells of the land, the church, the chapel, the school, the mills, the inn, the houses and other buildings, the roads, and some of the changes over the centuries up to the present day. It tells the story of some of the landowners and their families, including: the original Blore Family, Audleys, Bassetts of Blore, Duke and Duchess of Newcastle, Rivetts, Shores and Okeovers. It also tells of the residents, and ex-residents, who have been associated with the parish, where they lived, and events in which they have been involved.

ST BARTHOLOMEW'S CHURCH
Few Staffordshire churches can offer such a variety of interest and beauty as the picturesque church of St Bartholomew at Blore. There are two theories about the name of the church. One is, of course, that it is dedicated to St Bartholomew, one of the twelve disciples. The alternative view is that the name St Bartholomew is a corruption of St Bertram. Around Ilam there are many traces and reminders of St Bertram. He turned to a life of prayer and meditation following the killing of his wife and newborn baby by a wolf. In the Manifold Valley there are a number of churches dedicated to St Bartholomew, and this dedication is comparatively rare elsewhere in the United Kingdom. It has also been suggested that it might be a corruption of St Bertellin, or Bertelins or Bertelmus. Mr John Graves discounts this, because St Bettelin was a hermit of Crowland in Lincolnshire, nowhere near to or connected with North East Staffordshire.

No church is mentioned in Domesday 1086, but this is not surprising as the Staffordshire Domesday scribes appear to have been uninterested in recording churches. They only mentioned two churches in the whole of Staffordshire, with over three hundred named places of habitation. The church is very old, certainly of Norman origin. It was built around 1100, probably on the site of a previous place of worship. The base of the old cross in the churchyard is reputed to be of Saxon origin. When the moat was dug around Blore Hall, between the 12th and 14th centuries, the soil was dumped around the south side of the church. The depth of the gully along the south wall gives an indication of the amount of soil that was deposited. There is the outline of a door in the South Wall which is clearly late-Norman. This is level with the bottom of the present gully, in the centre of the south wall, just right of the porch. The blocked door comprises three quarter round columns and the worn remains of a scalloped west capital. As can be seen from the building line, with the old gargoyles and different masonry, the church was originally of lesser height. The typical bulging lower walls are about three feet thick and without the straightness and symmetry of modern structures.

The impressive tower stands on a base 20 feet square, with walls 5 feet thick and reaching a height of 45 feet. The tower is built of rubble with freestone dressings. The windows and bell openings have two lights with cusped heads and hollow reveals of perpendicular type. In 1857, the east wall of the tower started to lean. It was necessary to insert a screw pin through the tower, from west to east The characteristic "S" metal tie plates can still be seen. The entrance to the belfry is protected by an oak screen built by a Mr Stubbs sometime during the 19th century. In the bell ringing area, stands the iron safety chest. This chest was bought for £4.10s.0d, in 1846, as result of complaints by the Arch deaconry in 1830, 1837 and 1841 that a safety chest was needed. The nail-studded door leads up a stone stair, to an ancient door to the belfry.

There is a tradition that there were originally six bells in the tower, but there are only three bells hanging there now. The tradition probably emanates from an inventory of church ornaments in 1563, which records: two handbells, one sacring bell and three great bells. It is extremely doubtful that six great bells could ever have been in the tower. The oldest bell bears the inscription "GOD SAVE THE QUENE 1590"; this bell was bought from St Oswald's Church, Ashbourne in 1815, when St Oswald's acquired eight new bells. The second bell is inscribed "IHSVS BE OUR SPEED 1616" and the third bell "GOD SAVE THE CHURCH 1626". In 1952, the bells were re-hung. A significant donation, to carry out the work, was received from the Young Family, descendants of the Rev J.H. Young. He was Rector of this parish, from 1875 to 1915.

The stone stairs continue up to the roof, with its parapet and pinnacles. It is topped by an unusual ironwork weather vane, on curved supports. The entrance porch was built of sandstone in Early English style, around 1519, on top of a previous structure; the windows visible from the outside are level with the present floor. This could mean that there was an external flight of steps leading down to the church entrance instead of the present internal steps down into the church. Inside the entrance porch are the remains of a 14th century stoup, allegedly removed at the time of the Reformation. The stoup was a very important feature of the Catholic church and held the holy water into which the Communicants dipped their fingers and crossed themselves.

The main door symbolises the place of entry into the family of God. Near the door is the 16th century octagonal font of simple carved stonework. A drawing of the font was made by the artist J. Buckler in 1839 and is held by the William Salt Library. It shows that there used to be pew on the wall behind the font. In 1951/2, this pew was removed so that the font could be moved backwards into the corner and at the same time, repairs were carried out and a new font cover was provided. The lead lining of the font was stolen at the same time as the lead of the roof. The area around the font was re-concreted and made level with the entrance steps in 1968.

The roof construction is rather unusual. Externally, there is a single roof which covers the nave and north aisle. There is another single roof over the chancel and Bassett chapel. Internally, there are two separate coffered Tudor style timber roofs. There is one over the nave and aisle, and one over the nave and the chancel. Curiously, the main rafter on the north side of the nave is supported by brackets, at the apex of the orcade arches, but the brackets themselves are unsupported. There must be a secret support, in the upper part of the double roof. Back in 1818, the roof was covered in lead. In 1951/2, the external roof of the church was partially restored, and covered with copper cladding, at a cost of £1783.0.0.

It was common to have to stand in church although some of the select members of the congregation would bring their own seats. However the Bassetts, in the 15th or 16th century, installed the oak pews whose bone-aching discomfort must have helped to keep the congregation awake during many a service. This discomfort is due to the unusual design with the narrow seat and projecting ledge level with the seat in front. The ledges were installed before prayer and hymn books were used in church so the ledges were not book rests and they are too high for kneeling. Perhaps they were originally used for resting the elbows by worshippers kneeling on the ground. The box pews were installed in the 17th Century for the benefit of the Lord of the Manor, and those who were willing to make their contribution to the church, by payment of fees.

The floor originally was probably 25cm higher than at present, level with the blocked late-Norman door in the south wall and the remains of the stone floor behind the pulpit. Prior to the 17th century, it was not uncommon for burials to be made beneath the floor of the church. In 1975, shallow graves were found, whilst carrying out work on the floor, under the family pews. There were eight skeletons, packed side-by-side, two other burials and a lot of bones nearby. Some of these had been disturbed by a previous excavation around 1900 when 42 skulls were found. No record has been found to identify them or reason for such a shallow mass burial without coffins. Some of the burials were probably disturbed during the installation of a new heating apparatus in 1887.

The north aisle was added in the middle of the 15th century. The builders used some of the Early English cuspated windows from the original north wall of the church. As part of the major alterations, which took place around 1519, the present oblong Perpendicular windows of the nave were inserted.

These corresponded, in style, with those in the north aisle. The old east window is of Early English style, with a small trace of Perpendicular work.

The extension of the North Aisle was the result of more than one addition to the church. There is a break in the line of the wall, between the central and eastern windows. The eastern part contains a 15th century window of three lights under a three-centred arch. According to the Staffordshire Archaeologist, this was probably the position of a gable wall, at the north end of a transverse chapel. The north windows are square-headed with three four-centred lights and molded mullions. This might confirm a previous transverse chapel which, therefore, must have been built before the 16th century.

Up to the time of the Reformation, the altar was the focal point of all worship. However, following the Reformation the emphasis of the service changed, recognizing the importance of preaching the gospel. From the pulpit, built in the early 17th century, the preacher could be heard in all corners of the church. Around 1816 the water-colour artist Samuel Prout drew the interior of the church, and one of his drawings showed that the pulpit then had a handsome panelled sounding-board over it. The Prout drawings have disappeared and cannot be found.

In order to emphasise the holiness of the chancel and its separateness from the nave, a beautiful screen was erected. Hundreds of carved pieces of oak, all pegged together, created this exquisite example of Tudor workmanship. On close examination some of the original colouring can still be seen. Wrought iron gates were erected beneath the wooden screen during Queen Victoria's reign, further separating priest and parishioners.

Within the chancel, holiest of places in the church, stand the oak choir stalls with Tudor carving and unusual bench ends. Around 1519, when the stalls were erected, they were intended for the use of chaplains and monks for the singing of the daily offices. Singing and chanting were always an important feature of worship because the singing voice carries more clearly in the lofty church. The panelling on the wall behind the choir stalls was probably taken from elsewhere, as there are signs of much alteration to the woodwork. One panel, to the right of the blocked doorway, bears the almost invisible inscription "John Healde 1621". In his will, Sir William Bassett, who died in 1553, provided eight marks for a priest to sing the Vespers, every Thursday, and the Matins, every Friday for seven years after his death.

The central theme of Christian worship is the re-enactment of Christ's sacrifice by communion at the altar. The present altar rail, in front of the holy table, is of Jacobean origin. It has been suggested that the alabaster flags near the chancel gates may have been a much older altar. There may also have been a side altar for the performance of requiem mass where the Bassett tomb stands, which could be observed through the squint now hidden by the pulpit.

In 1563 an inventory of church ornaments includes: 1 silver chalice with paten, 2 silk vestments, 1 white satin cape, 1 altar cloth, 2 corporals (linen cloths used during Eucharist) with cases, 1 towel and 2 brass candlesticks. At the dissolution of Burton College, in 1544, Sir William Bassett bought 2 *"grett candlestyckes and one lytle peyr of organs"* for 13s.0d. He also bought a number of vestments and cloths. He probably donated some of those items to St Bartholomew's although there is no mention of any organ in the church inventory. Organs were becoming very popular, in the homes of the gentry, and he would probably keep those for his households in Blore, and Langley.

There is a 14th century low-side window in the wall between the Chancel and the North Aisle. This unusual window, only 2'6" by 6", with its ogee arch, is another puzzling enigma. As many as twelve different reasons have been put forward as to its purpose. One popular view is that it was a "lepers' window", in those days when this was the outer wall of the church. Another possibility is that it was an observation point and contained a sanctus bell, connected with some religious ceremony.

The north wing was built in the 15th century as a private chapel for the Lords of the Manor. Their private entrance into this chantry has been blocked up and there is another blocked doorway from the chantry to the chancel. The chancel was larger than now. The fine old carved screen was moved from its original position further down the north aisle. It once enclosed the heraldic window and the 15th century brass, in the aisle.

Over the original screen there used to be a rood loft upon which stood a crucifix and figures of the Virgin Mary and friends of Christ. Above the large squint in the north aisle is some evidence of a stone staircase. This led up to the rood loft where the musicians played. With the removal of the old choir, the church was also left without instrumental aid. This loss was particularly unfortunate. The congregation in those days only knew two hymns "All people that on earth do dwell" and "Glory to Thee, my God, this night". Jane Wood, the wife of the rector, tried to teach the choir to sing "Jesus Christ is risen today". At Easter Day service, Mrs Wood pitched the tune too high and after a vain attempt the choir broke down and began to giggle. The rector saved the day by telling his wife "Give over, Jane". He turned to the congregation and said *"Let us sing the hundredth psalm - All people that on earth do dwell"*.

In 1830 there was an inspection of the church during a Visitation of the Archdeaconry of Stafford. There was no organ. The need for accompaniment was soon filled by the acquisition of a so-called American organ, which cost £6.0s.0d. It was played for the first time by Miss H. Howell on Tuesday 29th August 1893. It is not known when the St Cecilia Organ was acquired. According to the plate, it was manufactured by Thomas Jones & Son, Marlborough Organ Works, Upper Holloway, London. The organ used to be driven manually and some members of the congregation remember pumping the organ as youngsters. In 1989 an electric motor was fitted in memory of Mr Drugan, a member of the congregation.

Sometime between 1618 and 1640, Judith, the widow of William (V) Bassett (died 1601) erected the magnificent tomb in the side chapel. This tomb was erected to the memory of her husband - the last of the Bassetts of Blore. Beneath the carpet, in the north aisle, is another Bassett memorial in brass which is also described in a later chapter.

Around 1830, John Flowers the painter said: *"Blore is just the sort of church that an artist is looking for - rugged and yet truly picturesque"*.

In 1845, the walls of the chancel badly needed repair. Mr Shore, the Lord of the Manor and patron of the Church, accepted responsibility for the repairs and erection of supporting buttresses. Ten years later his son Harrington Offley Shore installed the beautiful east window in memory of his young wife Isabel Emma, who died at the age of 25.

In 1994, the diocesan architects reported that there was need for considerable work on the external and the internal fabric of the church. The Bassett Tomb also needed renovation and repair. It was obvious that the likely cost was far beyond the meagre resources of the parish and financial assistance would have to be sought elsewhere. Mr Stuart Worthington, senior churchwarden and treasurer, volunteered to launch a national appeal for £100,000 and carry out the management of the whole project. Mr Worthington launched the appeal on the 1st August 1994 and by the end of the year had raised over £40,000. It had become obvious that the cost of the project would exceed £100,000 and so the target was raised to £120,000. By July 1995, half of the money had been raised and it became possible to start the work of restoration. Mr Worthington continued to pursue his goals and by 1996 the total appeal funds, received or promised, stood at £117,000, but the expected costs had risen to £125,000. In late 1997 Mr Worthington was able to announce with justifiable pride that the target had been achieved.

From the middle of 1995, the restoration was carried out in major phases, under the control and management of Mr Worthington. Rewiring the church and installation of new heating and lighting; external fabric repairs including reconstruction of roof of the tower; external fabric repairs including churchyard cross and paths and gates; internal repairs including organ and bells; replastering and redecoration including carpets, seat covers and furnishings; window repairs; repairs to the Bassett Chapel and Tomb.

On the 17th November 1996 the Lord Bishop of Lichfield, (The Right Reverend Keith Sutton) led a Service of Thanksgiving for the restoration of St Bartholomew's Church. Rev Peter Davey assisted in the service and the church was packed with people. The Donors and Grantors, the Architects and Contractors, the Clergy and the local Worshippers were all there to give thanks. In an unusual gesture the Bishop called upon the congregation to applaud the magnificent work carried out by Mr Worthington. The applause was loud and long.

Away from the crowds, St Bartholomew's Church has been renewed to its former splendour and stands in beauty as one of the remaining memories of a glorious and magnificent past.

The ancient stained glass in Blore church is a fine example of medieval workmanship. It is made more interesting by the jigsaw of fragments in the window of the chancel.

Elias Ashmole, upon whose collection the Ashmolean Museum in Oxford was founded, visited Blore in 1662. He recorded the heraldic arms in the church and the hall. At the bottom of the east window of the north aisle there was a picture of William (I) Bassett and his wife Joan, daughter of Richard Byron. Both were shown kneeling before Saint William with a scroll, in Latin, which is translated as "O HOLY WILLIAM, PRAY FOR US". William (I) Bassett was in his surcoat of arms and Joan wore the arms of Byron on her mantle. In the south window, there was a picture of Sir William (III) Bassett and his wife Anne, daughter of Thomas Cockayne. He wore his surcoat of arms and she wore the arms of Cockayne quartered with Herthull on the mantle, kneeling before a crucifix. Below was an inscription, in Latin, that translated as:

PRAY FOR THE GOOD ESTATE OF
WILLIAM BASSETT ESQUIRE AND ANNE HIS WIFE
WHO ERECTED THESE WINDOWS AND BUILT THIS CHANCEL AD 1519

This inscription, with a different coat of arms, was also placed at the bottom of the east window. In a chancel window, there was a picture of Christ, wearing a crown of thorns, and of St Anne, teaching the Virgin Mary to read. In a south window of the chancel, there remains a challenging jigsaw puzzle of glass, gathered from the remnants of the old windows. The figures of St Anne and the Virgin are still intact. St Anne is wearing a white dress with a red cloak. The cloak has a yellow border, containing lettering, which still waits to be deciphered. It has been suggested that the artist's name Piotri is represented within the inscription. The Virgin Mary wears an ermine robe and a yellow skirt covers her feet. Among the fragments is a kneeling figure with part of the scroll "O STE WILL... ...PRO ME". This corresponds to the Ashmole description. A hand and a foot impaled by a nail are obviously parts of the crucifix. There is a head of Christ surrounded by thorns and the head of another saintly figure. This other figure is probably meant to represent St Andrew, one of the twelve apostles, or St William mentioned in the inscription. In two fragments there is a box shape, coloured in gold on the upper half. This has variously been described as Blore Hall, the ark and a large altar; one of the latter two is more likely to be correct.

In a window in the north aisle there still exist nine of the coats of arms, recorded in 1662. With the exception of two, these coats of arms relate to BASSETT and to families whose daughters married a Bassett: COCKAYNE and MEVERELL. The non-marriage related coats of arms are those at the top left and the top right of the window: BLOUNT and STAFFORD. BLOUNT is most puzzling because so far there has been no trace of any direct connection between the Bassetts and the Blounts. STAFFORD was the overlord from whom the Bassetts held most of their lands.

In the east window of the Bassett chapel, there is a single coat of arms of BASSETT showing also the arms of BEKE and MEYNELL whose daughters married a Bassett.

The window in the North Aisle is as follows:
1. BLOUNT Quarterly of six
        AYALA Argent two wolves Sable with a bordure Or fretty Argent
        SANCHET Or a castle Azure
        HOLTE Argent three fleurs de lys Azure
        BLOUNT Vair
        WESTCOTE Agent a fess and in chief three covered cups gules
        BLOUNT Barry nebuly Or and Azure
2. BASSETT   Or three piles gules on a canton Argent a griffin segreant Sable
3. COCKAYNE   Quarterly 1 and 4 COCKAYNE Argent three cocks gules
                        Quarterly 2 and 3 HERTHALL Argent two bars Vert
4. MEVERELL   Argent a griffin segreant Sable beaked and legged Or
5. COCKAYNE   (as 3 above)
6. COCKAYNE   (as 3 above except fourth quarter has only two cocks)
7. STAFFORD   Or a chevron Gules
8. BASSETT   (as 2 above except there is no griffin on the canton)
9. BASSETT   impaling COCKAYNE

The East Window in Chancel
1. The Annunciation.
2. The flight into Egypt.
3. Christ teaching in the temple at 12 years old.
4. Christ's baptism by John the Baptist
5. Christ the Good Shepherd.
6. Suffer little children to come unto me.
7. The Last Supper.
8. The draught of fishes.
9. The raising of Lazarus.
10. Via Dolorosa - Christ with St Veronica.
11. The Crucifixion.
12. Mary by the tomb on East Morning - "Noli me tangere"

Inscription below the window reads:

TO THE GLORY OF GOD AND IN MEMORY OF ISABEL EMMA WIFE OF HARRINGTON OFFLEY
SHORE WHO DIED NOVEMBER 11TH 1863 IN HER 25TH YEAR

The magnificent alabaster tomb to the last of the Bassetts of Blore stands behind an ancient carved wooden screen, in the North Aisle of the Church. It has been suggested that Judith, widow of William (V) Bassett, employed Jasper Hollemans to create the sculpture. It was created in similar style to the monument to Queen Elizabeth I in Westminster Abbey. It is from the Bassetts of Blore that the descent of the present Charles Prince of Wales can be traced. Coincidentally through another branch can be traced the descent of Sarah Ferguson, wife of Prince Andrew.

The monument is in the form of a raised platform, with pillars at the head and foot. It measures 3.9m by 2.6m by 0.9m high, and the pillars rise to a height of 1.3m. They support a double cornice, divided by four square blocks of alabaster, each decorated with a Tudor rose. William Bassett lies on a central raised tomb with his wife Judith on his left. On William's right is Henry Howard, first husband of Elizabeth Bassett. Elizabeth kneels at the head of her husband Henry. The younger kneeling figure, Elizabeth (Catherine) Howard, daughter of Henry Howard and Elizabeth, kneels at the head of her grandmother. At the feet of Henry is the casket for a stillborn child, bearing the Howard Arms. The Bassett Arms are missing. Below Judith is the casket of James, son of Henry, bearing Howard and Bassett Arms.

The effigy of William Bassett shows him lying with his head resting on a helmet and his hands held in prayer. He wears a ruff above the pointed breastplate and overlapping shoulder and arm plates. Over the long breeches are the thigh protectors and long hinged leg armour with spurs over his boots. The hands, though now missing, were protected by gauntlets and a long sword lies by his left side. William (V) Bassett died in 1601.

Henry Howard lies on William's right, resting on matting, with the top rolled to form a pillow. Henry wears similar armour but with a flat collar rather than a ruff. His sword hangs from a sash over his shoulder.

Judith lies on the left of William, with her head resting on a cushion. She wears a long gown with full sleeves and bodice laced up the front and fastened with a bow. The figure of Judith is cut flat on both sides suggesting that perhaps that the stonemason made the figure too large for the available space on the tomb; the effigy of daughter Elizabeth is similarly cut on one side.

Elizabeth Bassett kneels at the head of her first husband Henry Howard. She wears a hood with a veil down to her shoulders. The gown she wears is long with padded shoulders, over which is a sleeveless bodice laced down the front and tied with a ribbon. The figure of Elizabeth (or Catherine) Howard daughter of Henry and Elizabeth kneels at the head of her grandmother Judith. She is similarly dressed to her mother and holds a prayer book in her hand. At each end of the tomb, on the pillars and rails, are the sculptured arms of the Bassetts. There are also the arms of families associated by marriage: CAVENDISH (1), BASSETT (2), HOWARD (3), CORBETT (4), AUSTIN (5), and HARPUR (6). A tribute to William Bassett is inscribed on the west end of the Tomb:

HERE LIES A COURTIER, SOULDIER, HANDSOME, GOOD
WITTY, WISE, VALIANT AND OF PURE BLOOD
FROM WILLIAM'S CONQUEST, AND HIS POTENT SWORD
IS THE SAME LYNE (FULL) MANY A NOBLE LORD
THAT TIME HATH LOST IN PAYING THUS DEATH'S DEBT
IN THIS UNPARALLELL'D WILLIAM BASSETT
BUT THY HIGH VIRTUES WITH THY ANCIENT NAME
SHALL EVER SWELL THE CHEEKS OF GLORIOUS FAME

Sir William Cavendish, later Duke of Newcastle, second husband of Elizabeth Bassett, wrote this inscription. His original draft is to be found among the Portland papers, in Nottingham University library.

The tomb was erected between 1618 and 1640. When Judith died in 1640, she left instructions in her will that her body should be buried in the vault below the monument she had erected. It is touching that she wished to be buried alongside her second husband, William Bassett, rather than her third husband, Sir Richard Corbet. The kneeling figures of Elizabeth and her daughter could have been added at any time during the period; both effigies are very similar though in slightly different poses. Elizabeth's daughter would be around 24 years old when her grandmother died.

Below the tomb, reached by a flight of steps, is the vault which used to contain the lead coffins, with the remains of the Bassetts. The vault was sealed off in the 19th century but not until after it had been plundered and the coffins stolen. There is even a story repeated by the Rector, Rev J.H. Young as from his predecessor's wife, Mrs Wood, that the vault has been used by a local farmer as storage place for potatoes!

Under the leadership of John Ruskin, Thomas Carlyle and William Morris, the Society for the Protection of Ancient Buildings was formed in 1876. Six years later, the Ancient Monuments Act was passed. Among the first monuments to be repaired in Staffordshire was the Bassett tomb.

As part of the restoration of St Bartholomew's Church, under the direction of Mr S.G.Worthington, Churchwarden and Treasurer, major work was carried out on the tomb by Harrison Hill Ltd. An account of the restoration is given in detail in Mr Worthington's book "The Restoration of St Bartholomew's Church, Blore Ray 1994 - 1997 - An Illustrated Record" published 1998.

In the north aisle a brass memorial plaque, measuring 2.2m by 1m is inlaid into a slab of marble-like purbeck stone in the floor. This brass is dedicated to the memory of William (I) Bassett and his wife Joan, daughter of Richard Byron. Like many others elsewhere, it was made to a stylised pattern and is not meant to be a portrait of the couple, although the style of dress is typical of the period. It shows two figures, male and female. The husband wears a sort of cassock, full in the sleeve and edged with fur. The lady wears a wimple on her head, to indicate that she was a widow. She wears a cloak fastened by tasselled cord, with some pleated linen around her neck. Earlier references confirm that the head had been removed prior to 1848. There is a local story that this vandalism was carried out by Cromwell's soldiers in the Civil War. Only two of the four emblems depicting Matthew, Mark, Luke and John still exist in the corners. At the head of the brass there is a BASSETT coat of arms showing also the arms of BYRON.

The Latin inscription is no longer completely legible, or intact, but it was recorded as follows:

ORATE PRO ANIMABUS WILLIELMI BASSETT ARMIGERI DOMINI DE BLORE ET LANGLEY ET JOANNE UXORIS EJUS UNIUS FILIARUM ET HEREDUM RICARDI BURYN ARMIGERI FILII ET HEREDIS JOHANNIS BURYN MILITIS. QUI QUIDEM WILLIELMUS OBIIT XXII DIE MENSIS NOV. ANNO DNI MILLIMO DLXXXXVII ET EADEM JOANNA OBIIT DIE MENSIS ***** ANO DNI ***** QUORUM ANIMABUS PROPITIERUR DEUS AMEN.

which is translated as:

PRAY FOR THE SOUL OF WILLIAM BASSETT ESQUIRE LORD OF BLORE AND LANGLEY AND OF JOAN HIS WIFE ONE OF THE DAUGHTERS AND HEIRS OF RICHARD BURYN SON AND HEIR OF JOHN BURYN KNIGHT WHICH SAID WILLIAM BASSETT DIED 12 DAY NOV 1497 AND JOAN DIED THE - - DAY OF - - MONTH - - ANNO DOMINI - - UPON WHOSE SOULS GOD HAVE MERCY. AMEN

Joan died after her husband and the date of her death was never inscribed in the blank space. It is possible that she was buried elsewhere.

In addition to the Bassett Tomb and Bassett Memorial Brass there are other interesting memorials and inscriptions inside the church, and in the churchyard. Mrs Eva Tuff of Ilam, in December 1994, produced a complete list of all graves and memorials of the church of St Bartholomew, Blore, Staffordshire. From the list, a great deal of valuable information has been extracted, for the present history of Blore-with-Swinscoe.

In the chancel, the second panel to the right of the blocked doorway, in the middle of choir stalls, bears the virtually invisible inscription - JOHN HEALDE 1621. It was only the eagle eye of Mr Philip Mottram, local historian for Ilam, and subsequently his infra red photography, that made it possible to decipher this interesting inscription. The purpose and source of the inscription are not known. Robert Healde, Rector of Blore, from 1570 to 1619, had three sons. One of his sons was John, born on 11th March 1596, and is mentioned in his father's will.

Behind the organ, there is a panel in the floorboards. Below the panel is hidden a brass memorial, 38cm by 20cm, bearing the following inscriptions:

> HERE
> LIES THE BODY OF
> CHARLES SIBLEY
> LATE RECTOR OF BLORE
> AND VICAR OF LONGFORD
> HE MARRIED ANNE DAUGHTER OF GEORGE GRETTON
> RECTOR OF STRETTON IN LE FIELD IN THE COUNTY OF DERBY
> AND LEFT ISSUE
> CHARLES ANNA-MARIA
> HE DIED MUCH LAMENTED MAY XXI MDCCXL AGE L
> ON THE RIGHT (hand) LIES CHARLES SIBLEY JUNIER
> HE DIED MARCH THE FIRST 1742 AGE 19 YEARES

On the wall of the North Aisle, there is a marble epitaph:

> DEATH'S A MIRROR NEVER FLATTERS
> ON MY EYES SUCH RAYES IT SCATTERS
> THAT THEREWITH I DAZZLED AM
> SEARCHING FOR THEE IN THE SAME
> BY SOME CHARME OR STRANGER CASE
> I SEE THY SPIRIT NOT THY FACE
> DEATH NEVER CAN THAT MAN SURPRISE
> THAT WATCHES FOR 'T WITH WARY EYES
> WHEN EVERY SOULE SHALL SEE WHAT T'IS
> TO HAVE LIV'D WELL OR DONE AMISS

Standing against the entrance porch is a memorial, which has a well weathered inscription:

> HERE LIETH YE BODY
> OF JAMES YATES
> WHOSE SOUL I HOPE
> IS WITH GOD
> WHO IN HIS LIFETIME
> LOVd A GUN A DOG
> AND A FISHING ROD

No date is given, so it has not been possible to identify this sporting gentleman. There has been more than one man named James Yates in the Parish. A James Yates rented land in Ox Leasow, Hinckley Wood, Blore and Mill Meadows from 1678 to 1687. The most likely candidate would be James Yates, who was the Landlord of the Dog and Partridge Inn in Swinscoe.

A large fragment of an alabaster memorial stands inside the Bassett Chantry. This memorial appears to show the lower half of a robe; the lettering is unreadable. It is reputed to have been a memorial to one of the Bassetts. It was fixed to the wall but was found lying broken on the floor, by Rector Sidney Roberts.

In 1844, Sarah Ann Taylor, spinster of Blore, left a bequest to pay for the cost and erection of two monuments, in Blore Church. These two memorials were erected, on the wall of the North Aisle, near the entrance to the Bassett Tomb. One is dedicated to Sarah Taylor, and the other to Samuel Robotham of Dog Lane.

CHURCH AND CLERGY

Blore church has always been different from other churches in the area. It is not mentioned in Wulfric Spot's Will, which gave very extensive lands, including Ilam and Okeover, to Burton Abbey, in 1004. Between 1178 and 1182, a judgment was given in the King's Court. This judgment confirmed that Blore church was free from the Abbots of Burton, and from their church at Ilam. The Lord of the Manor, Ralph de Blore, was required to pay one mark as compensation to the Abbots. Blore church continued to pay this sum to Burton Abbey until the Reformation. Subsequently, the equivalent amount of 13s.4d was paid to the church of Ilam, until the early 20th Century.

The Abbots, supported by the Diocesan Bishop, fought vigorously against the judgment. In the papal bull of Lucius, 1185, it was even suggested that Blore was part of Wulfric's gift to Burton. Nevertheless, the judgment held, and was again confirmed in a final agreement, in 1209. The Lord of the Manor possessed the advowsons and appointed his chosen clerics to the living.

Next to his patron, the rector was the most important and influential man in the parish. He held the rights to the use of the Glebelands, and the tithes were substantial. In 1612, the glebe terrier shows that the glebelands totalled twenty acres plus the parsonage, tithe barns and the two acres, on which they stood. The rector claimed grazing rights for fifty two sheep, one horse, one twinter [beast of two winters] and two beasts. The tithe was one tenth of the crop, plus a few pence for each foal, calf, and milking cow, not forgetting the geese and eggs. The rector made a charge for every baptism, marriage and burial but with such a small population, this part of his income was relatively small. There were only 59 weddings, 270 baptisms and 219 burials recorded from 1590 to 1640. From his income, it was the responsibility of the rector to keep the church in a good state of repair.

Most of the rectors of Blore were graduates from one of the universities. They were well versed in the law. They were constantly called upon as scribes, witnesses and executors and their signatures can be found on many of the documents and wills relating to the parish.

A curious arrangement was made in 1216. William de Lichfield, parson of Blore, agreed to pay to the church of Ilam a silver mark. As the parson was too poor to pay such a sum his vicar, William de Canoco, was instructed to pay the amount instead.

In the year 1325 Richard de Mefford was admitted to the church of Blore after the death of the previous rector, Hugh. The presentation was made by the patron Sir John Lestrange. The contentious issue of payment to Burton Abbey continued. In 1351 the rector, John Wylly, was specifically directed by the Bishop of Coventry and Lichfield to make the yearly payment of one mark to Burton Abbey. In December 1362 Sir Henry de Braylefford was the patron. Ralph Hychekok was instituted as Rector, following the resignation of Thomas Coyne. When Ralph Hechekoces died, Richard Grendon, priest, was instituted as vicar and canon. Sir Philip Bassett, knight of Cheadle, was stated to be the true patron of the church.

In 1398, at the presentation of the patron Sir John Bassett, Lord of Braylesford, William York was admitted to the church of Blore and instituted as Rector. William Bassett Esq., patron of the church of Blore presented Ralph Canterell following the resignation of William Sont, the previous rector. In 1425 at the presentation of Edmund Bassett, patron of the church of Blore, John Brokesby was admitted to the church of Blore. He replaced William Hancock, who had made an exchange with the vicar of Alspade. In 1532 there were over 120 people living in Blore. The church was served by a rector and two chaplains: Thomas Chadwyk, Henry Holgreve, Robert Gudhall. The rector received all the benefits and the chaplains were required to work for a mere pittance.

During the 16th and 17th centuries, the church wavered between Catholicism and Protestantism. The clergy had to face very difficult personal, moral and political problems. The puritanical observance of Sunday worship was enforced and the congregation included a larger than usual proportion of the community. In 1533 John Ward was appointed as rector of the parish. He appears to have thrived well during the very difficult period of religious and political change. Following his death on the 25th February 1577/8, his inventory was appraised and the value of his worldly possessions totalled £100.13s.4d - a very substantial amount. He names five maids: Ellen Tumkynson, Joane Hood and Margaret, Ruthe Bradbury, Mary Collear, and four servants: Edmund Derby and Thomas Fletcher, Richard and James Bradbury. He left bequests to each of them. He owned 179 sheep, 16 cattle, 4 horses and a large quantity of corn and hay. Only two rooms are mentioned in his will: "my parlor" and "my chamber". However, the size of his household suggests that he was not living in the Parson's cottage, behind the church. He may have been allowed to occupy Blore Hall, whilst his patron lived in the Bassett Mansion. He bequeathed to his "good Mr Bassett" a gilt goblet.

In 1535 Thomas Wright was the Rector of Blore. He was present when the benefice was valued at £8.8s 0d, plus the contentious 13s.4d. to Burton Abbey. On 23rd March 1577/8, Robert Healde was admitted to the parish church of Bloore, vacant through the natural death of John Warde, priest. In 1604, a survey of churches in Staffordshire was carried out, which recorded how well, or badly, the clergy were educated. Blore was recorded as having a parsonage worth £8 with 100 communicants. The parson Robert Healde, or Eld, was classified as ignorant, without a degree, and was receiving the stipend of £8.

The normal meaning of recusancy, especially after 1570, was acceptance of the Roman Catholic faith. However, strictly speaking a recusant was one who did not attend his parish church when it was legally compulsory to do so. In 1607 Rev Robt Heald, after 30 years as rector, declared that *"there is (nor never within my time) neither absolute nor half recusant in our parish.... but all, men and women, do usually frequent divine service"*. This declaration was questionable. The Bassetts, who were Lords of Blore Manor, during his period of office, certainly retained their Catholic faith, even if not openly.

Rev Henry Stubbs was born in 1589 and graduated from Oxford in 1616. He was presented as Rector in 1619, and held the post until 1643. In 1646, he was granted an augmentation of £14 to his stipend and in 1648 signed the testimony conforming to the Commonwealth settlement. He was presented to the rectory of Blore, which had been sequestered from the Earl of Newcastle. He died in 1650 and his will was proved at Lichfield. He was succeeded by his son, Josiah Stubbs, who graduated from Trinity College, Cambridge and was Rector from 1651 until 1657. Josiah left to become the Rector at Kingsley. Kingsley was another benefice which had been under the patronage of the Duke of Newcastle.

William Yates was Parson of Blore on two occasions for a total of twenty eight years. He was parson in 1657, and then from 1661 until his death in 1689. He married Anne Stubbing of Marston Montgomery in 1660, and his second wife Elizabeth Morris, widow of Noah Stine, on 5th May 1670. In the Hearth Tax, 1666, he is noted as having two hearths and probably lived in the parsonage behind Blore Church. In the Glebe Terriers the parsonage is noted as having four bays - approximately 4 x 16ft = 64feet long - plus a small barn of three bays. His inventory, in 1689 lists the rooms: his studdy and ould studdy, cheese chamber, chamber over the house, over chamber, nether parlor, buttery, milk house, kitchen parlor and kitchen. He had moved into Blore Hall itself. The total value of his inventory was £275, which shows that he was a man of significant wealth. The first item on his inventory, after his apparel and purse, were "8 pieces of hors flesh vallued at £20". These eight riding horses indicate a high standard of living. He died leaving one daughter, Elizabeth, of his first marriage and two sons and two daughters, John, Thomas, Anne and Dorothy, of his second marriage. He was buried at Blore on 24th April 1689 and his will was proved 26th September 1689.

Rev Samuel Smally was Rector of Blore from 1689 until 1708. He was a man of learning. The books and papers in his library were valued at £20, and his total inventory at £102.17.8d. The specification of individual rooms confirms that he, like his predecessor Rev Yates, also occupied Blore Hall. He left a wife, Ann, and three children: Mary, Dorothy and William.

After the death of Rev Smally, a Rector was not appointed but the Parish was ministered by two curates successively. Briefly, in 1708, by James Calton. In 1709 Aden Ley was appointed as curate and remained connected with the Parish for many years.

In 1718, just before the sale of Blore, the Tenants of Blore wrote to the Lord of the Manor, Lord Harley as follows:

To the Right Honourable the Lord Harley, Patron of the Rectory of Blore in Staffordshire. May it please your Lordship: Our Rector being lately dead We your Lordships Tenants and other inhabitants of the parish of Blore do humbly recommend to your Lordship choice Mr Ley our Curate who being a true member of the Church of England and having with diligence and care attended his duty here, for ten years together, we have no reason to doubt but he will continue so to do for the future and thereby render himself worthy of your Lordships favour. We presume not to direct your Lordship in this affair only with all humility beg leave to acquaint you that (in case you are not already engaged or have not any other person in your eye) he will be very acceptable to us who are Yr Lordship's Most obedient tenants and humble servants.

The letter was signed by: Ralph Waterfall, Richard Taylor, Philip Peach, James Kent, Humphrey Peach, Thomas Smith, Tho. Harrison, John Peach, Henry Milward, Jasif Millinton, John Bentley, William Alcock, Thomas Smith, Robard Dennis, John Smith, Ralph Smith, John Stubs, George Foster.

Although their letter is undated, when viewed with the following communication it is clear that they had been pre-empted. Their request was too late. Lord Harley had already agreed to the presentation of Mr Brailsford. The presentation in Latin dated 6th March 1718, has a postscript signed by Oliver Maston: *"Not knowing but My Lord might be willing to see the copy of Mr Brailsford presentation before ingrossed I have ordered Mr Gibson to bring it you for that purpose and can get it ingrossed in half an hour for my Lord and Lady to sign. Mr Brailsford will stay at the Coffee House in Dover street till Mr Gibson returns if my Lord and Lady are pleased to sign it this evening."*

Lord Harley was already negotiating with Thomas Rivett for the sale of Blore. It was to be another twenty years before Aden Ley was finally presented to the Rectory of Blore.

In 1720 the Rivett family acquired Blore. As Lords of the Manor, they had the right to present their own nominee to the rectory of Blore church. Thomas (IV) Rivett (1713-1762), during his lifetime, presented four different rectors to the living:

Rev William Blackwall	16th September 1728
Rev Charles Sibley	4th April 1732
Rev Aden Ley	22nd October 1740
Rev George Gretton	30th May 1752

The first of these Rectors, Rev William Blackwall, was probably related to Thomas Rivett's mother, Elizabeth Rivett née Eaton. Elizabeth's grandmother, whose maiden name was Blackwall, had a cousin William Blackwall. Rev Charles Sibley of Bath was nominated in 1732, and later his daughter, Anna Maria Sibley, married Thomas Rivett. After waiting for twenty years, in 1740, Rev Aden Ley became the Rector and remained at Blore for twelve years. George Gretton was presented to Blore Church in 1752, and was rector until 1769. The Glebe Terrier, dated 1755, confirms the size of the house, with stable adjoining, as about 3 bays, with a barn of the same size.

Rev William Bayliffe, whose memorial stone stands outside the church porch, was rector for fifty years, from 1786 to 1836. He was one of a family of nine children brought up in Sheffield. His father was for thirty four years perpetual curate of Eccleshall Church, Sheffield. This encompassed the Shore family estates at Norton and Meersbrook. It was Samuel Shore who presented Rev William Bayliffe as rector of Blore. For a large part of the fifty years as rector he lived in Ashbourne and rode on a pony to Blore for the weekly service. It was Rev Bayliffe who said: *"I have found by experience that a congregation cannot be depended upon except on Lord's Day."* He lived for the final years of his life in the old parsonage behind the church, being looked after by a local farmer, Mr Lees.

Around 1837 a new rectory, with coach house, stable, barn, cow house and cart shed, was built in the field called Terrace Croft facing the church entrance. Rev Hugh Wood was Rector from 1836 to 1869. In 1841 Rev Hugh Wood and his wife Jane were living in the Rectory with their twin daughters, Ellin and Catherine and two manservants: William Alsop and Joseph Frost and two maidservants: Ann and Sarah Hutchinson. His wife's older brother, George Jessop, was staying with them at the time of the 1841 Census.

Rev Hugh Wood's father, Rev John Wood, vicar of Pentrich, had succeeded his own father as Squire of Swanwick in Derbyshire. When John Wood died in 1858, Rev Hugh Wood succeeded him as Squire.

Two years later, in 1860, Rev Wood moved away from Blore to take up residence in Swanwick. He retained the rights of the rectory and installed two curates to carry out the ministry of the parish in his absence.

The first curate was Rev Joseph Dun Miller, BA, who came to Blore in 1860 with his pregnant wife, two children and his mother-in-law. He had moved around a bit before he came to Blore. He was born in Brazil and his wife came from Cheswardine. His two small children were born in Rotherham and Wessington and their baby boy, Ernest, was born in Blore rectory. He did not stay long and moved away after just over a year.

Rev J.D. Glennie (d.1903) was Curate-in-charge from 1861 to 1869. He was responsible for the building of the Swinscoe school and schoolhouse. Besides his great involvement with the school he achieved some fame locally as the first person in the parish to own and use a sewing machine. Unfortunately, he also achieved some notoriety among the villagers for allegedly having influenced the local landowners to give notice to two farmers, who had joined the ranks of the Methodists. This is possibly true, because the principal landowners were the Church Commissioners. As a result the villagers made an effigy of him and burned it publicly, which may have contributed to the fact that he left the parish, although he protested his innocence. His account was that he was driven away because he set up a Mission Service, in opposition to the Chapel, in Swinscoe. He moved to Croxton as Vicar, in 1869. The local schoolmaster referred to him, at the time of his arrival, as *"apparently a kind gentleman"*. However, Mr G.H.O. Burgess in his notes on Croxton says that the Rev Glennie was autocratic, crusty and did not suffer fools gladly - in fact, not at all!

The absentee rector, Hugh Wood, also resigned from Blore. He continued to live in the Hall at Swanwick and died in 1880 and was buried in Swanwick churchyard.

Rev C.E. Haslam was educated at St John's College, Cambridge, where he received the Bachelor of Arts, followed by a Master of Arts Degree. He came to St Bartholomew's from Kirk Ella, in East Yorkshire, in 1869. He only stayed three years, resigning as rector in 1873, and went to Frocester in Gloucestershire.

Rev Gray Granville took up the incumbency in 1873. He was the only son of Rev Granville of Stratford-upon-Avon. Before graduating from Christ Church, Oxford and becoming a priest, he was an officer in the Royal Marine Light Infantry. Rev Granville, with his charm and sincerity, was a very popular man. He was a friend to the poor and his first consideration was always the happiness and welfare of his people. From 1875, he was the vicar of Ilam for 22 years. In 1899, he moved to Wasperton in Warwickshire, where he remained until his death in December 1913.

Rev J.H. Young was rector of Blore for forty years, from 1875 to 1915. The Census of 1881 records Rev John Young, aged 40, and only two of his sons: Robert aged 1 year and John aged 2. His wife must have been away, as she is not mentioned. In the 1891 census Rev John Young, his wife and seven children are named: Allen, Cyril, Ethel, Evelyn, Margaret, Marian, Maxwell. He was well loved by his flock. He was sometimes regarded as a little eccentric, with his interest in local history. His sermons were often interspersed with anecdotes and his historical notes appeared in the Parish Magazine. This first appeared as "The Deanery Magazine" of the Deanery of Alstonfield, in 1890. After 1900, it appeared as "Our Parish Magazine". Rev Young was assured of a large and attentive congregation. He had thirteen children and his neighbours, churchwarden John Oldfield and his wife, had twelve children, of whom nine were living at Blore Hall.

In 1915 Rev T.J. Sidney Roberts M.A. became the Rector of the Parish. The late Mrs Frances Appleby used to recall that he often wore an old-fashioned mortar board on his head. He drove around the parish in an American Oldsmobile, with a young man called Clifford John acting as chauffeur.

When Rev Roberts died in 1945, Rev Horace John Graves, vicar of Ilam, covered the vacancy for five months. On the 19th February 1946, Blore Ray and Okeover were united with Ilam Church, by Order in Council. At the same time, Blore lost the right for calling banns, and the solemnisation of marriages. Rev Graves became the vicar for the united parishes of Blore and Ilam.

Five years later, in 1951, the church was re-licensed for marriages. In 1952 Rev W.D. Peck was asked to seek "appeal" funds for the renewal of the roof timbers of the church. In 1953, after Mr Peck left, Rev C.L. Chatham ministered at Blore for twelve months, and then moved to the Lichfield area.

Rev D. Nicoll-Griffith came to the parish from Barton-under-Needwood, around 1956, and remained for nine years. During his period of office he made Special appeals for funds to redecorate the church and restore the organ.

Rev J.A.S. Laurie joined the parish in 1965 and lived at Martin Hill, just outside the parish. Rev Laurie asked the Methodist Chapel in Swinscoe for permission to hold a service in the chapel once a month - this was agreed by the trustees. He was very concerned that so much money was being spent on the church. He felt that it was not justified in such a remote area to spend £2000 on repairs to the roof of the church. He believed that there were so many more needy places around the world. It was Rev Laurie who proposed at a special meeting that the church should be declared redundant. This proposition was rejected by Archdeacon Ven. G. Youell who said that the church could not be declared redundant, just because of its geography.

A new priest-in-charge, Rev S. Tittensor arrived at Blore. At the flower festival in 1972, he refused to allow refreshments or general goods to be sold. As a result the takings were reduced by half, which the parish council and local congregation found difficult to accept. In view of the poor attendances at the church, Rev Tittensor approached the Methodist Chapel in Swinscoe, with a view to combining their services. Rev Tittensor resigned in June 1973. He was replaced by Rev J.W. Bucknall who stayed in the parish for three years, until 1976.

In 1977 Rev R. Balkwill became the new priest-in-charge. It was Rev Balkwill who reported that there were seven clergy serving twelve churches in the Alstonfield Deanery, and forecast that the number of clergy would be substantially reduced in the next twenty years. How right he was!

In 1981 Rev A.O.L. Hodgson came to the parish. In 1982 he had the difficult task of advising the Parish Council that the quota due to be paid would be £515, a rise of 97% on the previous year. The Parish Council refused to accept this large increase and resolved to pay £300, an increase of 15%.

Rev Hodgson stayed with the parish until 1989. Rev Philip E.R. Hall joined the parish in 1989. After six important years, leading up to the plans for restoration of the church, he moved to Drayton Bassett, which also has interesting associations with the ancient family of Bassetts of Staffordshire.

On the 11th July 1996 the new Priest-in-Charge, Rev Peter W. Davey was licensed at Blore Church. Rev Davey had spent many years teaching art with the armed forces in Germany and came to Blore just as the restoration of the church was reaching its conclusion. In November 1996 he welcomed and took part in the thanksgiving service led by Rt Rev Keith Sutton. Bishop of Lichfield.

CHAPEL OF THE BLACK CANONS

During the reign of King Henry III, Sir Hugh de Okeover supported the King, during the Welsh War and the Revolt of the Barons. This commitment became a drain on his financial resources. He had to sell off large parts of his estates, including half of his land in Swinscoe, to the Abbot of Rocester.

Rocester Abbey was founded around 1146. The monks wore a long black cassock with a white surplice-like vestment over it. Unlike other orders, these monks sported beards and wore caps on their heads. This monastery of St Austin's Canons started with little revenue. As benefactions increased, and they expanded their activities, particularly in the raising of sheep, their income expanded considerably. References appear in the Rocester Abbey Cartulary, among the Okeover Papers, to "the chapel surrounded by ditches" and "an assart in Vecclehall and messuage near the chapel", in Swinscoe.

At the bottom of the fields belonging to Hall Flatts, not far from Ellis Hill Farm and New House Farm, is the probable site of the Chapel. During the 13th Century, the family of Bec held land in Swinscoe, and, it is possible that the reference to "Vecclehall" may well be "Becc-le-Hall". New House Farm, built on a rocky outcrop, contains within its structure a probable "Great Hall" and may be the site of Becc-le-Hall.

The name Hall Flatts may be of significance. It probably indicates Flatts belonging to the Hall. Wherever the name "hall" exists it is, commonly, found to have been the site of a hall. A possible but less likely meaning of hall is as a corruption of hill, indicating its position on top of Swinscoe Hill.

In 1438, the Abbot of Rocester sued Robert Tomkynson of Calton for breaking into his close at Swinscoe. Robert was accused of putting cattle on to the Abbot's corn and grass, and cutting down his

Barn between Hall Flatts and Rose Cottage - possibly an old chapel.

The Primitive Methodist Chapel, Swinscoe.

Interior - The Primitive Methodist Chapel, Swinscoe
Reproduced with the kind permission of the Ashbourne Advertiser

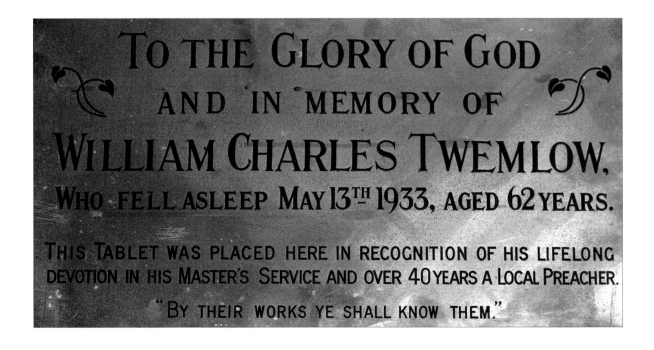

TO THE GLORY OF GOD
AND IN MEMORY OF
WILLIAM CHARLES TWEMLOW,
WHO FELL ASLEEP MAY 13TH 1933, AGED 62 YEARS.

THIS TABLET WAS PLACED HERE IN RECOGNITION OF HIS LIFELONG
DEVOTION IN HIS MASTER'S SERVICE AND OVER 40 YEARS A LOCAL PREACHER.

"BY THEIR WORKS YE SHALL KNOW THEM."

Ladies Meeting at Swinscoe Methodist Chapel c1930

Plate commemorating the first meeting at Mow Cop

Chapel entrance porch, 1935

trees. In 1519 William (IV) Bassett of Blore married Elizabeth Fitzherbert. As part of the marriage settlement, the Monastery of Rostett (Rocester) in Swinscoe is mentioned - the rent was 20 shillings per annum. The will of Richard Hood of Swinscoe, 1538, shows that one of his sons, Thomas, was one of the brethren of the Abbey. In 1532, according to the List of Families in the Archdeaconry of Stafford, Dominus Thomas Hude Capilanus was living in Calton. However, Thomas was not present at Rocester in September 1538 at the dissolution of the abbey. Sir William Bassett was a witness to the Deed of Surrender of the Abbey.

With the Dissolution the land was split up and sold off. In 1541 Frances, Earl of Shrewsbury was granted a pasture, called Elieshill, and a meadow, called Abbotts Croft, in Swinscoe.

PRIMITIVE METHODIST CHAPEL SWINSCOE

Hugh Bourne, one of the founders of Primitive Methodism, records in his journal, on the 17th April 1813, that *"I called at Swinscoe, and took tea and then rode in a cart rather above three miles to Ashbourne"*. He was there to discuss the setting up a local place of worship with Walter Swetnam. who lived in a cottage on the edge of the main road in Swinscoe. Two months later, on the 7th June 1813, Walter Swetnam registered his home as a place of worship for Protestant Dissenters. Mr Swetnam had become a member of the Primitive Methodists - a breakaway movement from the original Methodists.

Methodism had developed from John Wesley's preaching and his roving style of evangelical teaching. During John Wesley's time many of the evangelists were lay preachers and very few were ordained, notable exceptions being Wesley himself, John Fletcher of Madeley and Henry Venn. They kept their links with the Church of England, even occasionally preaching in its churches. The lay preachers were also clamouring for ordination and eventually Wesley broke with Anglican practice by, himself, "laying hands" on men who were to minister in Scotland and overseas missions. Shortly before his death, he began to make provision for areas in England where Methodists were denied the sacraments. These steps inevitably hastened the departure of his followers from the established church, although Wesley insisted that he did not aim at separation. At his death, in 1784, his authority passed to the Methodist Conference, represented by one hundred of its members. Unlike some other breakaway groups from the Church of England, Methodism maintained the doctrine of general redemption. They believe that salvation is available to all - not just the chosen few.

The founders of the new movement, Hugh Bourne and William Clowes, had been expelled from the Methodists, for taking part in the evangelistic gatherings, known as "camp meetings". Their new movement was named after the words of John Wesley: *"Wherever there is an open door enter in and preach the Gospel: if it be two or three under a hedge preach the Gospel: go out... and bring in the poor and the maimed and the halt and the blind, this is the way the primitive Methodists did it."* The first meeting of the Primitive Methodists was held on the 31st May 1807 at Mow Cop, in Staffordshire. The down-to-earth approach appealed to the men of the soil, especially those who felt that the church was too "high" for the ordinary people. The preachers were powerful and persuasive speakers. In 1823, Samuel Heath recorded in his journal: *"I preached at Swinscoe and the power of God came down like a mighty rushing wind. Two found the Lord."* The Primitive Methodists grew in number locally. In the early 1830s, regular contributions were made, towards the erection of a chapel, by local worshippers. These were collected by a treasurer, who travelled the district by pony and "tub". The Primitive Methodist Chapel in Town End Lane, Swinscoe, was built at a cost of £100:

> See down the lane, beyond the well,
> A country chapel, small and grey,
> It has no yew tree, tower or bell,
> But God is there its people say

(There is still a well down the lane, with low walls and steps where frogs used to sit, which provided drinking water for the local residents until 1961)

On the 23rd August 1835, the chapel was opened and the first sermons were preached by James Taylor, James Bourne and R. Jukes. The chapel was registered, for Primitive Methodists, by John Hampson of Swinscoe and Richard Jukes, on the 28th September 1836. A local builder and carpenter,

Anthony Stubbs, records an amount of 2s.0d rent for a seat in the chapel, for the year 1837. Initially, Swinscoe was part of the Ramsor circuit, but later, became part of the Ashbourne Circuit. Each Sunday, sermons were preached by visiting circuit preachers.

By 1851 the Primitive Methodists had achieved a nationwide membership of over 100,000 members. However, the strength of the movement did not apply to Swinscoe Chapel. In 1868, Swinscoe had become "low and feeble" and was relying upon a few stalwarts to keep things going - hoping for better days. Then, a man arrived on the scene, who, through his unpopularity, indirectly contributed more to the Primitive Cause in Swinscoe, than any other individual: the forceful and dogmatic new curate of Blore Parish Church, Rev R D Glennie.

The Rev Glennie was the driving force in obtaining grants and persuading the Okeovers to support the building of a school in Swinscoe. As an ex-school inspector, his views about instruction in Anglican religion and compulsory payment, were decidedly unpopular locally. The national, as well as the local, view of the non-conformists was in favour of free and non-denominational education. He also set up a Mission Service in Swinscoe School with the intent of trying to counteract some of the Methodist activity. The Methodists accused *"the Parson and the Devil"* of trying to stop their good work and the villagers became so incensed, by his apparent interference, that they burned an effigy of the parson.

Rev Glennie's actions and interference were so highly unpopular that he created a great deal of opposition. In doing so, Rev Glennie also caused an unusual solidarity among the local population which, unwittingly, furthered the Methodist cause. When Rev Glennie left the parish in 1869, the absentee rector, Rev Hugh Wood, also resigned. The Rev Glennie moved to Croxton where, even there, he obtained a reputation as *"a man of earnest and strong convictions which under all circumstances he never shrank from maintaining"*.

The society decided to hold a special camp meeting to support their members and try to revive the old enthusiasm. Preachers came from far and wide and preached powerful sermons. In all, twenty two people were persuaded to join the Methodist faith, among them several farmers, their wives and children and their servants.

With the absence of a permanent incumbent, there was a virtual vacuum at Blore Church during the next six years, which gave the chapel the opportunity to consolidate its own position. The Sunday School was set up to counteract the influence of the church-run school. The number of children who attended rose to a high of fifty, which is more than the thirty six pupils ever achieved by the school.

The Chapel continued to grow in strength and became an important part of the social and cultural life of the community. At Christmas and at New Year special efforts were made. The Camp Meetings on Whit Sunday and Love Feasts on Whit Monday were annual events and the numbers of people that attended them was often very large.

On New Year's Eve in 1893, a service of song was arranged entitled "Gems from the life of Squire Brooks". The Chair was taken by W. Austin Jr. The choir was under the leadership of Mr J. Twemlow, soloist Miss Phillips, harmonium Mr J. Phillips, clarinet Mr C. Twemlow, violins C. Philips and G. Moss, and violoncello Mr S. Clowes. On Whit Monday, 1893, the Chapel organised a Camp Meeting. There were addresses by T. Harrison, P. Needham, J. Bates and Rev W.H. Mason. Afterwards the Annual Tea Meeting was arranged by Mrs Tomlinson, Mrs Lees, Mrs Twemlow and Mrs Moss. There were recitations by Mr Twemlow, Mr Phillips and Mr Bott's children. These were followed by solos from Miss Stannah and Mr Phillips and a trio by Misses Moss and Miss Phillips. Under the leadership of Mr Twemlow, the choir and all those present enjoyed one of the most successful meetings ever held at Swinscoe.

In 1896, at the Camp Meeting and Tea Party on Whit Monday, the proceeds of the collection were used to provide the paint and varnish for Mr T. Ratcliffe of Waterhouses to decorate the Chapel. On the 11th June 1897, over 130 people sat down to tea presided over by Mrs Moss, Mrs Lees, Mrs Twemlow and Mrs Thurman. The camp meetings continued for a further twenty years. During the Great War, the number of those attending decreased and the meetings gradually died away. Efforts were made to resurrect the meetings during the Twenties but they never achieved anything like the success of earlier years.

The rift between the chapel and the church slowly began to heal and Swinscoe School was used by both groups. It was particularly useful for the chapel to use the school because it was often impossible to hold open air meetings during the hard winters of Swinscoe.

One important national and local issue continued to cloud relationships. The Methodists felt that they should not have to pay for educating their children at a school that was biased towards Anglican education. This matter was finally solved by an Act of Parliament, in 1907. The Rev John Young, Rector of Blore, during his 45 year ministry tried to heal some of the old wounds between the Church and the Chapel. In 1914, he offered his "dissenting brethren" the opportunity of taking confirmation from the Bishop, "All who have been baptized according to the rites and ceremonies of the Church of England (and many dissenters have been so baptized) come to ratify the Covenant made with God but it does not follow that they become any more a member of the Church than they were before". He assured them that he did not wish to proselytize, or gain converts. He wished to provide the privilege that John Wesley never intended his followers to neglect, or forego - to attend Communion.

The chapel was well supported by a number of families and particular individuals. Mr John Phillips was the secretary and steward for many years from 1911 to the 1920s. He was ably supported by Mr W.C. Twemlow as treasurer for much of the same period and Mrs Tomlinson was the organist for many years. Local residents were trustees of the chapel. In 1917, it was suddenly realized that the trustees of the chapel had dwindled from fourteen to three. It was necessary to call an emergency meeting, and make special efforts, to persuade members of the congregation to replace all those who had died.

The Sunday School was held at the chapel and children came from all parts of the district to attend. Up to fifty children attended each Sunday and each year the local community organised a Sunday School Treat, sometimes to places as far afield as Trentham Gardens. During the War, the visits were more local. In 1917, they were entertained at Calton Moor House by Mr J. Phillips and his wife. After tea, games and other amusements were organised and the children sang hymns. Just before departure they loyally sang the National Anthem. Music was always an important part of worship and local and visiting soloists made their contribution. For the Anniversary Service of the Sunday School in 1917, the visiting preacher, Rev W. Carrier of Sheffield, brought along his sister, who sang "Beyond the Dawn" and "Nearer my God to Thee".

When a member of the committee left or died it was necessary to find a suitable replacement. On the 13th June 1933, it was necessary to call an emergency meeting of the committee to find a replacement for the treasurer, Mr W.C. Twemlow of Forest Farm. Mr Twemlow had made major contributions to all the chapel's activities and would be sorely missed. A plaque was installed on the wall beside the pulpit in the chapel, in recognition of his work.

In his place, Mrs Wilson was elected as Trust Treasurer and Mrs Twigge as School Treasurer. These ladies were also entrusted with the task of collecting for the erection of a new entrance porch. In 1935, in celebration of the centenary of the chapel, the porch was built. It cost nearly as much as the original building of the chapel.

The ladies of the parish made major contributions to the chapel activities and held meetings of their own. The sound of their voices, accompanied by a harmonium, could be heard all over the village. As at church, it was the custom for the ladies of the chapel to cover their heads and this resulted in the wearing of the magnificent creations to be seen in the group photograph taken around 1930.

During the Thirties and the Forties, the children looked forward to the annual Sunday School treat which went by coach to Alton Towers. Long before it became a theme park Alton Towers was a popular destination for visitors, with its gardens, parkland and boating lake. Ken Twemlow recalls an incident during a Sunday School visit when he and his friends, Arthur Hayes and George Morris became marooned in their boat and had to be rescued by the attendants. On another occasion Miss Annie Morris remembers going to a farm, near Uttoxeter, owned by Mr Prince - a staunch Methodist.

The chapel was registered for baptisms, weddings and funerals. A register containing, only two baptisms, is held in Matlock Record Office:

"July 21st 1963.
Elaine daughter of Joan Irene and Thomas Frederick Clowes of Green Farm, Swinscoe Born July 1st 1963
12th September 1965.
John Antony daughter (sic) of James David and Margaret Rose Bradbury of Calton Born 27th June 1965"

The register containing the rest of the baptisms, including all the Morris family, cannot be traced.

The Register of Marriages for the period 1921 to 1954, contains only ten marriages. Weddings were always important events within the community and especially welcomed by the children. If the wedding took place on a school day, the children were allowed to leave school to go and watch the event. They were also eager to attend because of an old custom; part way down Town End Lane (previously known at Chapel Lane) there were two large wooden farm gates. The local children "roped" the entrance to stop the wedding car and would not let it pass until coins had been thrown to them. Miss Sheila Allen recalls the wedding of Miss Phillips of Ellis Hill to her cousin, Mr Stanley Phillips, from Calton Moor House, when pennies were thrown to the waiting children. Jean Thompson, daughter of the licensee at the Dog & Partridge, was married at the chapel. Graham, her husband-to-be, had to come by bus from Manchester but the bus was late and he had to run down the lane to get to the chapel in time.

During the 1940s and 1950s, Mr Charles Phillips used to run the Sunday School with fifteen or twenty regulars. Among the families whose children attended Sunday School were: Allen (Martin Hill), Bailey, Bradbury (Waterings), Briddon, Lees and Phillips. He was not averse to giving a little tap with a light cane, to those who fidgeted or allowed their attention to wander. Later, Frances Appleby (Mycock) carried on the good work and walked from Woodhouses, up the Cliff every Sunday morning. At Whitsuntide, the children used to give little recitations and were rewarded with a book. Those who attended regularly were given a better book than the rest, but everyone got one.

In those days, long before unification of the churches, it was common for the young people to go to both Chapel and Church. They would go to Sunday School at the Chapel at 10.30am, the Service at Blore Church at 2.30pm and the Service at the Chapel at 6.30 in the evening.

In August 1954, it was again necessary to review the trustees.

The chapel badly needed renovation and redecoration. Mrs Salt of Calton Moor House worked very hard to collect over £50 towards the cost. On the 11th April 1955, after the renovation had been carried out, the chapel was filled to capacity for its reopening. This was an opportunity to unveil a plaque in recognition of lifelong service of Mr Charles Phillips. He died in 1955, and his wife Annie Phillips died in 1953. They both lived at Ellis Hill Farm. The plaque was unveiled by Mr William Walker of Alton, the oldest local preacher, who had been closely associated with Mr and Mrs Phillips for over fifty years. Mr Fred Cotton of Waterhouses spoke of the good work of Mr Charles Twemlow, Mr Charles Clowes and Mr Charles Phillips. The members of the church gave an oak communion table and holy communion vessels as a sign of their respect for Mr Phillips.

The population of the parish had reduced over the years from 299 in 1841 to half that number in 1951. It was becoming increasingly difficult to maintain local support. Special efforts were made to increase the involvement of those members of younger generation, who were still around. On the 12th May 1957, the chapel was well filled. The local young folk took a prominent part in conducting the service. Mr Arthur Twigge was the chairman, the Rev Barker gave the address, Miss Margaret Clowes and Mr Ernest Allen read the lesson and Miss Beryl Cotton of Waterhouse was the organist. The chapel was also used for the Women's Mission Service on the 15th August 1957, when Mrs Wilcocks of Mayfield made an eloquent address.

Over the next few years, the attendance at the chapel dwindled even further. The good old stalwarts, Mr and Mrs Twigge, Mr and Mrs Phillips, Mr and Mrs Shaw, Mr and Mrs Salt, Mrs Bradbury kept Methodism alive in Swinscoe. In 1962, it was agreed to install electricity and a fresh water supply. However, it was agreed to postpone appointment of preachers for the following Whit and Harvest Festivals because of poor attendance. The small band of the faithful was further reduced in 1970 when Mrs J. Phillips died. In 1964 the organist and member of the chapel, Miss Lizzie Phillips, was taken to hospital never to return.

Both St Bartholomew's Church, at Blore, and the Methodist Chapel, at Swinscoe, were experiencing poor attendance. In 1965, Rev Laurie of Blore Church asked permission to hold a church service in the chapel once a month to which the trustees agreed unanimously. Rev Laurie was appointed as the preacher for Whit Saturday and Whit Sunday 1966. In 1972, the new vicar of Blore Church, Rev Tittensor, and members of the Parish Church Council, began discussion with the trustees of the chapel. They discussed and agreed to hold united services. Rev Tittensor would take the first service and the Methodist Minister would take the next. It was also agreed to hold alternate services in the summer months in Blore Church.

Mr David Shaw died in 1975 and two years later Mr J. Phillips also died. This left Mr and Mrs Twigge, Mr and Mrs Salt and Mrs Shaw to soldier on. In 1980 Mr and Mrs Twigge decided to move to Ashbourne and this effectively meant that the chapel could no longer remain. The final service was held on Sunday 28th June 1981. The chapel was closed and bought by Mr Tom Clowes of Green Farm for use as a storeroom. The Methodist Bible and other items were returned to members of the Phillips family and the communion sets were distributed to other chapels.

The Primitive Methodist Chapel, its leaders, trustees and congregation made a significant spiritual, moral, cultural and social contribution, to a small Staffordshire community over a period of 150 years. The chapel building still stands - as a memorial to a dedicated band of people.

SWINSCOE SCHOOL

The people of the parish have always recognized the importance of education and even the poorest tried to send their children to school. There were, however, problems for the poorer families, who were at a disadvantage when the family needed extra income. The children were needed to help in the home as well as maintaining the family gardens and working for local farms and factories.

Early in the 19th Century, the cobbler's shop in Swinscoe was used as a classroom. It is recorded as a free school for boys and girls and in 1850 Mrs Fenton is recorded as free school mistress. Some children attended the schools at Ilam and Mayfield but these arrangements were never really satisfactory.

In 1861, Rev R.D. Glennie, the young and enthusiastic new curate, led a movement to establish a school for the parish. With the generosity and support of Leake Okeover, who provided the land, Rev Glennie was responsible for building the school and schoolhouse for the teacher in Swinscoe. A photograph of Rev Glennie and one of the Rector, Rev Hugh Wood, used to hang on the wall of the classroom. The school was associated with the Church and licensed for divine worship. It was designated C.E. but the initials C.E. meant Certified Efficient and not, as often thought, Church of England.

According to a plan of the school preserved in the Stafford Record Office, there were nine six-foot long desks in the school. Even if the children were packed four to a desk this meant that not more than thirty six children could attend. The maximum recorded number, at any time during its one hundred years of existence, was thirty six.

The school had two entrances to the same classroom, one for girls and one for boys as well as separate playgrounds at the back. The facilities were primitive by modern standards; water was drawn from the well and it was only in its later years that special delivery of water was made in churns.

The school opened in 1864 and its first teacher was Miss Eliza Edwards. Among her pupils were the following: Hannah Allen, Betsy and Louisa Barnes, Ann Beresford, Emma and Ellen Bott, Herman Fielding, A. Gerrard, Frances and Ann Harrison, Annie and Betsy Lees, Helena Thurman and Rachel Smith and George Stubbs.

John Farmer, garden labourer, and his wife Eliza were very poor but still tried to send their children to school. Mary, age 10, and Emma, age 8, started school but sometimes their parents could not afford to pay the fee, so the children did not attend. The eldest son Thomas, at the age of 14, was working as a factory boy at the mill in Mayfield, and baby George was at home.

Another poor family of the village was the Sutton family of four children: Sarah, Fanny, Rhoda, and Fred. They were sometimes absent as mother could not pay the fees. In the school register it is reported that they also did not attend because they had no shoes to wear. On one occasion, young Fred was sent home again to get his face and hands washed.

Every school has one! Walter Gould was always the one in trouble; playing truant, absent for all kinds of reasons. He was up to all kinds of mischief including playing with the girls in the playground, for which heinous crime he was punished by the rector himself! He obviously lacked the influence of his elder sister who was working full time at the mill. His father, William Gould, was in constant trouble with the local authorities and on one occasion was jailed for two months hard labour, for leaving the youngest daughter, Emma, without proper care so that she had to be looked after in the Poorhouse in Ashbourne.

Initially, the school taught the three "R"s: Reading, Writing and Rithmetic, and being a church school a fourth "R" - Religious Knowledge (Gospel and Catechism). Geography was another subject, and the older girls were given instruction in Domestic Work. Children were eligible to attend from the age of three. In 1866, three children under the age of six were admitted; Elizabeth and David Howson and Christine Gould.

In 1871, Mrs Annie Dawson was the schoolmistress and was living in the school house with her husband Henry Dawson. During the 1870s and 1880s, the attendance at the school remained constant between thirty three and thirty six children. Those who received prizes for regular attendance, in 1884, were: William Harrison, William Holden, Frank Smith, Harriett Smith, John Smith and Lilian Smith. Good attendance was important, especially when the children left school, and were looking for a job. The school leaving report showed the standard of work, and attendance, which has always been important to potential employers.

In 1881, Fanny Laurence was the school mistress and was living in the school house with her young sister Alice Laurence who also attended the school.

Miss Mary Ann Barlow was schoolmistress for six years. On 20th February 1888 the snow was so deep that only three children arrived at school out of the thirty five who were registered. Miss Barlow died at the age of 29 years on the 6th September 1891 and is buried in Blore Churchyard. She was replaced by Miss Fanny Gamble, who took up residence in the school house.

The school has always been used for a variety of parish activities. In 1886, a meeting was held to choose candidates for the positions of Overseers of the Poor. The meeting was chaired by the Rector, the Rev John Young and was attended by the following inhabitants:

William Stannah	New House Farm
Thomas Stannah	Hill End Farm
Rd Phillips	Calton Moor
Henry Harrison	Common End
Henry Harrison	The Myre
Sam Clowes	Common End Farm

A list of householders was submitted to the Justices of the Peace, for the Division of Leek:

Capt Alfred Charles Duncombe	Calwich Abbey
Ralph Webster	The Waterings
Mr Twigg	Town End
Frederick Thompson	Golden Fleece

Mr Webster and Mr Thompson were elected as Overseers, whose duties were to collect the poor rate from the inhabitants and to arrange for its distribution among the poor of the parish.

A heart-rending note in the school register, concerns the three Winson children, Thomas, William and Elizabeth. On 12th May 1890 it is recorded that they have *"gone to the Union as their mother is dead and they have none to keep them"*. The Union was the local workhouse.

The school was a charity school, run by the church and the parish with the backing of Squire Leake Okeover. As it was built by the parish, not under the Education Act of 1891, only local children could attend. The teachers were probably not trained until after 1900 when teachers leaving training colleges, set up by the Act of 1891, were taking up posts at schools like Swinscoe School. Gradually as the education of children of all age groups became free of charge, children came to school from outside the parish.

The Primitive Methodists were unhappy about the influence of the Church. They formed a local Sunday School to counteract some of the influence.

The remoteness of Swinscoe, and difficulty of getting to and from the area, made it difficult to keep school teachers. In 1892, Miss Gamble resigned as school teacher and was succeeded by Miss Emily Naish of Sutton Very School, Warminster. In the following year there were four different teachers.

In 1894, the school inspector carried out a census of the local population and found that there were 154 souls and that, in the year of 1894, only 24 pupils attended the school.

The financial support of the school depended upon grants from the County Council, aid from the church, and local subscriptions, but Swinscoe School being so small often received very little help from outside. In 1900, the Voluntary School Association, under the Chairmanship of the Bishop of Lichfield, granted aid of £162. This was distributed to schools in the Deanery of Alstonfield, but Blore received the smallest allocation of £5. In 1903, Mr Joseph Robotham, of Town End Farm, and Mr D. Howson, of Blore Hall, were elected members of the committee of management. In that year, the County Council made no grant and the school had to rely upon local subscription. The Rector, through the columns of the Deanery Magazine, wrote impassioned pleas for parents to subscribe to the upkeep of the school.

In September 1903, after six years as schoolmistress, Mrs Shaw resigned. At the time of her leaving she was earning £45 per annum plus £10 efficiency allowance. She and her husband lived rent free in the partly furnished school house and received five tons of coal each year as part of her wage. The vacancy was advertised on three separate occasions without success, and Miss Oliver conducted the school on a temporary basis. There were applicants but most of them refused the position when they found that Swinscoe was too far from a railway station.

Whooping Cough was a scourge and, because of a local epidemic, Swinscoe School was closed for three weeks in 1904. The children must have been dismayed when they heard that the Managers had made a request to the Education Authority for the school to be opened, during the Easter holidays, to compensate for the time lost.

During 1906, Miss Storey was employed as school mistress, at a salary of £90 pa but she only stayed until the following year. In 1907 Mr H.E. Okeover retired as chairman of the School Managers, after more than forty years service. This was the year that Miss Margaret Young became school mistress. The earliest photograph of the school, looking just as it does 85 years later, was taken in 1910 and is seen as the frontispiece of this book. In the centre, the schoolteacher, Miss Margaret Young, is holding a small baby, Alice Clewes. Behind her long skirt, another member of the Clewes family is hiding - John Clewes. The assistant teacher, Miss Mary Gerrard, smartly dressed in a long skirt and blouse with tie, is standing besides the ten boys all wearing britches, with an older boy wearing a cap. The thirteen girls are all wearing aprons over their dresses, a style that was still a school standard in the 1930s.

The Clewes family in the photograph lived in the schoolhouse. The house was furnished rather sparsely: 2 bedsteads, 1 bed, 1 bolster, 4 chairs, 1 chest of drawers, 3 tables, 1 dresser, 1 toilet service with a badly cracked basin, 1 corner cupboard, 1 pair of blankets, 1 counterpane, 2 pairs of sheets, 1 badly worn bolster case, 6 pillow cases, 2 toilet covers and 4 towels. Later, in October 1912, when a new teacher was expected, Mrs Clewes was given notice to leave the house and she and her family moved across the road to the cottage next to the Dog and Partridge. Mrs Louisa Clewes, aged 29 at the time, continued to carry out her duties at the school; cleaning, washing towels, tidying playground and emptying and cleaning the closets.

A collection was made among the parents and local residents when Miss Young resigned in 1911. She was presented with a solid silver teaset bought specially from Elkingtons of London. After her departure, Miss Gerrard asked for an increase of salary and although the School Managers supported the increase of £10, it was turned down by the Council for Education. The School Managers generously gave Miss Gerrard an increase of £2.10s.0d out of their own pockets.

In 1912, the school had 12 boys, 13 girls and 10 infants. Two years later, there were 19 boys and 18 girls at school from a population of 148. The following year 1915 there were 35 pupils from a population of 176.

During the War everyone was encouraged to help the war effort. In 1914, £1.0s.0d was used out of school funds, to buy wool for the school children - to make heel-less socks for the soldiers.

By the 1920s, the school had installed modern equipment and teaching methods, and a number of its pupils won scholarships to the grammar school in Ashbourne. In May 1920, Miss Martha Seals, a local resident and one-time pupil at the school, was appointed headmistress. Mrs Beard was appointed in June 1922 and stayed in Swinscoe until 1936. Miss Annie Morris, who still lives in the village, started school in 1923 and remembers Mrs Beard well. It was during this period, in 1933, that the Ditchfield family left Calton and moved to Swinscoe. Their children, Laura Irene, Violet and Alice May joined the school. Mrs Beard used to play the organ at Blore church. When she left the parish, she was given a purse of notes, in recognition of her faithful and capable service to both school and church.

June Rowlinson (Little Moor Cottage), Eileen Howson (Fleece), Margaret Clewes, Jimmy Bradbury (Cottage Opp school), Leslie Mellor (Waterings)
Arthur Twigg (Latham Hall Farm), Ernest Allen (Martin Hill), Max Bailey (School House), Enid Bradbury (Waterings), Charles Clowes (NewHouse)
Nancy Bradbury (Waterings), Neil Jackson (Hillcrest), John Salt (Calton Moor House), Christine Robotham (Town End), Sylvia Clowes (New House), Margery Allen (Martin Hill)

SWINSCOE SCHOOL C1941

Louis Hill (Fleece) Jimmy Milward (Corn Park) Tommy Grindey (Littlemore) Graham Wallace (Common End) Bill Prime (Bull Gap) Ken Twemlow (The Mire) Geoff Prime (Bull Gap)
Middle: C.Tony Bradbury (Waterings) Joan Clowes (Latham Hall) Sheila Allan Post Office Mabel Howson (Fleece) Pamela (Evacuee) Joan Briden (Pub Cottage) Freida Hodge (Common End) Mary Briden (Pub Cottage) Tommy Clowes (The Green)
Front: Enid Cotton (Forest farm) John Bradbury (Waterings) Ron Twemlow (Hill End) Doris Mellor (The Cottage) George Prime (Bull Gap)
Derek Hodge (Common End) Arthur Mellor (The Cottage)

Miss Prince lived at the School House with Mr & Mrs Bailey

Swinscoe School c1951

Jimmy Bradbury (Waterings) Leslie Mellor (Cottage) Malcolm Ratcliffe (Common End) ?? Stanley Phillips (Ellis Hill) June Rowlinson (Little Moor) Cynthia Clowes (New House) Mrs Smith (1951-56)
Kevin White (Stanton) Bogue Carnegie (The Cliff), Ken Allen (Martin Hill), Jennifer Feeley (Croft), Nancy Bradbury (Waterings) Christine Robotham (Town End)
George Finney (?) John Robotham (Town End) Louis Hill (Fleece) John Salt (Calton Moor)
Alex Carnegie (Cliff) Keith Mellor (The Cottage) Peter Wallis (Common End) Sylvia Robotham (Town End) Nancy Morris (Calton Moor Farm) Rita Richardson (Bull Gap) John Clowes (?) Doreen Bradbury (Waterings)

Combined school trip to Trentham gardens

In the classroom
Sylvia Clowes, Ken Allen, George Finnet, Bogue Carnegie, Jim Bradbury, Doreen Bradbury, John Clowes, Mrs Smith
Neil Jackson. John Salt, Stan Phillips
Rita Richardson. Jennifer Feeley, Peter Wallis, Alec Phillips
Keith Miller, Michael Feeley, Dennis Salt, Glynis Wallis

John Salt, Miss Watkins, Malcolm Ratcliffe, Leslie Mellor, Jim Bradbury, Miss Smith
Neil Jackson. Bogue Carnegie, Nancy Morris, Jennifer Feeley, Nancy Bradbury, Rita Richardson, Sylvia Clowes, June Rowlinson Christine
Robotham, George Finney, John Robotham
Peter Wallis, Keith Mellor, John Clowes, Doreen Bradbury, Sylvia Robotham, Glynis Wallis, Michael Feeley, Denis Salt, Alec Carnegie,
Kevin White, Stan Phillips.

The schoolhouse was let to Mr and Mrs Bailey at 4s.0d. per week. When Miss M.H. Prince accepted the post of schoolmistress in 1936 she used to drive from her parents' home in Osmaston each day, in an old Mayflower car. This was a source of amusement to the children because Miss Prince was small and could barely be seen over the steering wheel. After a while the long drive became too much and she decided to lodge with Mr and Mrs Bailey. Miss Prince was a graduate of Manchester University and she set a high standard of teaching. She was also a strict disciplinarian, and believed in the use of the cane and that the pupils should sit up straight with their hands behind their backs whilst she was teaching. Through her methods of teaching, many of the pupils at Swinscoe School managed to obtain entrance to Ashbourne Grammar School - one as early as the age of nine. Some children were subjected to constant punishment, but no-one escaped entirely. Spare the rod and spoil the child, was the motto. Sometimes Miss Prince could be quite human. She would took the children round the village to study the animals and flowers and plants and there were dancing classes when the sound of "The Dashing White Sergeant" would echo round the schoolroom. The ancient gramophone would play other dances like "The Scotch in China" where three children would hold hands and weave in and out. Christmas was always a special time with parties and fancy cakes and balloons.

Miss Bull was the infant teacher and lived at Cauldon Low. She travelled to Swinscoe on her motor bike. A lady on a motor bike was a very unusual sight in those days. Mr Charles Phillips, of Ellis Hill, was one of the school managers for over thirty six years. In 1946, a letter of appreciation was sent to him, in recognition of his long service.

During the next 30 years, the number of pupils dwindled. A school photograph in 1948 shows sixteen pupils. As Swinscoe was a farming community, the children were allowed to take ten half days to help with the harvest. It was all done with rake and fork in those days and the farmers needed as much help as they could get.

In 1951, Mrs Helen Smith from Mayfield was appointed teacher and remained with the school until 1955. She is seen in a photograph, with her twenty pupils, taken around 1953. Mr J. Wilson held the post on an interim basis during 1955 and early 1956 until the arrival of Mr White. On the 23rd January 1956, Mr Graham White was appointed as the head teacher. In a letter from Mr White in 1995, he recalls: *"sixteen relatively happy pupils, aged four to fourteen years, in one classroom, with one teacher, working together as a family in what was quite a unique setting."* Among these pupils were: Doreen Bradbury, George Finney, Keith Mellor, Rita Richardson, John Robotham and Marilyn Clowes. Mr White recalls a school outing jointly with another school, and provided a copy of a photograph showing the teachers and pupils.

In 1957, the school was changed from all-age 4-14 years to primary-only 4-11 years and the senior pupils transferred to Waterhouses Secondary Modern School.

In 1958, the Staffordshire Education Authority proposed that the school should be closed and that the remaining four boys and two girls should be transported on a daily basis to the school at Calton. The Authority stated that the school was costing £2000 per year to maintain which, with only six pupils, was a waste of public money. The parish council opposed this recommendation because of the travelling time and effect upon the children. Mrs Pyatt of Oakamoor was appointed as teacher. One year later, on the 3rd November 1959, notice was given that the Education Authority would no longer maintain the Blore-with-Swinscoe C.E. Primary School. Mrs Pyatt held the post until the actual closure in 1960. Unfortunately, although the earlier registers and records have been retained in the Staffordshire Record Office, the more recent school logbook has disappeared and cannot be traced.

With the permission of Sir Ian Walker-Okeover, the school was converted to the village hall, so continuing its valuable service to the community.

Swinscoe School

The Dog and Partridge

DOG AND PARTRIDGE

The Dog and Partridge has served the inhabitants of Swinscoe, and travellers passing through, for almost three hundred years. The building was built around 1690. Although it has undergone a lot of change, it has always served refreshments, food and rest as an alehouse or inn. In 1768, an Act of Parliament was passed authorising the turnpike road up Swinscoe Hill. Firstly, the thirsty workmen building the road learned of the pleasures of the local brew. Then, those who used the new road, found at the top of the long steep hill, a haven of rest for themselves and their weary animals.

In 1792 and 1793 the proprietor was James Yates who served meals to his customers. A copy of a bill for meat was found under the floorboards of the building, during major reconstruction, in 1960.

Mr James Yates		To Joseph Hodkinson DR
Hart		0. 0.10.
Head & Pluck		0. 0. 4.
Beef	35	0.11. 8.
	9¹/₄	0. 2. 8.
Nov 30 "	12	0. 3. 0.
Dec 20 "	10¹/₂	0. 2. 6.
1793		
Janry 8 "	19	0. 6. 4.
		£1. 7. 4.

The landlord's wife, Mary Yates, dispensed the ale while her husband looked after the farm and the lime quarry and kiln across the road. The Dog & Partridge, like the pub at Calton Moor crossroads, charged 4d per pint for ale. In 1838, the inn also provided a nine-pin bowling alley for its customers.

The turnpike through Thorpe and Blore gradually became disused. In 1831, the passenger and mail coaches stopped using the old route and came up the hill through Swinscoe. The Dog & Partridge claimed more of the traffic coming up from Ashbourne and this caused the Red Lion Inn at Calton Moor to decline. With the increase in passing travellers, another public house was opened in the village. Unlike the Dog and Partridge it changed its name on three occasions, first it was called the "Golden Ram," then the "Spotted Cow" and then the "Golden Fleece". The building is still locally called the Fleece.

In late 1838, Anthony Stubbs, the local joiner builder, did a fair amount of work for Robert Yates. The bill totalled £18.16.5d. Anthony received payment in cash against this bill of £17.16.5d, plus 14s.9d for ale provided, and three days work valued at 6s.0d. He also carried out a large amount of subcontracted work at Robert Yates house, raising stable building and raising room, etc. for which he charged the main contractor Mr M. Vaughan £28.16s.0d. Members of the Yates family continued to act as victuallers and combined these activities with those of farming. Robert Yates was at the Dog & Partridge in 1850.

Frederick Thompson was at the Golden Fleece in 1884. In 1886, he was elected as one of the Overseers of the Poor, for the Parish. Benjamin Salt was licensee of the Fleece in 1888, but obviously he recognised that the local and passing trade was not sufficient to support two public houses so he moved to the Dog & Partridge around 1892 and took over from Sarah Yates. The Fleece closed its doors as a public house. In 1918, Benjamin Salt and his wife Eliza were still at the Dog & Partridge.

From 1939 John William Howson and his wife Gladys were at the Dog and Partridge and Bertram Smith was with them. When her brother John moved to the Fleece, Mabel Blore (née Howson) ran the pub. Grandma Howson lived with her and used to sit in a room at the back. Grandma never moved about very much, but she enjoyed visitors, particularly those who were willing to play cards. The Howson children from the Fleece liked accompanying their father, because Grandma always produced the "sweetie" tin.

In 1954, Mr Herbert James Thompson, and his wife and daughter, were living at the Dog and Partridge. Daughter Jean Maria married Graham Lomas at Swinscoe Chapel on the 4th December 1954.

Around 1958, the Dog and Partridge was acquired by George Gage. The cottage where the Briddons used to live, was incorporated into the structure and the motel was built. With its new size and image, including a tiny dance area and stage, it started to attract people from far and wide. The fame of its cabaret spread and stars such as Tommy Cooper, Jimmy Edwards, Ronnie Hilton, Hutch, Tommy Trinder, and Dianna Dors, gave performances here. Diana Dors became such a frequent visitor that the cottage next door became known as Diana Dors Cottage. As the years passed, the Dog and Partridge had many famous visitors: the Brazilian Football Team 1966, footballer Georgie Best and Miss England 1967. It also achieved some notoriety with customers such as the Kray Brothers from London gangland. Most of the members of the Mellor family worked at the Dog & Partridge and remember George Gage as a very charming rogue.

The business was bought by Mr and Mrs Kassam, who ran it for a few years.

David and Christine Coxon then became the owners and ran the pub, restaurant and motel for years. The electoral registers record their names, along with their daughter Tina, in 1984. David and Christine later moved to the Bluebell Inn on the main road near Tissington.

In 1987 it was bought by Mr and Mrs Stelfox. Not far away, the attractions of Alton Towers draw lots of visitors, and many of them call at the Dog & Partridge for accommodation and refreshment.

OTHER INNS

After a hard day's work in the fields, there have always been places where a man can go for a drink and enjoy the convivial atmosphere of an alehouse or inn. In 1598 there was an alehouse in Ilam called Getlifes, which was used by men from both sides of the river. Crossing the river by the stepping stones could be a perilous journey after a few pints, even though there was a handrail.

It was the usual practice for publicans to act as sureties for each other. John Getliffe is mentioned in the Quarter Session Reports as victualler or surety to the nomination of other victuallers.

In 1621 a man called George Gatclife or Getclife late of the parish of Bloore died. Actually there is a bit of a mystery concerning the death of George Gatcliffe - he disappeared and his wife claimed that he must be dead. This happened in February, the worst month of the year for bad weather and deep snow. Shortly afterwards his wife died and an inventory was made of the estate of George Gatcliffe against which Peter Tumpson claimed one pound for arranging the burial of Agnes Gatcliffe.

George Crychlow, a salter from Blore, used to call in at Getlifes on his way home from Longnor and decided to set himself up in that trade. George Crochle (Crichlow/Crichley) of Blore was licensed each year, for ten years, to keep an alehouse. He provided lodgings and entertainment for travellers. This classified him as a victualler, rather than a tippler who kept a mere drinking shop.

At Blore Hall in 1652 they had their own brewhouse, with two lead cauldrons for the ale, for the use of the Lord of the Manor, his visitors and his servants.

At the foot of the Swinscoe Hill, the Queens Arms and the Royal Oak were normally too far away from the Parish, especially with the hill to climb afterwards. One of these public houses, the Royal Oak, achieved some notoriety as standing on Hanging Bridge. Local folk lore attributes the name of the bridge to the hanging of Scottish Rebels, caught stealing, in 1745. Actually, the name of the bridge is much older than that. The name used in 1745 was just a perpetuation of an older name. The Hanging Bridge is mentioned, in 1710, as needing repair. Even earlier, among the Okeover Papers, it is referred to in Latin as the "bridge hanging (inclining) in direction of Acover".

According to Anthony Stubbs account book, John Smith was at the Ram (Golden Fleece), from 1834 to 1841. Obviously, the publican needed to protect his property and his ale because he was charged for installing guard windows. In addition, John Smith was charged 8d for repairing a cheese ladder because, like many others in the village, John Smith made his own cheese.

THE MILLS OF BLORE-WITH-SWINSCOE

According to the Domesday Survey, there was a Mill at Ilam with a rent of 10s.0d per year. This is confirmed by a terrier from the Burton Abbey Chartulary dated around 1113. This mill was on the Blore side of the river, near the site of the present bridge into Ilam village.

In the 13th to 14th Centuries, the mill of Ilam retained one sixteenth of all grain as payment for milling. At the Okeover Mill, the tenants were only required to give one twentieth of the grain.

The watermill is again mentioned, following the death of William (V) Bassett in 1563, as being in Blore. In 1609 the Miller Thomas Austen died and the inventory of his estate states that the rent of the mill was £3.6s.8d per year. The Austen family were not only millers but also carried on a considerable

The Queen's Arms. Hanging Bridge

The Royal Oak, Hanging Bridge

trade making buckets and tubs, and pewter and copperware. Thomas's son William took over as Miller. In 1612, it is recorded that the Parson of Blore collected 3s.4d in tithes for the mill called Ilam Mill in Blore Parish. After 30 years in the business, William sold out his milling business to a family called Bagnall and moved to Waterings Gate. Here his son continued to trade as a cooper and supply his wares to local people and travellers passing along the old road, below the Waterings, to Ashbourne. In 1656, the Bagnalls were tenants of the mill and mill meadow at a rental of £12. They continued as miliers until at least 1689.

A watermill is shown on the Blore side of the river, near Ilam, on William Senior's Map 1631 and is mentioned in 1652 as part of Blore Manor. In 1718, there is a rental for Blore of £7 but it states that the mill is not wrought [worked].

The mill was built on a diversion channel, called a leat, which cut across the corner of the river bend. A depression remains across the field, which at times of drought has been clearly identified as the old mill leat. The mill was built on a leat, rather than the river, so that it was possible to stop the flow for repairs. Around 1895, although the leat had been filled in, stepping stones were still in existence and a building on the site was being used as a cowhouse. On the Ordnance Survey Map dated 1929, a building is still shown on this spot. An old millstone was recovered from the site of the old mill and lies in the yard of the farm now called Ilam Meadows.

The only known windmill stood not far from the crossroads at Calton Moor, along the road towards Blore. In 1823, a serious accident occurred at the windmill when one of the sails struck Thomas Hill on the head, fractured his skull and killed him. His body was carried back to his home at Caldon Grange in Waterfall and laid to rest in Waterfall Churchyard. The windmill is marked on the earliest Ordnance Survey Map and on an estate map dated 1844. By 1894, only a cowhouse and barn remained to mark the site of the windmill; the barn remains and is still being used.

Nearby Calton Moor House was an Inn, then called "The Honest Miller". Innkeeping was not a full time occupation, especially in a remote location, and it may well be that the landlord was also the miller. The miller's opportunities for cheating were very great. What is more, he had the virtual monopoly of milling for all tenants who held land from the Lord of the Manor. The "Honest Miller" has been a joke since time immemorial; the man whose honesty could be attested by the hair growing from the palm of his hand!

There may also have been Mills in Swinscoe at one time or another; it was a long hard path from Swinscoe to Okeover or Ilam Mill. In the Rocester Chartulary, relating to the 13th Century, there is reference to land belonging to Owen the Miller. In the 16th Century, there is a reference to Ground Rent, paid by M. Berysford, for land in Walkemyl Close. The name of the close possibly indicates the place where a fulling mill stood. Fulling is a very important process used in the thickening of the wool by compressing the wool in water to shrink it and increase its density. This was initially carried out by treading by foot or beating with clubs. The process also cleaned the wool and by the use of Fullers Earth removed any oil in the wool before spinning. The fulling mill, or walkmill, had two wooden hammers attached to a revolving drum, on the lift-hammer principle. The revolving drum was driven by a water wheel, thus replacing the need for manual labour. Though not strictly a mill, as it did not involve the grinding process, it was similar in action to a watermill.

The monks of the ancient chapel in Swinscoe must have built the mill close to the stream in order to use water driven power. No evidence has been found of a possible location for such a mill.

TRADES, CRAFTS AND INDUSTRY

Trades and Crafts within the community were usually carried out in conjunction with normal farming activity. In the inventories, tools of the trade are always found along with livestock and farming implements. Tradesmen were vital to the farming community and were usually more affluent that their fellow farmers, probably because they were able to maintain some income from their trade during the winter months.

In the first half of the 16th Century, Richard Eyton (Eton), along with his son William, was carrying on the trade of wheelwright, which kept not only himself and his son busy, but also two labourers, William Flixon and John Grene. When Richard died, in 1544, he left a very extensive inventory of the tools of his trade: saws, axes, hatchets, adzes, augers, chisels, bills, spoke shaves and planes, together with timber and a half cwt. of iron. He had taken on his daughter Ann's son John Toples as an apprentice. Richard instructed his son to honour this obligation until John Toples was the age of 15 years. His son William carried on the business until 1553 when he also died. In addition to the wheelwright trade, they also owned a lot of livestock. Richard had 113 sheep, 2 pigs, 4 cows, 1 bullock, 3 heifers, 1 calf and 3 swine at his death. William left 91 sheep, 4 cows, 1 calf, 2 oxen, and 5 swine. As now, it was common to combine a trade or craft with farming. The Eytons probably carried on their trade on the site of the old mill down by the river.

Widow Joan Hood of Swinscoe, who died in 1628, left all the "instruments and toales belonging to a Wheelwright" to her sons Richard and Thomas; these most probably belonged to her husband. The presence of a wheelwright in the Parish, undoubtedly contributed to the finding that most of the farms owned a wagon. By comparison, in Leicestershire, according to Professor Hoskyns, during the same period very few farms owned their own wagon or plough. In the censuses of 1851 and 1861, Phillip Sutton, who married Hannah Stubbs of Swinscoe and went to live with her parents, is described as a wheelwright.

In the 17th Century, the mill was the site for another trade besides corn milling. The Austen family carried on the trade of cooper, making wooden ware, pewter and brassware. The inventory of Thomas Austen in 1609 shows his timber valued at £4.1s.0d, and pewter and brass valued at £2.10s.0d plus the tools of his trade. A wide variety of manufactured goods obviously represented his stock in trade: coffers, coffers with locks, barrels, wooden tubs, etc. The site was previously used by a wheelwright whose inventory included half a cwt. of iron and Thomas Austen also left an iron shewing horne, both of which confirm that there was a forge on the site. It also poses the possibility that there may have been a water-driven hammer. Thomas Austen kept seven head of cattle, ten sheep, two horses and a couple of swine. He had a large quantity of hay from the rich meadowland down by the river. There was more than one building on the site. The house was fairly large because two fetherbeds, one flockbed, four chaffe beds, two bedsteds with testers (ceiling of bed) and four bedsteds are mentioned. It is possible that some of these were for sale. The Austen family later moved to Waterings Gate and continued to operate their business as coopers.

A very important aspect of local farming was the ready availability of limestone for use as fertiliser, road making and rough walling. Lime was also used for whitewashing farm buildings and for making mortar. Within the Parish are a number of old lime quarries and kilns. Their sites are readily accessible for easy carting, and on suitable slopes from which the limestone could be fed into the kiln. They are generally close to woodlands to provide fuel for burning the lime. The earliest kilns probably date from around 1760.

In 1812, Brian Hodgson renewed a mining lease with Michael Saxelby of Mayfield that included the liberty to erect lime kilns and quarry limestone. On the 3rd September 1825, Chas. Weston of Ipstones wrote to Brian Hodgson giving notice of his intention to quit the lime kiln and quarry in Swinscoe. In 1844, the lime works, consisting of a lime kiln and quarry which was occupied by Mr Robert Yates, was put up for sale. At the time it was producing a rent of £30 per year.

In addition to lime quarrying, the Parish has seen extensive efforts to find lead, ironstone and coal. On the top of Hazleton Clump are signs of the search for lead ore. The disturbed land near the church cottage, at the entrance to Blore Dale, may be a site of similar searches. According to the Ordnance Survey Map of 1900, there is an old, now capped, lead mine on the lane to Calton opposite Latham House.

As early as 1375, the Rector of Blore, Ralph Hichecok, was accused by Sir Henry Brailsford of taking lead value £10 from Sir Henry's land in Grendon. In 1643-45, Mr John Gregson of Biggin employed miners to search for and mine lead in the Lordship of Blore. John Millington of Blore, was the Barmaster whose job it was to settle disputes over lead mining and William Yates of Blore succeeded him later during the period of the Civil War.

Where lead is found, sometimes copper is also found. In 1692, a series of leases were arranged for the opening of small copper mines in the neighbourhood of the Parish. Articles of Agreement in 1732 show that the mines in Swinscoe were sub-let to Jas., Duke of Chandos. It is interesting to note that in the

Bronze Age Top Low burial mound on Common End Farm, a small bronze clasp was found; whether the copper was from a local source is not known.

In 1804, Brian Hodgson leased an allotment of nineteen acres on Swinscoe Common to Michael Saxelby of Mayfield. The purpose of the lease was to allow mining for lead and coal, and included the erection of suitable buildings. On Forest Farm, then known as South Side Farm, there are two pieces of land called Upper and Lower Coal Pit Pieces. The two adjacent fields between the farm buildings of Ellis Hill Farm and New House Farm, are both called Colliers Ley. The depressions, which are still in evidence, are most probably the old mineshafts.

Another interesting activity in the Parish is indicated by the map of 1631. The map shows a field called Brickkiln Close, near to Blore Hall. As the Hall is built of old bricks, as well as the internal beehive oven, there is little doubt that bricks were made locally.

In 1861, according to the Census, three boys aged 11 to 14 and nine girls aged 9 to 17 were working as factory boys or girls. They were working at one of the textile mills on the River Dove. In 1784, A.Bradley & Co. opened a cotton spinning mill in Mayfield. In 1793, John Cooper also set up a mill.

Some of the children worked part-time but still went to Swinscoe School in the afternoons. When there was a clash of interest between work and school, the overlooker at the Mill insisted that the children change to Mayfield School. One family in particular, the Farmers, moved house from Swinscoe down to Mayfield rather than lose this chance of work.

In 1994, Mr and Mrs Woodley of the Old Post Office, Swinscoe, were working in one of their bedrooms. They found a cavity in a wall that contained an account book belonging to Anthony Stubbs, the carpenter, joiner and builder who carried out a lot of work locally. His activities included work on Blore Hall, Blore Rectory, Okeover Hall and Ilam Hall and he built the house and other buildings at The Waterings. In addition, he carried out many minor jobs including the building of coffins and making clothes' boxes; these boxes were mainly for children's use when they were away from home. He employed a couple of labourers and Sampson Stubbs, who was a highly regarded carpenter. Sampson was probably the builder of the screen and door to the vestry in Blore Church.

Mr J.W. Howson ran a large haulage business - an account can be found in the chapter describing the Fleece. A number of houses along the main road offered drinks and food to passing travellers: Calton Moor, The Yew, Mellor's Cottage, Rose Cottage and the Old Post Office.

PREHISTORIC BLORE-WITH-SWINSCOE

Hidden away from the main routes, with moorland only suitable for the hardy sheep, North East Staffordshire has always been sparsely populated. The people, who lived there, were scattered over the area in small farmholdings.

North East Staffordshire is well endowed with archaeological evidence of small settlements from the prehistoric period. A large number of burial mounds have been discovered in the area. Most of these burial mounds have remained undisturbed because the terrain is less suitable for ploughing and cultivation. By comparison, centuries of cultivation have destroyed much of the evidence in the Staffordshire Lowlands.

Within Blore-with-Swinscoe itself, a number of burial sites have been found, confirming that people have been living here for over 3500 years. Many of these burial sites were excavated during the middle of the 19th century. They are described in the book by Mr Bateman, "Ten Years Diggings in Celtic and Saxon Grave Hills in the Counties of Derby Stafford and York from 1848 to 1858".

An interesting discovery was made, in 1849. A burial mound was opened on Common End Farm, in Swinscoe by Mr T.W. Bateman, historian and archaeologist and Mr S. Carrington, a schoolmaster from Wetton. In this oval shaped mound thirteen human skeletons were found, with the burnt remains of a wild boar in the centre. The wild boar was probably a sacrificial offering - the swine was worshiped by people of Wales and Ireland during the same period. The human skeletons were from the Beaker Period of the Bronze Age, around about 2000 BC. Arrow heads and a bronze drinking cup were also found.

In 1929 the mound was opened again and one remaining skull and a number of other bones were found. These were sent to the British Museum who confirmed that they were 3000 to 4000 years old. The

Barn on the site of
the windmill

Millstone found on the site of Ilam Mill in Blore
Parish, near the present bridge into Ilam on the Blore
side of the river. The stone is now stands in the yard
of Ilam Meadows farm.

Ilam schoolmistress Mrs Beatty in
front of the barn which stands on
the site of the old watermill.

The Ginny Ring, Blore Hall

Lime kiln between Waterings and Blore

skull belonged to a 28 year old woman, about 5 feet tall. The male bones indicate a man of strong muscular build with a large head and strong jaw for ripping his food, about 5 feet 8 inches tall. They lived during the late bronze age, and belonged to the race that introduced the bronze leaf-shaped sword into Britain. A number of flint flakes and a polished green axe head were found which were presumed to be of the Early Bronze Age. After examination and recording the remains were placed in a wooden box with a bottle containing details of the discovery and restored to the original mound.

There is little evidence that can be related to life in Blore during the following two thousand years. However in the surrounding countryside a number of discoveries have been made relating to the period after Christ. The Romans had a camp near Okeover. There were Roman Burials in Ilam, where an urn of coarse pottery and a brass of Constantine the Great (291 AD) were found.

During the fifth and sixth centuries, the Anglo Saxons began their migration to England and gradually spread throughout the land. There is evidence that Anglo Saxons settled in Blore. An iron ring of Anglo Saxon origin was found in one of the burial mounds. According to the Domesday Survey, four Saxon Thegns held Blore prior to 1086. The base of the cross in the churchyard is generally accepted as of Saxon origin.

In the 8th, 9th and 10th Centuries, the Vikings invaded large parts of North and Eastern England which became known as Danelaw. Some of the invaders travelled up the River Trent to Newark and on into Derbyshire. There is proof of their visits in the cremation cemeteries near the river. Blore-with-Swinscoe is just across the River Dove, near the extreme borders of Danelaw. The origin of the name Blore is doubtful; it possibly means "windy place". The name Swinscoe is of Scandinavian origin, "swin" means swine and "scoe" was Norse for wood.

FARMING IN BLORE-WITH-SWINSCOE

The Limestone Moorlands of North East Staffordshire, with shallow top soil and a short growing period, provide good sweet grass for grazing livestock but are difficult to cultivate. Within the parish the soil varies. On the highest ground it is dry due to the limestone rock. On the lowest ground it is wet with a subsoil of clay. In the middle level it tends to be wet due to drainage from the upper level of limestone.

Two ploughs are recorded for Blore in the Domesday Book 1086. One plough belonged to the Lord of the Manor and the other was shared by two farmers. The plough itself had a shaped board that cut the soil and turned a slice over in a continuous furrow. The team of oxen which pulled the plough were difficult to turn so the land was divided into separate strips of land, normally a furlong in length, each held by the lord or a villager. On the long narrow strips of land, oats and sometimes corn were planted on the drier ridge, and peas in the furrow. In 1248, there was an agreement between William de Audley of Blore and Sir Hugh de Okeover which refers to the carrying of hay and corn. The ploughman ploughed about an acre a day, in comparison with the present acre an hour.

Evidence of ridge and furrow ploughing, probably in some cases dating back before Domesday to the Anglo-Saxon period, still remain in many places in the parish. There is evidence on the slopes below The Waterings Farm, within an observable enclosure and in the field sloping down from Hall Flats in Swinscoe. In the field on the Okeover side of Blore Hall, the 'S' shaped curvilinear form is of the type that was formed by the bladed plough, rather than a plough with simple rod, to penetrate the surface. The ridge and furrow on the slopes on Waterings Farm, and at Hall Flatts, obviously took advantage of the sloping terrain to use the furrows for drainage.

In the 13th Century much of the land in Swinscoe was owned by the Okeover family. Thirteen tenants are recorded as holding twenty eight bovates of land. In 1241, Sir Hugh de Okeover leased two bovates of land in Swinscoe to Richard de la Forde.

The early settlement was centred around the flatter hill top; its nucleus coincides with the centre of the present village. This can be seen by examining the field boundaries, with the later extensions to the North West and South in straighter lines.

When Sir Hugh de Okeover got into financial trouble he sold off a lot of his land to the Abbot of Rocester. Sir Hugh retained the Lordship of the Manor, and the right to hold court. His successors preserved these rights into the 20th Century, even though the Okeover proportion of the land was only a

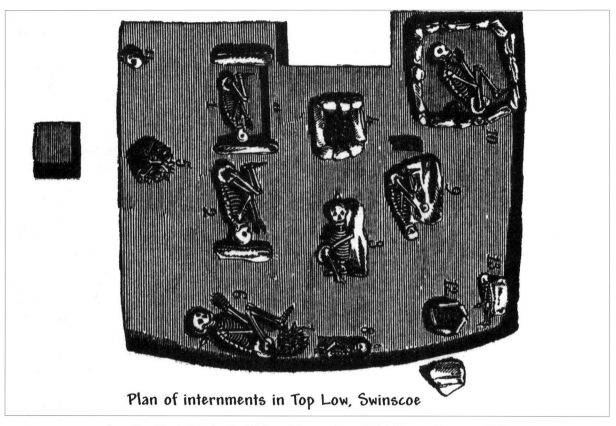

Plan of internments in Top Low, Swinscoe

from 'Ten Year's Digging in Celtic and Saxon Grave Hills', Thomas Bateman, 1861

Mr Mellor with scythe

Norman Richard Phillips with Lincoln Long Wool sheep

small part of the total in Swinscoe.

The Abbot and Monks of Rocester built a chapel in Swinscoe, and farmed the land there for 300 years. The Abbots and their tenants gradually reclaimed more and more of the Swinscoe woodland and commons. Some of the common land was enclosed for pasture. In 1302, Roger the Abbot of Rocester claimed that three acres of common in Swinscoe had been wrongfully taken from him. In 1438 Henry the Abbot sued Robert Tomkynson, of Caldon, and John Alynforde, of Combrigge, for breaking into his close at Swynysco. He accused them of cutting down his trees, and underwood, and depasturing cattle on his corn and grass.

In 1538, Rocester Abbey was dissolved and 320 acres of land was acquired by Henry Talbot, son of the Earl of Shrewsbury. When Henry died in 1596, he left three houses and over 200 acres of land in Swinscoe, Blore and Rocester, to his two daughters Gertrude and Maria.

From the beginning of the 16th century, oats are frequently mentioned in the probate inventories of the period. In 1609 Thomas Austen the miller of Ilam Mill in Blore Parish died. He left one corne stacke of oats estimated to be fyftie thraves (12 sheaves = 1 thrave) at a value of 50s.0d. His land lay in the more fertile land down by the river, and his hay in all places was valued at £4.10s.0d. In April 1689, from the previous year's tithes and crops, the parson left thirty-three strikes (bushels) of oats at 14d a strike. Richard Hood, in 1538, left to his son, John, "one grett ark to put corne in". These great bins, for storing the oats, are commonly found in the inventories, along with dasons (vessel for preparing oatmeal). Oats formed the staple diet of the hill folk, providing porridge for breakfast and oatbread which was eaten with homemade butter and cheese, plus an onion from the garden. Oatmeal cakes were sometimes toasted in front of the fire using a small fork with a long handle. This fork was called a pickle. Such a fork was found in a Romano-British burial mound at Wetton. It is probably from the pickle that the name pikelet was derived - the muffin that is toasted on a fork.

The value of a diet full of fibre is now being recognised by modern dieticians. It was obviously a contributory factor in the hardiness and health of the local people. They needed to be strong and healthy - most of the work was only accomplished by toil and sweat. Peas are not mentioned in any of the wills or inventories. However, it was reported that stacks of peas were burned down, during the siege of Blore, in the 1450s. Arable farming provided the food on which the inhabitants subsisted but it was the rearing of animals that provided the income. In 1447, Sir Sampson Meverell of Throwley was accused of taking twelve oxen, and twelve cows from Blore Hall.

In the Probate Inventories of the parish, every family owned some form of ox, cow or calf. The word most commonly used for cows in the 16th century inventories was kyn. Twinters were beasts two winters old. Stirks were young bullocks or heifers, between one and two years old. Even poor old Alice Philip, who lay in bed for 5 to 6 years until her death, "helpyd with charyte by hur son Henry," owned a calf and three sheep - but little else. Three of the twenty-two inventories did not include sheep. Giles Button in 1543 left twenty head of cattle; with such a large herd he probably concentrated his farming solely on cattle. Richard Hood in 1538 left nine cattle, and a poor farmer John Hamson who died in 1598, left only two cows, one bullock, a year old calf and a half share in a calf. These two may have only stocked cattle. Their inventories were taken in February and March and they may have sold their sheep at the previous Michaelmas, before the start of the winter. It was common to sell off surplus sheep, which would have been difficult to feed, during the winter months. This may also account for the larger than normal amount of money owing to Richard Hood - 20s.0d and 23s.4d due from the Abbot of Rocester, £6.0s.0d Agnes Turner and 25s.4d others.

Around 1640, Gilbert Markham declared that the cattle bred in Staffordshire were the best in England. The cattle were of two main types, the Staffordshire Longhorns and the black moorland cattle. Dairy farming provided the milk, cheese and butter as food for the family. It was used for additional income by sale locally, and in the market at Ashbourne. Thomas Austen, the miller, in 1609 left butter and cheese valued at 6s.0d. Obviously Richard Hood of Swinscoe was producing for sale. He left butter and cheese valued at £5.0s.0d, which is more than the normal household needs; his inventory was taken towards the end of the winter in February 1637. In 1689 the milk house at Blore Hall contained churns, tubs and vats for making cheese, and a cool larder for storing the dairy produce. The tithe small dues payable in Calton and Swinscoe (except Ellis Hill) was one penny for every milking cow.

In the earliest inventories, before 1550, the value of cows was around 15s.0d. The value rose steadily in the third quarter of the century to double that price. Further price rises followed, reaching £2.6s.8d by 1598. The rise in values in the second half of the century was, undoubtedly, related to the bad harvests in 1557, 1558, 1586 and 1588, and then between 1591 and 1596. These caused serious food shortages and inflation. All prices have been derived from inventories taken at different seasons of the year. They do broadly agree with figures from other sources.

In the 17th century, the rise in value of cows was not as dramatic as it had been in the 16th century. At the beginning it remained relatively steady around £2.10s.0d. By 1630 it was past the £3.0s.0d mark, and by the end of the century had risen to around £3.10s.0d each.

Fully grown oxen were widely used as beasts of burden, and for pulling ploughs and hay wains. The wains were very simple open carts. They usually appear in the inventories with ploughs, coulters and shurs (iron plough blades), harrows, yokes (for coupling two oxen) and teams (harness chains). During the 16th Century, eight out of twenty-two inventories show no plough. Two of these belonged to tradesmen, Richard and William Eton, two to widows, Alice Phylyp and Margery Hood, and the other to the parson, John Ward. The absence of ploughs in the remaining three cases, would seem to indicate that not all farmers grew their own oats. Perhaps they borrowed their neighbour's ploughs, or hand cultivated just sufficient land to produce their own food and bought or traded for the rest. An ancient custom in the Blore area survived into the early 20th century. At certain festivals, it was the custom for a group of young men to haul a "fool-plough" through the village, performing a silly play and begging for pennies. Woe betide anyone not making a contribution, their garden would be ploughed up - there is no record of the threat being carried out.

The need to cultivate the land, even though normal facilities were not available, did not stop the hardy cottagers. It is told that an old resident, with his wife in the harness and him pushing, used to plough their land in this most basic fashion in the mid 1800s.

Most farms owned a horse or two, called cawpuls in those days, for pulling the haywains, and as pack animals. Although the transition was slow, particularly in such a hilly area, horses gradually replaced oxen, as the beast of burden. Saddle horses called nags were means of getting around the farm and to the market, but only in a couple of cases are bridle and saddle mentioned. In 1689 William Yates, the Parson of Blore, owned eight pieces of horse flesh valued at £20 - horse flesh indicated live horses, not meat for eating.

The rearing of poultry and their eggs have always been a source of income as well as food for the family; hens and geese are to be found everywhere. A local farmer tells of keeping chickens during wartime and feeding them on fishmeal. In spite of the resultant fishy flavour, he was still able "to earn a few bob".

Sheep have always been an important part of farming in the Moorlands. Sheep were known by a number of different names: sheersheep, gelde sheep, oyes (ewes), hoggs (6 months up to shearing) and weders (wethers - male sheep). In the late 18th century, there were two main breeds of sheep; the small Gritstone blackface sheep with horns and the heavy white-faced Limestone breed. The black-faced short horned sheep provided a coarse fine wool, which was especially useful to felters and hatters. The wool was also used within the home, probably as part of a home industry. In 1698, a spinning wheel is recorded in the inventory of William Bentley of Swinscoe. By the middle of the 19th century, the selection had been improved and the principal breeds were Leicesters, either purebred, or crossed with Cotswolds or Lincolns. The large ancient pastures of Blore were obviously used as sheep runs. On the Croxden estates, which included neighbouring Musden Grange, in the 15th Century there were over seven thousand sheep. Wool was fetching between twenty and thirty marks a sack. In 1573, the inventory of Elizabeth Bassett, widow of William (V) Bassett, Lord of Blore, shows three hundred and forty sheep. The Parson of Blore John Ward, who died in 1577, left one hundred and seventy one sheep. Other farmers in the parish kept from one to one hundred and twenty sheep. The value of sheep during the 16th Century changed very little. Early in the century the value was around two or three shillings each, and by the end had only risen a few pence, to just over three shillings. However, the importance of sheep is clearly shown, by the way in which the farmers made bequests of sheep to their families, children, godchildren, friends and relations.

The evidence from the 17th Century is sparse but the value of sheep appears to have fluctuated wildly; 2s.9d in 1607, 4s.6d in 1610, 6s.4d in 1620, 2s.3d in 1623, 5s.0d in 1665, 4s.0d in 1684 and then down to 3s.6d in 1689. In general, however, through the 16th and 17th Centuries, prices rose. This is shown by the growing incomes of the farmers of the parish. The values of inventories increased, and their standard of living improved. This is clearly seen by the greater number of household goods. But it was still a hard life.

From 1375 to 1601, all the land in Blore was held by the Bassetts. Elizabeth Bassett inherited the land and in 1618 married Sir William Cavendish, later Duke of Newcastle. The Duke commissioned a survey of his land, and the map and survey drawn by William Senior shows in detail the park and each field and piece of land.

The Land farmed from Blore in 1631 was as follows:

	Acres	R	P
Hall	5.	0.	0.
Blore Park	212.	0.	0.
Harlton Pasture	32	0.	0.
The Waterings	53.	0.	20.
The Waterings Meadow	25.	2.	0.
The Waterings Pasture	17.	0.	30.
Bloar Dale	32.	0.	0.
Brickkiln Close	28.	3.	20.
Hinckley	15.	0.	17.
Hinckley Spring	32.	3.	0.
Hinckley Head	1.	3.	20.
Hinckley ...Thisle Close	28.	3.	0.
Bloare Oxe Leasow	31.	2.	0.
The Cote Close & Parson Stubbs	23.	2.	20.
Robert Croft		0.	20.
Robert Croft?		2.	20.
Rushon Pingle			
Kent Rushon Pingle			
Grinley Meadowe	22.	3.	20.
The Parsons Grinley Meadowe	6.	2.	10.
Grinley Pingle		2.	30.
Parsons Yarde	3.	2.	16.

In 1644, the Duke was Commander of the Royalist Forces in the North of England. The Royalists were defeated at Marston Moor and the Duke fled into exile to the Continent. All his lands were confiscated by the Commonwealth and the land in Blore was leased to Richard Mellor. When King Charles II returned to the throne, the Duke returned to England and reclaimed his land. However, Richard Mellor continued to farm a large part of Blore. In 1678, he was paying £161.10. 0d for Blore Hall, the Demesne, Grindlow and Thisle Close. The rest of the land was rented out to various smallholders - for a total yearly rental of £99.4s.4d. They were: Phillip Austin, James Yates, Henry Mellor, Ralph Phyny, Wm Yates, Wm. Millington, John Stubbs, Wm. Kent, Wm. Bukham.

The 18th Century was the century of basic improvement in farming methods and good farming practice. Some of the land in Swinscoe was still owned by the Okeover family. For greater control over their lands, and the rents they collected, they changed their tenancy agreements from number of years to a year-to-year basis. The rents in the parish varied considerably. In 1776, Thomas Hodgkinson was paying 15s.0d per acre for 147 acres in Woodhouses. Almost a century later, Samuel Archer, of Swinscoe, was paying £2.0s.0d per acre for 20 acres (plus an additional £20.0s.0d per acre for ploughing up the Hill). To ensure their tenants good farming practice, each tenancy agreement contained clauses specifying minimum requirements: *"not to break more than 'n' acres in any one year...... not to keep any part in tillage more than 3 years successively......... in one of the 3 years the same shall be in summer fallow........ shall sow 12lbs of clover seeds in the 3rd year of tillage"*.

Fetching the water from the well

The well in Town End Lane

Lime was widely used as manure. Lime kilns were built in all parts of the parish, usually into the side of a hill, close to a quarry. The bottom of the lime kiln was covered with a layer of sticks, with lump coal on the sticks. Then a layer of small lime stones was added and another layer of sticks, and lump coal, and so on, until the kiln was full. The size of the limestone was increased on the way up the layers. The top was covered with the old rough lime, plus any stone not properly burnt through on previous burnings. This waste was made into a putty-like substance, with water, and plastered over the top layer of limestone, to keep in the heat. When lighted, great heat would gradually spread through the kiln, burning the stone in the process. After the fire had burnt out and cooled down, carts were backed under the arched area of the kiln. The lime was taken from the bottom of the kiln, with any unburnt stones being thrown to one side. Carts were loaded with shovels, and then taken to the farms, where the load was tipped into heaps, and left to swelt (breakdown into powder). This powdered lime was loaded and taken into the field for spreading from the back of the cart with a shovel. A typical example of such a kiln stands on the right, halfway between Blore and where the Waterings cattle grid used to be, at the bottom of the dip. It can be easily spotted with its fireplace arch built of brick.

These continued improvements made the land sweeter for the grazing cattle and sheep. The amount of dairy farming increased. Butter and cheese are mentioned, directly, or indirectly, in most of the inventories. Ralph Smith in 1730 left cheese valued at £12.0s.0d. He also had a great variety of dairy equipment; milking pails, tubs, churns, cheese presses, cheese shelves and a cheese cratch (a rack for curing cheese).

From 1700 to 1740, prices of cows fluctuated between £1.15s.0d and £3.0s.0d. Then a series of bad harvests and severe winters forced prices up to £4.0s.0d and £4.10.0d.

The exceptionally hard winter at the beginning of 1748 caused great losses of beef and dairy cattle. Tenants on the Okeover estates suffered badly, and were asking for reduction in rents. It was not only the farmers that suffered. Three years later, the Lord of the Manor of Swinscoe, Leake Okeover, fled to the Continent to avoid his debts. This was partially as a result of reduced rentals and increased costs, but also his excessive overspending. All the horses and cattle were sold and the deer reduced in number, to provide money to satisfy his creditors. His wife, with help from his agents and friends, sorted out his problems. The debts were repaid and he was able to return to England in 1753.

Cash became increasingly more important, and bequests were made in money, rather than giving cattle and sheep. Every inventory mentions "money in the purse". Thomas Smith in 1745 left "Purs and apperell and Gold in the Cofer £14.0s.0d".

There was not much money for the workers. Ordinary labour such as digging, walling or tiling, was paid at 8d or 10d per day. Even the more skilled thatcher received only 1s.0d to 1s.3d per day. In 1793 the price paid for beef varied between 3d and 4d per pound. With such prices, the farm workers could rarely afford meat. Many other foods were unlikely to be part of their diet, unless they grew their own. According to accounts kept in 1765 by Wm. Rowbotham, Parish Clerk of neighbouring Calton, the price of 2 lbs potatoes was 2d, 2 lbs butter 1s.0d and a cheese 1s.9d. There would always be the dilemma of whether to use their home-made produce themselves or sell it at Ashbourne or Leek Market. It is no wonder that oats and oatcake were the staple diet for the Moorland people.

As the 19th century progressed, there was some improvement in wages - but not much. The poorer families used to rely upon farm labouring as their source of income. By the 1860s, they started to send their children down to the cotton mills of Mayfield, as factory boys and girls. The wages of factory hands were higher and less dependent upon the season than farmworkers. The children tended to stay at the mills into adulthood. Three of the families: Allen, Birch and Farmer all sent their children to Mayfield, and later, each one of the families moved down the hill away from Swinscoe. In part, they were forced to move because the Factory required that those children who were still attending school should change their school to be closer to work.

The farming community for centuries had relied upon the poorer members of the community, as well as their own large families, to provide cheap labour. This move away from the land, and loss of cheap labour, undoubtedly affected the local farmers. The move, away from Swinscoe caused some of the decline in population of the parish. In 1861, the population was 248 but in each of the following decades it reduced so that, by 1901, it was only 176.

In the 18th to 19th centuries, the horse began to play a greater role. With a history going back almost a thousand years, hunting, and riding for pleasure still went on, in and around the parish. The Throwley Hunt was still going strong in the early 1900s. The Okeover family and their Royal visitors, even now, still enjoy this beautiful countryside on horseback. Of course, the farmer rode to market on his horse. Rector Bayliffe rode to St. Bartholomew's Church from his home in Ashbourne each Sunday. Rector Young did the rounds of his parishioners on his horse. The stage coaches and the carrier carts, and the waggoners, all passed through Blore and Swinscoe. Horses replaced the oxen to pull farm wagons and ploughs and harrows. In the early 14th century, reference is made to "oxen and horses of the plough". When they installed the Ginny Ring at Blore Hall, it was a horse that provided the power. It was with great pride that horses were specially bred, reared, cared for, groomed and exhibited. A photograph of Mr Prime shows his prize winning horse and cart at Ashbourne Show in 1913. On New House Farm, and on Forest Farm, prize certificates still adorn the old barns and stables, preserving memories of awards at local shows.

Elsewhere in Staffordshire, the 19th century saw the adoption of mechanical reapers and traction engines. There was little need for such technology in Blore-with-Swinscoe, with the relatively small area of arable or meadow land. The harvesting was mainly carried out manually by scythe, sickle and flail. A photograph of Mr Clifford Mellor of The Cottage, Swinscoe, shows him wielding a scythe. At Blore Hall a horse-wheel, known locally as a Ginny Ring, was built. According to John Weller in his "History of the Farmstead", a horse-wheel driven by two horses could thresh, and dress, one hundred and twenty bushels in a day. This meant that the work could be done in days rather than months. The use of a flail only produced seven bushels a day, although it did provide work for the farm workers during the winter months. Alternative feeds for cattle decreased the dependence on hay, and, in doing so, released more pasture for cattle. Slowly, but surely, there was an increase, and an improvement, in cattle farming.

In the late 18th Century, three quarters of the land in Swinscoe was owned by Brian Hodgson, Esquire. In 1781, the seven tenants of Mr Hodgson paid £4.7s.0d in land tax, out of the total £6.14s.3d assessment for the whole of the Township of Swinscoe. The remaining quarter of the land was held by five others: W. Okeover, John Alcock, John Heath, Thomas Smith and Thomas Hodgkinson.

In a survey carried out in 1802, Mr Hodgson still held the same proportion of land: 450 acres of the 604 acres, in Swinscoe.

Around 1197/8, one of the earliest surviving documents confirmed the rights of the villagers of Swinscoe to use the common land. Over the centuries the smallholders and villagers used the common land for grazing cows or sheep, and the woods for foraging their pigs and their chickens. The produce from the commons often supplied the income that made the difference between poverty and starvation. There was also some encroachment on the Common Land by squatters struggling to survive.

The ancient rights were maintained until the beginning of the 1800s. The Lord of the Manor, Haughton Farmer Okeover and other landowners, Brian Hodgson, Charles Bill and John Smith, got together. They decided to enclose three hundred and sixty acres of common land: Swinscoe Common, Swinscoe Moor, Town Fields and others. The Napoleonic Wars gave them the excuse for taking advantage of every available piece of land. The landowners stated that the common lands were incapable of any significant improvement, and requested that they should be divided, and enclosed. A notice, of intention to enclose the commons was posted in the church porch for three Sundays in August 1801. Parliament was asked for permission to enclose, a Bill was brought and, in 1802, the Act was passed. As the landowners held more than 75% of the land in the village, objections from the villagers were likely to be ignored by the Commissioners. However, the task of assessment and measurement of the land, and its allocation, was a long, complicated and fraught affair. It was not until 1815 that the final award was made. However, the enclosure of the common land also involved the redistribution of the land tax assessment. This affected the smallholders, and squatters. It was not until 1826, that the smallholders agreed to pay their proportion of the land tax assessment and the wrangling finally died away.

According to a survey carried out in January 1802 before the Act, there were sixty eight milking cows and ninety sheep kept in the village. Of the 604 acres of occupied land, 56 acres were under the plough and 120 acres were mowed for pasture. In the previous year, prices had reached a peak; oats were selling at 37s.0d. However, there was a lull in the War, thanks to the signing of a Treaty of Peace, and prices had dropped. Oats were down to 20s.4d. With the resumption of hostilities, prices rose again. Ten years later, the price of oats had doubled to 44s.6d a quarter.

Even though the final award was years away, the landowners immediately began to take advantage of the additional acreage, and not just for agricultural purposes. In 1804, Brian Hodgson leased 19 acres, on Swinscoe Common, to Michael Saxelby of Mayfield, for mining lead ore and coal. A reminder of this attempt to find coal remains in the old field names: Upper and Lower Coalpits, Colliers Lea and Colliers Pingle. There are depressions in fields on New House Farm which are undoubtedly the remains of the coal shafts. The lease was renewed in 1812 for a further nineteen years. Saxelby was given a licence to erect the necessary buildings and machinery to mine coal. The mining of coal was not successful. In the middle of the 19th century, most of the coal was brought from Kingsley Moor on the backs of mules and asses.

Brian Hodgson put up the rest of his Swinscoe Estate, of 604 Acres for sale by auction. After prolonged negotiation, the sale fell through due to problems of title. Certain deeds were missing for the period 1685 to 1744 and there were problems regarding the non-payment of tithes for Ellis Hill Farm.

Following the War with France, and the Battle of Waterloo in 1815, there was a post-war slump which continued for more than twenty years. It was during this period that three government commissions were set up to study ways of beating the depression. They were unable to come up with satisfactory solutions. The farming community suffered badly from the lower prices. Eventually in 1829 the Hodgson estate allowed a 10% reduction in rentals, and these new rents continued at the lower level for at least eight years. In order to compensate for the loss of income, the Hodgson estate restricted the assistance given to individual farmers for repairs and extensions. Such luxuries as wining and dining the farmers on half-yearly rent collecting days were restricted, and the expenses claimed by the agent to the estate were severely curtailed.

The Swinscoe Estate remained with the Hodgson family until the death of Rev Edward Hodgson, in 1844. The estate had been increased in size by the enclosure of common land. It comprised 835 acres, a limekiln, and a limestone quarry, and was split and sold off in lots. Part was sold to the Okeover estate. Ellis Hill was sold to the Ecclesiastical Commission. Around 1866, both the Okeover Estate and the Ecclesiastical Commission, (under the name of the Rectory of Shelton), took advantage of land improvement acts. They carried out substantial drainage schemes in Swinscoe. For Ellis Hill, the work was carried out under the supervision of a local man - Mr Fielding. It was a difficult task in limestone country. Kevin White reports that he has found evidence of this early drainage in his fields on New House Farm.

The burnt remains of a swine were found in a burial mound on Common End Farm, dating back three thousand years. The name of the village of Swinscoe could refer to Swine. It seems appropriate that, as late as 1840, at least four farms had their own piggeries: Common End, Forest, Leesows and New House. There is also an old pigsty at Blore Hall.

In Staffordshire, as a whole, sheep farming was on the decline; 317,000 in 1870, down to 210,000, in 1914. However, in the Moorlands, there was still a concentration upon producing high quality sheep. More sheep were kept for mutton to feed the growing population of the towns. There were weekly sheep markets at Leek and Ashbourne. Many farmers bought sheep at the sheep fairs for fattening and selling; such a fair was held close by Calton Moor House. The most popular breeds were the Oxford and the Lincoln Long Wool Sheep. Many farmers in the area belonged to the Leek Agricultural and Horticultural Society. During the years 1906 to 1911, at the Leek Agricultural Show, farmers from the parish of Blore-with-Swinscoe won the cup in each successive year, for the best Long Wool Ram Lamb. There is a photograph, taken in 1911, of a young boy, Norman Phillips, of Calton Moor House, with two prize-winning sheep.

Dairy farming was an important aspect of Moorland farming. The best milking cows produced around three gallons a day. Three gallons a day could produce three pounds of cheese, at about £3.0s.0d per cwt. In 1802, in Swinscoe, there were sixty nine milking cows, giving a fair potential income to farmers of the village. Around 1860, when the Gallimores farmed Ellis Hill they milked thirty cows, and in summer made four cheeses a day. Not all the milk was turned into cheese and butter. The consumption of milk itself had steadily risen, and milk was carted to Ashbourne and Leek. The moorland farmers always had the problem of distance from major centres of population. By the end of the century, milk trains were running on a regular daily basis, to take the milk to large cities. Egginton Junction, near Burton on Trent, became a collection point for milk, for the 150 mile journey to London.

At Derby cattle market, in March 1893, the prices were:

Beef	6d-6¹/2d per lb
Mutton	7d-8d per lb
Veal	7¹/2d-8d per lb
Pigs	10/6d-11/3d per score

At the cheese fair, in the same month, the average price for cheese was between 50s.0d and 55s.0d. cwt.

In October 1911, the local farmers held a meeting at Swinscoe School, under the chairmanship of Mr Charles Philips to discuss the rising prices. They agreed to form a local association, for the wholesale purchase of corn and cereals.

During the Depression of the 1930s, farmers had serious problems in finding a market for their milk, and often had problems getting paid. The National Farmers Union were responsible for encouraging the formation of the Milk Marketing Board. This ensured that the farmers had a ready market. There was a guarantee of payment and the milk cheques were usually received by the last week of month. Churns are no longer used to hold the milk. Nowadays, bulk tankers collect, on alternate days, which saves labour and reduces the cost of transport.

During the War, and time of rationing, butter and cheese making was prohibited. Butter was still made illicitly and sometimes sold on the black market. The wartime period saw the appearance of the Ministry of Agriculture Inspectors. Their task was to identify evidence of poor farming, such as fields over-grown with thistle and weeds. Their job was also to ensure that farmers ploughed sufficient land to grow corn and potatoes.

After the Second World War, there was an increase in the number of cows kept on the farms. Although milking machines had appeared pre-war, they did not come into general use until the 1950s. This innovation meant that one person could do all the milking, instead of the several people needed previously. Now the machines automatically remove themselves from the cows, which further reduces the labour involved. Even the feeding of cattle has become computerised with the feed being automatically calculated on the basis of the cow's yield.

The area of activity in agriculture which seems to have grown the most in recent years is the production of paper. Mounds, and mountains, of paper and forms are produced, not only for British bureaucrats, but for those of the Common Market as well. Many things have changed, and continue to do so. The one thing that, so far, neither scientist nor bureaucrat can change is THE WEATHER.

NAMES OF PLACES, FARMS AND FIELDS

The most commonly accepted meaning of Blore is "a windy place", which illustrates its position very well. Blore can also mean "a blister" or "top of a hill", which is also descriptive of its location. Like most names, the spelling has varied over the centuries: Blore, Bloware, Bloor, Bloore, Bloer, Blower and Blora. The ecclesiastical parish is sometimes referred to as Blore Ray. This may be a corruption of the sound of Blora. Most authorities suggest that the Ray could be derived from Roy or Roi meaning King, but as Blore was never held of the King this is unlikely.

The name Swinscoe means Wood of Swine. Scoe is a word from Scandinavia meaning wood or forest; Swin is a common word throughout Northern Europe meaning swine. Swin could refer to the wild swine that roamed the woods of Swinscoe - the burnt remains of a swine were found in Top Low burial mound, indicating special significance for the swine. It could refer to a landowner, or tenant, called Swin. The name Swin (Swein) appears in Domesday at Wootton and in six other places in Staffordshire.

With three exceptions, the names of the Farms themselves are only relatively recent. Only the names of Blore Hall, Ellis Hill and The Waterings are found in documents before the early 1800s. The fields and strips of land were each given a name, and farmed as individual units. They were not grouped together into major contiguous units until the enclosure in 1815, and the sale of the Hodgson Estate in 1844.

Names of fields, and farms, are often quite simple to explain. They usually relate to physical features or to the owners or tenants of the land and they are most frequently in the form of two words. Swinscoe stands at 1000 feet, above sea level, at the top of the hill from Mayfield and Ashbourne. It is no surprise to find the name Hill End Farm. Relative positions, are shown by Back of the Hill, Near Side, Far Side and Hill Side and Common End.

Swinscoe was an old Township, with well-marked boundaries. It has Green Farm, The Green and Town End Farm, and Little, Big, Upper and Lower Town Meadows. Extensive woodland covered the Swinscoe area. The plantations still remain, with names like Swinscoe Wood, Big Wood, Little Wood, Rough Wood, Long Wood and Lime Tree Piece.

One of the most ancient and interesting names is Low. The prehistoric lows in the Parish have retained the ancient Gothic word low in Top Low, Upper, Lower and Back Low on Common End Farm, and Dun Low behind The Waterings. There is the Netlows which, at one time, was corrupted to the Nettles; the upper part of Swinscoe Hill is still known as Netlows. There are a wide variety of names for the different enclosures: Field, Meadow, Pasture, Croft, Close, Land, Piece, Paddock, Ley (lea), Pingle, Acres, Green, Greaves (bushwood), Slang (small piece). Piece is very frequently used, and refers to the time when the Common was enclosed, and pieced off. Leasows is the old Saxon word for pasture and in both Blore and Swinscoe this name appears. Ilam Meadows in Blore used to be called Ox Leisure or Ox Leasow Farm and there is The Leasowes, or Leisures, in Swinscoe.

There are names which describe the type of vegetation or a natural feature: Withy Meadow, Rushy Meadow, Vetch Piece, Rye Grass Piece, Ferny Ley, Dry Knobs, Clay Pit Piece, Saw Pit Piece and Bull Pit. A number of fields are named after people; Millington's Close, Salt's Nursery, Blackshaw's Field, Hurd's Common Piece, Heath's Croft, Baddaley Meadow, Woolley's Croft, Dennis's Common Piece; and their occupation: Parson's Flat, Smithy Field and Colliers Ley.

Upper and Lower Coalpits are reminders of the attempt to find coal and there are all the Lime Kiln Pieces. There are Upper and Lower Barn Pieces. Well Piece and Spring Close indicate the source of water.

On Town End Farm in 1844, there was Salt's Nursery and Clough Nursery and Lane Nursery Plantation. The nurseries were plant, or tree, nurseries. There were similar nurseries, not far away, at Cheddleton. Swinscoe is 900 feet above sea level. This is rather high and cold for success in such activities, dependent upon the varieties of plants, shrubs and trees. There remain a variety of old trees, and bushes, in this area, which confirm the existence of a nursery for hardy plants.

Most of the field names illustrated here are those given in the sale notice of 1844 but since that time some of the names have changed. On New House Farm, Top of Blackshaw Field is now known as Sweps but no reason for this name has yet been established. Lower Blackshaw is now Pump Field; Barn Close is Back Meadow. The Rushy Piece, the field over which it was impossible to take a horse, is now called the Rough.

ROADS AND TRACKS

The Parish is criss-crossed with roads and tracks and paths that have served the travellers, the tradesmen, the farmers and the people of the parish. One of the more ancient roads of the parish, long since disused and disappeared, came up from Okeover to Blore. It climbed Yerley Hill for half a mile then left the line of the present road to go behind Lees House Farm; there is some evidence of paving in the section above Lees House Farm. It followed the contours to join the valley and continued up below Blore Rectory and into Blore Dale. An examination by archaeologists from Staffordshire and Peak Park in 1980 identified evidence of an entrance roadway into Blore Hall in the south east corner of the property.

For many centuries one important road came from Ashbourne to Thorpe across the River Dove to Coldwall, through Blore, around The Waterings, across Calton Moor and on to Blythe Bridge. From Thorpe, the road went, past Thorpe Church, down the lane to the bridge. By the side of the lane, hidden in the undergrowth, there is a signpost indicating 11 miles to Cheadle. This is a relic of the old Turnpike Road, which was used by the early stage coaches. Before a bridge was built the river was crossed by the ford. This ford is still used today to drive cattle across the river to graze. When the heiress to the Bassett Estates was abducted from Blore in 1502, Roger Vernon and his band of 100 men rode off across the river through Thorpe. In 1717 there is an early reference to repairs to a wooden bridge. Like other bridges over rivers between counties, Coldwall Bridge was the source of dispute between Staffordshire and

Derbyshire. Each County accused the other of so creating the bridge supports that the current of the River was cast upon the opposite side. This continual bickering was partially solved by the setting up of a joint committee to oversee the upkeep and repair of all bridges, between the two counties. In 1726, the bridge was replaced by the stone bridge. This now stands, unused, in splendid isolation, known only to those who tread the footpath, by the side of the River Dover. The bridge spans not only the river itself but also the meadowland whose frequent flooding enriched the land and made it ideal as pasture.

The road curved up to Coldwall Farm. A row of trees and shrubs in the field on the left show the original line of the road from Coldwall to Blore. The road turned left just before Blore Hall, around the west side of the moat. It went straight up over Church Green, past the Church, and on down to Blore Dale, to join the ancient road from Okeover. It rejoined the line of the present road as far as the site where there used to be a cattle grid and then curved right along the track behind the Waterings Farm, then back to the present line and on across the Calton Moor crossroads towards Blythe Bridge.

In 1762, an Act of Parliament authorized the construction of a urnpike, from Thorpe, through Blore, to Blythe Bridge. The old road was re-routed and straightened out along the line of the present road. To pay for the improvements, toll gates were placed at Blore, Waterings Cattle Grid, and near Stanton. The toll house near Stanton still stands. The toll gates were leased out. The traffic along this road, known as Green Lane, was relatively small, and the rent charges at the tollgates were only minimal. In 1765, Blore Tollgate rent was £23.0s.0d. per year. Although it fluctuated a little over the thirty years, by 1786, the rent was down to £15.0s.0d. per year. Toll-keepers were employed to collect the toll fees and they were paid 2s.0d. per week for the job. The repair and maintenance of the road was a continuous activity. In 1838, charges were made by the local joiner for the repair of wheelbarrows. In 1844, there was a Toll Bar on the West Side of the Calton Moor crossroads, towards Cheadle. In 1851, Samuel Maskeray and his wife Hannah lived at Blore Gate. The precise location of the toll house is not known, probably on the corner of the crossroads leading down to Ilam. There were special exemptions from the paying of tolls for the villagers of Blore and Swinscoe. In particular, they travelled free of tolls if they were collecting furze and turf as fuel, or they were going to the market. The local inhabitants became fed up with the tollgates at Calton Moor and Blore Gate and made a special proposal to the Trustees of the Turnpike that the tollgates should be abandoned. In return for this concession, the Inhabitants agreed to accept full responsibility for the maintenance of the road.

Nowadays the most important road in the parish is from Mayfield, up Swinscoe Hill, through Swinscoe, and on to Calton Moor crossroads. It is now part of the A52, the major road leading west to the Potteries and North West, as the A523 to Leek, Macclesfield and Manchester. It was by this route that part of the army of Bonnie Prince Charlie marched on its way towards Derby, in 1745.

The original route passed, to the left of the Queen's Arms Hotel at Hanging Bridge, right through Upper Mayfield, and up the hill. In Swinscoe, it passed in front of the Dog and Partridge Inn, down Town End Lane and, in a curve, back to the line of the present road. In the same year as the Blore Turnpike Act, 1762, another Act of Parliament also granted the right to construct a turnpike road along this route.

In 1786 the road was re-routed from Hanging Bridge straight up to Upper Mayfield and a toll house, which still stands, was built on the corner of the lane to Okeover

There was unrest in the mills of the North West in the early 1800s. In 1817, a meeting of over 10,000 people assembled in Manchester, planning to march to London and petition the Prince Regent. The Riot Act was read to the crowd, and the mob dispersed. However, between 300 to 1000 did set off carrying only blankets for their protection. Only a mere handful of these "Blanketeers" walked down Swinscoe Hill to Ashbourne where they broke up and returned home. This left only one solitary walker, to complete the journey.

Stagecoaches stopped using the turnpike road through Thorpe in 1831. In preference they turned to the road up Swinscoe Hill, which reduced the journey from Ashbourne by twenty minutes. On a plan of Swinscoe School dated 1863, the road is called the Manchester and Ashbourne and London Turnpike Road. An account of the "Manchester and Glasgow Road" describes the road: *"up a long staggering hill out of the valley of the Dove and comes again to grim uplands"*.

Swinscoe Hill has been the site of a number of horrific accidents, especially in the days when teams of horses were used. On the 1st January 1830 whilst descending the hill a coachman and a passenger, rather the worse for drink, fell, or were thrown, from the coach. The horses and coach careered on downhill, across Hanging Bridge, into the wall of the pub. They ended up against the gatepost of a Tollhouse, at Green Lane.

Sometime in the early 1900s, a steamroller descending the steep slope from the top, smashed into some old houses close to the side of the road. The houses were so badly damaged it was necessary to pull them down.

In 1844, a proposal was made to build a new Turnpike, through Swinscoe, to avoid the steepest gradients on Swinscoe Hill. It was planned that the road should run from west of Calton Moor House, parallel with the present road, in a line down between Ellis Hill and New House Farm. The civil engineer Thomas Telford surveyed and planned this new highway but due to the high costs involved the project never came to fruition.

Outside the parish are two ancient tracks that may have been connected with the parish. In the Burton Abbey Cartulary, in the 13th century, there is mention of Viam Comitis - Earl's Way, which is subsequently referred to as Yarlsway and Erlysway. It was along this route that the Earl of Chester's tax collectors travelled, to collect taxes from the Earl's estates. There is an ancient trackway up from Calwich Abbey to Swinscoe, known as Rice Lane, parallel with the present road up Swinscoe Hill. This probably connected with Ellis Hill - Erlys Hill? Within the parish, the old road from Blore to Ilam went down from Blore to the steepest part of Ilam Meadows. With a slight curve it reached Wood Lodge, which has been known as Blore Lodge, Ilam Lodge and Wood Lodge. It followed the river to St Bertram's Bridge which was then the main road. Ryk Eton, in his will of 1544, left a contribution of 3s.4d for the "making of a bryge oer the water at Ylm". It would be of particular importance to the Eton family to have access across the river to their mill and coopering business on the Blore side.

The material for the building of Ilam Hall was carted over St Bertram's Bridge - it was this heavy traffic that finished off the old structure - it collapsed one evening, luckily, just after some people had passed over it.

Further along the river, opposite the old mill near to the present bridge, stood the stepping stones. They were very dangerous during the winter floods. In 1598 a rather drunken labourer almost fell into the river but was saved by clutching the handrail. In February 1633 Elizabeth Buxton, a maid at the Hurt household in Casterne, was swept away and drowned whilst crossing. Close to the stepping stones was a small cottage known as Ilam steps, probably on the site of the old watermill, which from 1841 to 1851 was occupied by Edward Thompson, his wife Ann and their daughter Mary. The well-trodden stepping stones were subsequently removed to the turning point of Dovedale where they now stand.

The three-arch bridge over the River Manifold to Ilam was built around 1828 by James Trubshaw the Staffordshire builder for £600.

There is a track from Stanton, via Bullgap, and across Swinscoe, into Field Lane and on to Blore. It was probably this route by which the stone was carried from the Stanton Quarries to Blore, for the building of part of the Church. It was along this lane that the churchgoers of Swinscoe used to return after Sunday service. On the way to Blore Church, they used the steeper footpath from Hill End Farm in Swinscoe, up over Feenie Lee, down the Cliffs and across Blore Dale to the church.

The original track leading to Ellis Hill Farm from the North, came along Town End Lane via Leasow Farm, east of Ellis Hill and into the farmyard. By agreement with the owners of New House Farm, the occupants at Ellis Hill were allowed direct access to the Main Road, first of all, through New House stackyard; then, a road was built which curves north of New House Farm. The Ordnance Survey Map of 1879 shows a footpath through the middle of the stack yard. There appears to have been a bridle path, following a similar route to the present farm road, from Ellis Hill Farm to the Main Road. It is shown on the 1844 Map of Sale as Jagg Way. It came from Stanton, through Ellis Hill Farm yard, north of New House Farm and, in a loop, over to the North of Martin's Hill. The jagger was a very common sight with his string of ponies, carrying lead, coal and other materials to all parts of the region. It was not unusual for pack animals carrying salt from the Cheshire Salt Mines to cross the Moorlands and return with Malt for the North West Brewers.

The Old Coach Road leading down from Thorpe to Coldwall bridge

Milestones around the parish

Ilam bridge

Coldwall bridge

St Bertram's Bridge, Ilam

The Stepping Stones - moved from Ilam to Dovedale

HOUSES AND THEIR RESIDENTS

The farms in the parish have been well documented. For early periods deeds for some of the properties still exist. Stafford Record Office holds some deeds for Ellis Hill. The late Mr Bertram White and his wife kindly allowed me to examine the deeds for New House Farm and Hall Flatts. Mr John Robotham and his mother, Mrs Joyce Robotham, have kindly allowed me access to deeds in their possession. Mr and Mrs Dear showed me copies of documents relating to their property.

Over the past one hundred and fifty years, some details of farms and their residents can be traced in documents preserved in the Public Record Office, the Stafford Record Office and other archives. Land Tax Records 1783 to 1832, Census Records 1841 to 1891, Electoral Registers 1832 to 1996. The period around 1840 is well served by three main sources. From these sources, it has been possible to identify most houses in Swinscoe and residents at that time. These are the Hodgson Estate Sale 1840, the Tithe Survey, 1844 and through Mr and Mrs Woodley of the Old Post Office, Swinscoe, who allowed me to consult and copy the account book of Mr Anthony Stubbs, 1840 to 1850.

It has been difficult to identify some houses. A house name for the smaller houses (and even some farms) is often not given in the records. Farm and house names have changed - in some cases, many times. It has been difficult to relate surnames with a particular place. A number of the families have common names, and it is often not clear which is the particular family, But I have done my best. Please forgive me for the errors and omissions that I have made, but please write to me and tell me about them.

PEOPLE, FAMILIES AND NAMES

In December 1905, the Reverend J.H. Young, Rector of Blore, wrote a fine epitaph, to the men of the Parish of Blore-with-Swinscoe: *"Within the last 30 years I have buried the generation of those who were born in those hard times. Such a generation of men we shall never see again in our country parts - men who at 80 had teeth of iron, and sinews like thongs, giants at all labouring work; who deftly wielded scythe and sickle, shear and flail; men of shift who were never at a loss to tide over a difficulty; rough and untutored, but withall having a kindly genial corner in their hearts for all whom they believed to be true men."*

During the 20th Century there have been many changes in farming methods, education, and way of life. The men and women of this moorland parish still work hard, they are always ready to give a helping hand, and, like their forbears, are still the very salt of the earth.

It has been common for the residents of the parish to live to exceptional age. Wander round the churchyard, or browse through the Parish Registers, and you will see a host of examples. Page 72 of the Parish Register reads: Sarah Haywood aged 68, Elizabeth White aged 85, Mary Ward aged 92, Elizabeth Radcliffe aged 91, William Smith aged 92: an average age of 83. In 1998, out of a population of less than one hundred, there are three ladies over 80 years old and still going strong: Grace Bailey, Annie Morris and Joyce Robotham.

The ALLEN family have lived in and around the parish for a long time. Mrs Margaret Allen of Offcote has been working for years on the history of the Allen family in North East Staffordshire. Mr and Mrs Allen lived at the Old Post Office from the early 1900s. This Mr Allen was the local cobbler, grave digger and clerk to the parish council, and his wife Hannah ran the old Post Office. Another Allen family lived at Martin Hill Farm just outside the parish boundary. Their children went to Swinscoe school, and one of them, Mr Ernest Allen is now at the post office in Alstonfield. In the 1930s, Mr Frank Allen and his wife Ellen lived at The Netlows, now known as Hillcrest

Around 1700, one branch of the GALLIMORES were living in Tean and they gradually spread out. The Gallimores lived in this parish during the 19th Century. Thomas Gallimore was baptised at Ellastone in 1757, and lived his early years in the Old Hall Farm, Mayfield. After his marriage in 1784 to Mary Wood of Lower Ellastone, he went to live at Corn Park Farm just south of Swinscoe. Although Corn Park continued to be farmed by the family, Thomas moved to Ellis Hill Farm and lived there with his wife and nine children. Thomas died in 1842, and his unmarried children, Thomas, William and Mary, continued to farm Ellis Hill until 1857 when the eldest son Thomas died. His brother and sister gave up the farm in 1859 and retired to Rose Cottage. John Gallimore married Sarah Barnett of Upper Ellastone around 1813, and went to live at The Green (Chapel Farm) in Swinscoe. He kept eight cows on the twenty eight acres.

Eight years later he sold The Green and moved to Calwich. Ellen, another of the nine children, married Matthew Lees a farmer of Blore. William Gallimore sold his house and three acres at the Netlows in 1839, and moved to a public house in Kedleston. His son, John Gallimore, sold his house and farm of twenty nine acres at Woodhouse. A descendant of the Gallimores, Mrs K.M. Prince, kindly supplied most of the information relating to her ancestors.

HOWSONS have moved in and out of the parish for at least one hundred and fifty years. William Howson was farming Common End Farm in 1829, and lived there until the 1840s. When he died, his sons, John and Thomas, carried on at the farm. Thomas was still at Common End Farm in the late 1860s. When Blore Hall Farm became vacant in 1890, David Howson took the tenancy and farmed there for twenty years. In 1939, Gladys and John William Howson were at the Dog & Partridge. John William moved to the Fleece, where he developed a very successful road haulage business, with up to eleven lorries. After nationalisation, when all the vehicles were take over by the British Road Services, Mr Howson retired to Clifton. His son, John Howson, after an equally successful career, is now living near Hanging Bridge.

Of all the families, with the possible exception of the Smiths, the name PHILLIPS has had the longest connection with the Parish. The earliest will which has survived, is that of Alice Phillips in 1538. She probably lived in a little cottage by the entrance to the church green, where her descendants were living in 1631. Among the archives at Lichfield Joint Record Office, are a number of other wills and inventories relating to the Phillips family:

1542/3	Wm Phylyp	Calton
1556	Henry Phylyp	Calton
1607	Edw Philips	Swinscoe
1684	Rob Phillips	Calton
1718	Edward Phillip	Swinscoe
1742	John Phillips	Blore

Around the turn of the 20th century, the Dove Valley hounds used to meet at Throwley Hall. Old George Phillips rode up to the Master of the Hounds, and asked: *"Have you ever, in your experience, known a man begin to hunt after he was ninety years of age?" "Most certainly not."* replied the Master, Mr Tinsley. *"Well, then, I'm ninety two and this is the first day's hunting I have ever done in my life."* announced Old George, and galloped off to join the rest of the hunt. Old George Phillips was then living at Wetton. One day, he was seen by the Rector of Blore looking around the gravestones in Blore Churchyard. When asked which grave, he was looking for, he said: *"My old friend John Oldfield's grave."* Standing silently at the grave for a little while, he then announced he was returning home. The Rector asked how he was going to get there, and Old George replied that he would be walking back the way he came. Wetton is a good stiff seven miles each way - not bad for a ninety year old. Old George had a brother, and a sister, both of whom were also in their nineties. In the first half of this century, Charles Phillips farmed Ellis Hill in Swinscoe, whilst his brother John Phillips was at Calton Moor House.

The POYSER family has been closely connected with the Parish for centuries. The earliest reference found is in the List of Families in the Archdeaconry of Stafford, in 1532/3. Thomas Poyser was living in Blore with Agnes his wife and their children, William, George, Ellen, Isabel and Jeffery. His son Jeffery was possibly the Jeffery Poyser who in 1558 witnessed the Will of Nicholas Bamforth, the steward of the Bassett Lands in Blore. Galfrid (George?) Poyser was one of the Appraisers of the Inventory, after Nicholas Bamforth's death.

The Rent Rolls for Okeover Woodhouse, in 1579, show that George Poyser was paying 2 shillings per year for the "sprynge". It is not certain where his land lay, but George and his family certainly lived close to the church. They were obviously very friendly with the Rector, John Ward. When Rev Ward died in 1575, he left George one silver spoon worth 6s. 8d, and George's wife, his greatest cauldron, and each one of their children, one sheep. George had a son Roger who was born 3rd April 1581.

Richard Poyser married his wife Elizabeth in the early 1590s, and he farmed his land in Woodhouses. Between 19th March 1595 and 9th March 1616 they had eleven children, 6 girls and 5 boys:

Elen born 19th March 1595
Ann born 26th February 1596.

Elizabeth born 23rd January 1598.
Isabell born 2nd July 1600.
Thomas born 15th August 1603.
Raphe born 18th August 1605.
William born 11 Nov 1607.
Jeythe born 11th February 1610.
Hellen born 14 March 1612.
George born 31 March 1615.
Dorothy born 9 March 1616.

Richard got himself into a spot of bother with a neighbour in Woodhouses called Royley. He was arrested, taken to court, and found guilty of assault. After a very fruitful life, his wife Elizabeth Poyser died and was buried 13th August 1639 in Blore Churchyard.

In April 1975, Mr John Poyser of Mayfield, was carrying out repairs and renovations to the old family pews in Blore Church. In doing so he discovered that the floor was only a very thin layer of cement and below that lay eight skeletons packed closely together, and another two burials nearby. The burials were without coffins. There was no way of identifying them, but they probably originated from the 15th/16th Centuries, around the time when the first Poysers were recorded in the Parish!

ROBOTHAM is a Scottish name that has been known in these parts for centuries. John Robotham of Town End Farm reckons that the name came down from Scotland with the Jacobites, when Bonnie Prince Charlie's men passed through Swinscoe in 1745. But the Robothams were already here. In 1720, when John Waterfall of Blore died without a will and left underage children, Daniell Rowbotham was witness to the deed of guardianship. The exact date is not known, but before 1755 according to the Glebe Terriers of Blore Church, Edmund Robotham was paying 11 pence as a composition for tithe hay, for Cliff Top Farm, Swinscoe. Mr Robotham held Doglands, in Calton, which was then in the Parish of Blore. A party of the Scottish Soldiers came to the farm, just as an old butcher, Joseph Mellor, was riding into the yard, with a side of beef tied across his horse. Robotham gave a warning to Mellor, who immediately threw the meat, from the horse, and galloped off to the safety of Musden Woods. The warning nearly cost Mr Robotham his life. One of the soldiers drew his sword, and rushed at him, blaming him for allowing the horse to escape; luckily another soldier parried the thrust. To appease his unwelcome visitors, Mr Robotham offered food and a pan of milk covered with cream. One of the soldiers took a spoon, and began to stir the milk, remarking that *"the best were at the botham."* The earliest surviving Register, in Calton Church, is an old pocket book, which was given to William Robotham on the 6th March 1789. William, as Churchwarden, was required to keep a record of all baptisms, weddings and burials. He used the book for his own personal notes, and accounts, and one of the earliest entries in his hand, reads: *"William Robotham is my name Eingland is my nashon Caulton is my dwelling plase and Christ is my salvashon."*

Like his father and grandfather before him, John Robotham farms at Town End Farm and his mother Joyce lives at Peak View Cottage.

Like everywhere else in Britain, the name of SMITH has been common in the area. In the neighbouring parish of Calton, in 1532, more than half the population of 170 people were called Smith, although in Blore there was only one Smith. The very first name recorded in the Blore Parish Registers is *"Jane Smithe the daughter of John Smith baptised the first day of April 1558"* and Smiths continued to be recorded over the centuries. Thomas Smith was a churchwarden of Blore Church in 1686. There is a will of John Smith of Blore, dated 1773, in Lichfield Joint Record Office. On the wall of the North Aisle of the Church is a memorial inscription to three Smiths: Thomas Smith died 1790, William son of John and Mary Smith died 1797; and Elizabeth Smith died 1802. There is a "true story" about Smiths, at Blore Hall, in the chapter on Local Tales and Folklore. There were Smiths at Martin Hill for centuries. Mr Ian Smith and his family are now, in 1998, living in Ilam Meadows Farm. Of course, not all the Smiths were paragons of virtue. In March 1866, Job and John Smith of Swinscoe were summoned by Mrs Martha Buxton of Mayfield, for assaulting her at Mayfield. Job was fined 2s.6d, plus costs, but the case against John was dismissed.

In 1676, there were three families named SWETNAM, in Swinscoe: Henry Swetnam and Ellin with a daughter Ribiccah; George Swetnam and Ellen; and another labourer called Swetnam and his wife,

Elizabeth, with a daughter called Susanna. Again, in 1841, there were three families of Swetnam, in the village. Elizabeth Swetnam, a 45 year old widow had her two daughters living with her. Elizabeth was looking after two children, Hannah Stubbs (4) and Henry Ayre (2) as a child nurse. Walter Swetnam lived by himself, and at the age of 80 was still actively working as a Nailer. Back in 1813, Walter registered his own home in Swinscoe, as a place of worship for the Primitive Methodists. Over the following twenty years, he went round the parish collecting subscriptions for the erection of the chapel in Town End Lane. Walter died in 1845 and was buried at Blore Church.

Dun Low

Blore Hall c1910, and below, Blore Hall in 1997

Blore Hall under snow

Blore Hall

Blore Cottage

Above: The Moat, Blore Hall - the depression is the southern part of the moat.

Blore Rectory

Letter from Sir William (III)Bassett to Thomas Cromwell.
Reproduced by permission of the British Library CLEO E1V 285

Blore Hall

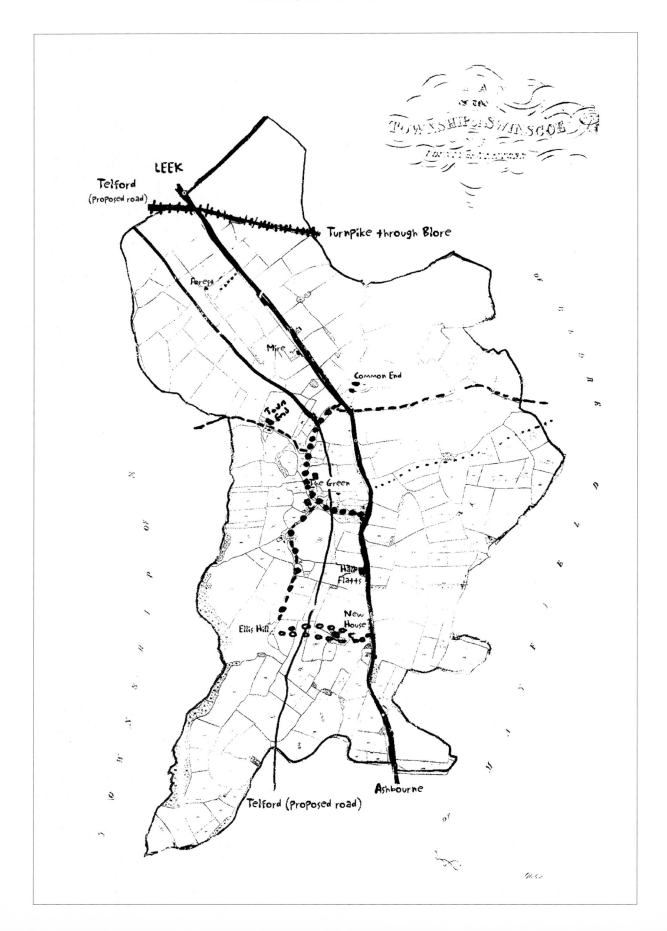

TWO
SWINSCOE AND CALTON MOOR

The village of Swinscoe is situated on a hilltop on the main A52 Turnpike Road northwest of Ashbourne. Most of the residents of the parish of Blore-with-Swinscoe actually live in Swinscoe village, with the others in farms scattered around the parish.

For thousands of years Swinscoe was covered by woodland and wild swine roamed the woods. Swinscoe means "wood of swine"; "scoe" is the Norse word for wood or small forest; "swin" was a common word throughout Northern Europe including Scandinavia meaning swine.

Ever since written records were kept, and undoubtedly before that, the land in Swinscoe has been farmed and fought over, divided and enclosed. During the first half of the 13th Century, Sir Hugh de Okeover got himself into financial trouble supporting King Henry III in his military campaigns. Sir Hugh sold off twenty acres of land, twenty acres of wood and three acres meadow, representing half his land in Swinscoe, to the Abbot of Rocester. He was also involved in transactions relating to the lease and transfer of land to other individuals.

A few years later, the Abbot of Rocester sued Robert Okeover, the son of Sir Hugh, for half of the Manor of Swinscoe. The Abbot also took action against local inhabitants for using three acres of common land which he said belonged to Rocester Abbey. The local people were able to prove their right to use the common land, and the Abbot withdrew his complaint. In the late 13th century, Lucian, son of Ralph of Stanton, granted to Rocester Abbey the right to graze their flocks of sheep and herds of cattle on Stanton Moor. Rocester Abbey benefited by further gifts of land from the Okeover family. A dozen or so charters in the Okeover collection at Matlock Record Office detail the extent of the Rocester Abbey holding, and describe some of the boundaries and the tenants of the land.

The names of the tenants and their holdings in the 13th Century were:

Hugh de Acova	12 Bovates
William Armiger	1 Bovate
Geoffrey de Bec, Margaret de Bec	2 Bovates
Robert le Blunt	1 Bovate
Edith the Widow	1 Bovate
William le Fureis	1 Bovate
William Kinton	1 Bovate
Alvered de Monias	1 Bovate
Ralph de la Mees, Robert Morsel	2 Bovates
Cecily Multuno. Own the Miller	1 Bovate
Saniel	1 Bovate
John le Tureis	1 Piece Land
Ulfkel, Henry de Wittona	1 Bovate
Hugh de Wodehouse	2 Bovates

The Rocester Abbey holding in Swinscoe remained for over 250 years until the Dissolution of Religious Houses in 1538. In this year, Richard Hood of Swinscoe left twenty shillings to the Abbott as his herriott due on death to the Lord of the Manor. He also left 3s.4d to the Brethren to pray for his soul.

In 1541, Francis, Earl of Shrewsbury was granted a pasture called Elieshill, and a meadow called Abbotts Croft in Swinscoe.

According to the inquisition, following the death of Henry Talbot Armiger, who died 20th June 1596, he held three messuages, 200 acres of land in Swinscoe and Blore. His daughters Gertrude and Marian were his heirs.

Some of the land in Swinscoe was regained by the Okeovers and it continued to expand and contract with the fortunes of the family and their tenants. When Humphrey Okeover died in 1537/8, he left seven houses and 230 acres of land in Swinscoe and Woodhouses. The Okeovers have always been Lords of the Manor of Swinscoe. It is therefore an interesting and as yet unsolved problem why Swinscoe is associated with Blore as a parish, rather than with Okeover. The parish is called Blore-with-Swinscoe.

In 1762, a major change occurred in the Parish. A road was built up the hill through Swinscoe. Although the hill was steep and dangerous, the time of the journey from Ashbourne to Leek was reduced by at least thirty minutes. This was obviously more attractive to the horse-driven passenger and mail coaches that now used the route. As a result the turnpike road via Thorpe, over Coldwall bridge and through Blore was gradually abandoned and in 1831 the coaches ceased to use it. With the re-routing of the main road and the loss of means of communication and transport, Blore became more isolated. The population reduced even further and Blore became the lost village of today.

Swinscoe was the natural resting place after the long hard climb up Swinscoe Hill. The local inhabitants took the opportunity to serve the travellers and their horses. Two inns appeared in the village and the population increased. The traffic was, however, insufficient to support two inns and so only one survived - the Dog and Partridge. With the advent of modern vehicles, the improved road and more efficient clearing of snow in the winter, cars now speed up Swinscoe Hill and on through the village. Travellers now stop, not out of necessity, but to enjoy the attractions offered by the Dog and Partridge.

BARNFIELDS
Mr Reginald Bailey and his wife Grace spent much of their life in Swinscoe. During his early life, Mr Bailey worked at Blore Hall Farm and lived at the tied cottage at the entrance to Town End Lane - The Croft. Then at the beginning of the war they moved across the main road and took up residence in the school house. Mr Bailey was a member of the local Home Guard Unit who used to carry out their practice and drill in the school yard.

In 1951 Mr Bailey bought five acres down Town End Lane from Peter Gregory, landlord of the Dog & Partridge. He used part of this land to build a bungalow. His son Max lives next door at the bungalow called Sonley, and Mr Bailey's grandson moved into the school house which had been the home of Mr and Mrs Bailey for such a long time. He sold some of the land as building sites for new houses - Gilman House and Oakfields. In a field on the right of Town End Lane there was a large barn. In 1990 he converted this barn and he and his wife moved in - they called it Barnfields. Sadly Reg died in 1996, but his wife Grace continues to enjoy the property. Mrs Grace Bailey, like her husband, has been an enormous help in providing information relating to the parish and its residents.

BLUNDER COTTAGE - *possibly Clod Hall Springfields Blunder Castle*
There is a capped old lead mine shaft near the entrance to the property. This mine passes under the road and the field of Latham Hall Farm opposite. The line of the diggings can be recognised during summer months, by a yellow band across the fields. This is limestone country and even the heaviest rainfall soon runs away down the large shakehole on the property.

In 1732, in the will of Thomas Bennitt of CLOD HALL, he is called a miner. As there is no other reference to Clod Hall within the Parish and because of its association with the lead mine, it is a guess that this may be Clod Hall. Thomas Bennitt's inventory was valued at £18.11s.6d. There is a headstone in Blore churchyard which reads:

> Death never can ye man surprise that watches forth with wary eyes
> Then every soul shall see what its to have lived well or done amiss
> In memory of Thomas Bennet who died June ye 13 1739

Mr Forrester and his wife lived at The Springfields; he worked for the Phillips at Calton Moor House for many years. Mr Phillips had a very high regard for Mr Forrester and was present at Mr Forrester's funeral as one of the principal mourners.

In 1964 the land associated with the property was measured as 28a.3r.8p.

The cottage seems to have acquired the name Blunder Castle around this period but was renamed Blunder Cottage by Mr and Mrs Douglas Holyoak the present occupants.

CALTON MOOR COTTAGE - *Calton Moor Farm*
The earliest reference to Calton Moor Cottage or Farm, as distinct from Calton Moor House Farm, is in the Survey for the award of rent charges in lieu of tithes, which took place in 1844. Elizabeth Riley is

shown as farming 15a.3r.0p. The cottage is shown on the Plan of the Township of Swinscoe, together with the three fields, at the top end of the lane towards Calton: Big Common Piece, Little Common Piece and Far Common Piece.

A few years later, in 1851, James and Mary Critchlow and their three children John (7), George (6) and Harriett (4) were living there. The farm was stated to be 14 acres in extent. From around 1870 until 1883, Joseph Harrison was living there with his wife and two daughters Ellen and Sarah. Both girls attended Swinscoe School but left there and moved to the school at Calton in 1882.

Edwin Charlesworth moved into the farm in 1883, and stayed there for over ten years. His name appears in the Electoral Registers as eligible to vote in the local elections.

At the end of the First War William Fitchett and his wife took over the property. It was conveniently placed at the crossroads to offer teas to passing cyclists and travellers. When William died, Mary continued to live on the farm until around 1940. Later, Mrs Fitchett moved to the home of Tom Finney at Newport in Shropshire, where she died in 1953 at the age of 81.

Tom Finney farmed at Calton Moor.

Around 1948, George William Morris and his wife Sarah lived at Calton Moor and their daughter Nancy went to Swinscoe School. When George died in 1975/6, Sarah left Calton Moor and moved to Ashbourne. In 1964, the farm was recorded as 35a.0.35.

Reg Twigg farmed nearby Latham Hall Farm for thirty years, and when he retired in 1978 he bought Calton Moor Farm and lived there for three years.

Mr Pain who worked for Rolls Royce somewhere in Scotland, expected to move to the Derby Factory. He bought the cottage but, after three years of ownership, never got the chance of living in it. There was no alternative but to sell the cottage.

Gilbert and Christine Meyrick farmed here in 1984; they bred goats and pigs and sold the goats milk and produce.

Part of Calton Moor outbuildings were transformed into extra living accommodation and in 1996 Michael Dickinson and Karen Oldknow were living at the farm. The farm has now changed from farming goats to a herd of deer, which are admired by visitors en route to Dove Dale.

CALTON MOOR HOUSE - *Honest Miller, Red Lion*

Calton Moor House stands at the junction of the Ashbourne to Leek and the Froghall to Blore roads. It was built around the middle of the eighteenth century and with its location at Calton Moor crossroads has frequently combined its activities as a farm with those of a public house and as a provider of accommodation. Over the years Calton Moor House has sometimes been recorded as being in Swinscoe, and at other times in Calton. Even the post office has had problems with two different postmen passing the door.

As a public house the first recorded name was the Honest Miller: *"the man whose honesty can be attested by the hairs on the palm of his hand"*. A landlord, with a sense of humour, may have had some interest in the windmill which used to stand half a mile along the road towards Blore; the farm was 105 acres in size and could have encompassed Windmill Piece.

Yates Map of Staffordshire, published in 1775, shows the Red Lion Inn prior to the opening of the turnpike road from Blythe Marsh to Thorpe. Even though it was such an important intersection, no tollgate was erected until 1827.

In 1806 John Hambleton Innkeeper of Calton Moor died. He was obviously a very successful man, like some of his successors, because he left to his three grand-daughters, Mary, Ellin and Edith, the sum of £150 to be divided equally among them. His children John, William and Sarah Hambleton were appointed as executors to his will.

In 1827 the price of ale was four pence per pint. The provision of ale to farmworkers was an important part of their wages. From the evidence of surviving farm accounts, it appears to have been common for farmworkers, whilst on farm business, to call for a pint and charge it to the farmer.

The turnpike through Thorpe and Blore became disused and in 1831 the passenger and mail coaches stopped using the old route and came up the hill through Swinscoe. The inn served the local community and also acted as a centre for display of notices of sale of property and animals. The sale of the Hodgson Estate in Swinscoe in 1844 was advertised at the Red Lion Inn Calton Moor. Calton Moor Sheep Fair was held on adjacent land.

It was, in 1844, that an incident occurred which was recorded in the Blore Parish Registers, and described, in detail, in the Deanery Magazine, in March 1894:

"A gang of mules and asses in charge of "Old Stout" were passing Blore Lime Kiln after having delivered coal to Ilam Hall. "Old Stout" found a gentleman lying exhausted and unable to carry on. The ganger put him on the back of a quiet mule and took to the inn at Calton Moor kept by a family named Gilman. The stranger asked to stay for a few days as he felt very unwell. Next morning he was no better and after first consulting a cow-leech, who could do nothing, it was suggested that a doctor should be called but the stranger refused. However after a few days, the situation became serious and Dr Hall was called. The doctor carried out his examination only to find that the stranger was a lady. At that time the Rev Frederick Day was private tutor to the sons of John Russell at Ilam. The Rev Day was called and he talked to the lady who admitted to being of noble birth but pledged him to secrecy. Her death occurred a day or two later and a special messenger was sent to a Country Seat in Cheshire. Her funeral at Blore Church was attended by a heavily veiled lady who arrived in a hired coach from Leek. Who or what the deceased lady was, is not known but an entry in the Parish Register reads as follows:

Ellen H—- of C—- aged 21 buried 10 March 1844. Frederick Day Officiating Minister.

This young woman had wandered about in the disguise of a man's clothing for several years, through England Wales and Ireland and died at Calton Moor House. Since this entry was original made in the Register, the name and place has been completed:

Ellen HATFIELD (alias HADFIELD) of Chapel-en-le-Frith.

After a few days the grave had sunk and it was assumed that the body had been stolen. The Rector Rev Hugh Wood instructed the Sexton, George Bott, to re-open the grave. Mr Bott always swore that he found the coffin burst, and saw the hand of the corpse. Two others, Robert Yates and Thomas Stubbs of Swinscoe, both firmly believed that the lady's friends had taken the body away.

In 1851 James Critchlow and his wife were farming the 104 acres of Calton Moor Farm. They also provided accommodation for passing travellers and, at the time of the census, two lodgers, James Fox and John Steel were staying at the Inn.

John Fernyhough and his wife Ann followed the Critchlows. John died in 1861, and his wife carried on until 1864 when she too died. The licence was taken away, but Calton Moor House was still referred to as the Red Lion on the map of 1881.

The Phillips family moved to Calton Moor House around 1870, and their descendants continued to occupy the farm for over one hundred years. Richard and Elizabeth Phillips were married at Blore Church in 1864. They had a four year old daughter, Annie, who sadly died on 21st December 1876. According to the census of 1891, Richard and Elizabeth were at Calton Moor House with three of their children: John, Charles and Sarah. They were entertaining a visitor, Mr George Weaver, and had a young servant girl called Sarah Parker. Richard continued to farm at Calton Moor House into the 1900s and died on 4th December 1904 at the age of 69, and his wife Elizabeth died 15 years later in 1919 at the age of 83. She was buried beside her husband in Blore churchyard. John Phillips married Frances Austin of Waterhouses in 1903. A photograph taken in the 1920s in front of Calton Moor House shows Mr John Phillips standing with two young boys in the background - probably local lads who worked on the farm. Mr John Phillips, as Justice of the Peace, was involved in all local matters.

There was great rivalry between John Phillips and his brother, Charles Phillips of Ellis Hill. John and Charles were members of the Leek Agricultural and Horticultural Society. Each year at the Leek Show, members competed for the cup for the best bred Long Wool Ram Lamb. In 1906, John Phillips won the cup; in 1907, his brother Charles won; in 1908, John won again, but in 1909, David Howson of Blore Hall won, and then in 1910, Charles won again. The rules specified that whoever was the winner of the cup on three separate occasions would hold that cup forever. In 1911, John Phillips, of Calton Moor House, won for the third time, and the cup is now proudly owned by his grandson, Richard John Phillips of Culland Farm Brailsford. A photograph shows John Phillip's five year old son Norman Richard Phillips with two of the prize-winning Lincoln Long Wool sheep.

The Phillips of Calton Moor House and the Phillips of Ellis Hill were Primitive Methodists and very involved in all the activities of Swinscoe Chapel. Mr John Phillips was the Superintendent of the Sunday School. During the Great War, when travelling any distance was difficult, he invited the children from the Sunday School to visit Calton Moor House for their annual treat. On 9th August 1917, fifty children with some of their mothers and teachers, were entertained by Mr and Mrs Phillips. They played on the swings, and took part in organised games and amusements, in spite of the showery weather. They sang several hymns, and as they were sitting in their conveyance ready for departure, they sang the National Anthem. Mr Phillips had a fine voice himself and trained the children of the chapel in singing.

During the Great War, Mr Phillips allowed one of his fields to be used by the local battalion of the Volunteer Regiment for training. In May 1917 a group of forty local volunteers from Ellaston, Stanton and Swinscoe, demonstrated their marching drill to a large group of spectators.

Frank Harrison worked at Calton Moor House. On 3rd November 1926, he and Lilian Gertrude Bradbury from The Waterings were married at Swinscoe Primitive Methodist Chapel.

On the 6th February 1937, Stanley John Phillips, 27, chartered surveyor of Carlisle, and originally from Calton Moor House, married his cousin Ethel Phillips, 31, from Ellis Hill. Stanley's brother Norman Richard Phillips was one of the witnesses and his father, John Phillips, as an important member of Swinscoe Methodist Chapel, helped the officiating minister Mr John Price. After the wedding local children "roped" the gates on Chapel Lane and only allowed the couple to leave after the due throwing of pennies. Locally couples did not consider themselves as properly married until they had been roped. The Phillips family left Calton Moor House around 1941 and moved to Heathy Close, Langford.

The Salt family moved into the farm when the Phillips left. According to the Electoral Registers, Samuel B.Salt was living at Calton Moor House in 1945, and in 1948, Sarah, Clifford and Thomas Salt are recorded as eligible to vote. Mrs Salt was a very active member of the Swinscoe Methodist Chapel and in 1957 was responsible for collecting over £50 toward the restoration of the chapel. John Thomas Salt died on the 5th January 1983, and Doris Sarah Salt died on the 16th February 1993. They are both buried in Blore churchyard.

CARAVAN - *Countess Caravan. Mire Farm. Mitre Farm.*
Mr Sidney Jackson was a driver in the Royal Army Medical Corps. After the War he went to live with his brother at Hillcrest. When his uncle, Tom Stannah, died, Sid acquired the site called Mire or Mitre Farm. The name is more probably Mire because the farm included the house on the opposite side of the main road - Clough House, formerly The Mire. He bought a Countess Caravan and installed it behind the large barn on the property. Here he lived until his death, when his nephew, Neil Jackson, inherited the property. In 1997, Neil Jackson sold the land to Mr Cotterell from Stanton.

CHAPEL FARM - *Chapel Cottage, The Green*
Many years ago, Chapel Farm was known as The Green which has caused some confusion with the similarly named Green Farm across Town End Lane.

In 1813 John Gallimore left Ellis Hill and moved to The Green at Swinscoe where he remained for eight years. In 1821 he left The Green and moved to an eighty acre farm, The Hutts at Calwich, living there until his death in 1838.

According to the Notice of Sale, in 1840, The Green was ten acres in size. Thomas Smith and his wife Mary were living there with a five month old baby, Mary, and Hannah Wibberley, age 4. Thomas and his wife continued to live there through the 1850s and 1860s with a variety of relatives from the his wife's sister's Wibberley side of the family: When Swinscoe school opened in 1864, Levi Smith from The Green attended the school. The local builder Anthony Stubbs carried out some work on the property, for which he charged £2.14s.6d.

According to the census in 1881, George Bott, his wife Emma, their daughter Louisa, and eight-month old baby, Samuel, were living at Chapel Farm.

1893, Mr Arthur Tomlinson of the Green was appointed as one of the Overseers of the Poor. He was involved with the activities of Swinscoe Primitive Methodist Chapel, and frequently took the chair at the Tea Meetings. His wife was also involved as one of the principal organisers of the meetings. Mr Tomlinson continued to live at The Green into the early 1900s. In 1903 the farm was twenty eight acres in size and Mr Tomlinson had eight milking cows.

In 1914 Chapel Farm was put up for sale. It comprised two pieces of land: Homestead of 2.62 acres and the Meadow of 2.727 acres - a total of 5a.1r.14p. It was rented by Richard Naylor, with his wife Fanny, at £14.0s.0d per year and the adjoining owners were Okeover and Tomlinson. On 19th January 1922 Chapel Farm was again for sale and is described as a stone house with parlour, kitchen, scullery and two bedrooms. There was a cowshed for four cows, and a pigsty. The farm had been extended and there was a stone barn in one of the four fields which made up the eight acres. Before the sale, the farm was let in separate lots to Richard Naylor and John Howson. In 1939, Frederick and Nellie Hall lived at Chapel House, and stayed until 1950.

George Warrington retired from Hill Top Farm and moved to Chapel House in 1954. While he was there the house came up for sale, but in his retirement he did not wish to buy, so his nephew Ken Twemlow bought the cottage. Mr Warrington stayed at Chapel House until his death in 1976. In 1984, Mr Kenneth Twemlow and his wife, Jean, and their three children John, Janice and Leon, moved into the farm. Mr Twemlow built a new house on his land across the lane. They were only there for a short while and left Chapel House for their children, John Twemlow and his wife, Freda, who are now living there.

CLIFF TOP FARM AND SWINSCOE CLIFF

Situated near the very steep slope down to Blore Dale, the aptly named Cliff Top Farm has been there for at least three hundred years. As one of the more remote farms, difficult to reach, it has remained relatively small.

In the 17th century it was known as Cliff Top or as Swinscoe Cliff and a family called Wood lived there for at least seventy years. Like many smallholders, the Wood family combined their farming with another trade. John Wood of Clifftop is recorded as being a nailer. He may have worked at the mill on the Blore side of the river where the Austin family carried on their trade as millers and makers of barrels and ironmongery. According to the Glebe Terriers for Blore Church prior to 1755, Edmund Rowbotham was paying 11d as a composition for tithe hay for Cliff Top Farm.

In 1841 it was farmed by 20 year old William Harryson and his wife Ann. It was too much for William to handle by himself. He and his wife moved to a cottage at Lease Head, and he hired himself out as an Agricultural Labourer. William Harryson was a very pernickety man, always insisting that everything around was tidy and well ordered. When he died his widow insisted that his ghost came back to haunt the cottage and make sure everything was kept ship-shape. Apparently this haunting was the reason for the cottage being empty for a long time. In 1844 the tenant was Michael Rose: Cottage Farm House with Parlour, Kitchen, Dairy, Bed chambers, Garden, 2 Cow Houses, Barn, stack Yard, Piggery etc.

Short Rakes	Turf & Arable	3.2.21
Cliff Top Meadow	Old Turf	4.1.38
Cliff Top Farmhouse, outbuildings yard and garden		0.0.24
Dale Meadow	Old Pasture	4.3. 5
Back Of Hill	Old Turf	2.1. 5
Back of Hill	Turf	1.2.13
Cliff Top Hill	Old Pasture	6.1.36
		23.1.22

In 1845, Cliff Top Farm was sold by the Rev Edward Hodgson to the Trustees of the Okeover Estate. The Farm comprised Cottage, Farmhouse, two cowhouses, barn, stackyard and twenty three Acres comprising Short Rakes, Cliff Top Meadow, Dale Meadow, and Back of the Hill, Cliff Top Hill. William Smith was offered the tenancy of the farm on a year-to-year basis.

In 1851, William and Ann Smith and their five children lived there and farmed thirty eight acres. The two eldest girls, Elizabeth and Frances, and son, Arthur, had left home by 1861. Mr and Mrs Smith were still there with four children; two more children had been added to their brood. By 1871, William and Ann were still living at Cliff Top with two of their children Ann and Elizabeth. They were also looking after two of their grandchildren, Sarah and Annie Millward, who both attended Swinscoe School. William died on the 25th April 1875 age 76. Ann moved to Archers Cottage with her 16 year old grand-daughter Annie, and there Ann Smith died six years later, on 17th September 1881, aged 69. Ann was buried with her husband in Blore Churchyard.

A barn in a neighbouring field was used as a home in 1885. Francis Radcliffe (Ratcliffe) with his wife Ann held the tenancy. In 1891, William Wilson, and his wife Alice, and their one year old baby Alice, lived there and had two farm servants living with them. When the building stopped being used as a home, the roof was replaced and the chimney was removed.

The Smiths continued at Cliff Top; William Smith and his wife Sarah Ann, with their three sons, Frank who worked on the farm, and Arthur and William who were still at school. In 1893, William Smith was appointed as one of the Overseers of the Poor. Around 1894, Mrs Sarah Smith was suffering from a disease at the back of the nose, which was gradually closing up her throat. Her doctor recommended that she should be taken into Derby Infirmary for treatment - but without success. As a last resort, she was taken to see Dr Stewart, a specialist in Nottingham, who carried out a tracheotomy and the insertion of a silver tube into her windpipe. Although she was only able to speak in a whisper, this prolonged her life for six years. On 10th January 1900, Sarah Ann, died, at the age of 53, and was buried in Blore Churchyard.

From 1908 to 1918, Arthur and Lucy Smith lived at Cliff Top. The long run of Smiths ended in the 1900s and Thomas and Mary Grindey became tenants, and farmed the forty five acres. According to Kelly's Directory, George Gold was living at Cliff Top in 1940. He was followed by Captain Shute and Owen Hand.

In 1950, Mr G. Finney took the farm and remained there for twelve years until 1962. Mr Turner held the farm from 1962 until 1968. Jim Warrington followed for three years from 1968 until 1971.

In 1971, Mr Charles Bowden and his wife Joyce came to live in the house. Charles became closely involved in all the activities of Blore Church. He moved from Swinscoe in 1993 and died in 1994. His ashes were placed in the churchyard of St Bartholomew's Church which he loved so much. Mr Edwards and his wife Rachel now live at Cliff Top with their two children, Benedict and Edmund.

CLOUGH HOUSE - *The Mire*

This cottage, built prior to 1840, has had a large number of tenants over the years. From the map and survey of 1840, it appears to have been two, or even three, cottages which were occupied by Dorothy Howson, David Pegge and Isaac Smith. According to the census in 1881, Elizabeth Berrisford, farmer's wife, was living there. Ralph Adams of Roston owned the property in 1888, and Henry Harrison lived there. Henry was one of those who attended a public meeting to choose suitable persons as Overseers of the Poor for the parish. Ralph Webster of The Waterings and Frederick Thompson of the Golden Fleece were elected.

William Stannah of New House Farm bought the property. In 1891, Edward Smith, farmer, and his wife Elizabeth and two children, Frederick and Mary, were his tenants; both children attended Swinscoe School. By 1908, John Renshaw was the tenant.

At the end of the Great War, William Anson Warrington and his wife Eliza were living at the cottage. George Warrington was in the army during the Great War, and was awarded the George Medal for bravery. His bravery was never in doubt. One local story tells of his being attacked by a bull and lying on the ground, pretending to be dead, with the bull above him. The Warringtons continued to live at the Mire until the mid 1930s. William then did a swap with Thomas Stannah and moved to Hill End Farm. Thomas Stannah, and his two daughters, who rarely left the house, lived there. Thomas's niece, Gladys Lily Jackson kept house for him until her death in 1952.

Mr Poole, a baker from Leek, moved into the cottage. Unfortunately, Mrs Poole was knocked down and badly hurt outside the house when she crossed the road to a travelling tradesman's van. She was taken to hospital, with serious injuries to the leg. Mr Sherratt carried out major internal work on the cottage, knocking out one of the main walls to enlarge the rooms. Mr Geoff Prime and his brother George, of Forest Farm, bought this farm of twelve acres, and their sister, Mary Salt lived in the house with her husband Samuel. George and Geoff Prime farmed the land as part of Forest Farm. Mr Salt, and his wife, occupied the house from the 1970s and stayed there. His wife died in 1991 and Mr Salt stayed till 1993.

In 1993, Mr Smith from the Red Lion at Waterfall was doing some work at Town End Farm. John Robotham told him that Sam Salt had heard that Mr Smith had sold the pub, and wondered whether he would be interested in buying Clough House. Mr Smith went to look at the cottage and then, with the encouragement of Sam Salt, he fetched his wife to see it. They both liked what they saw and, in May 1993, they took possession. Unfortunately the first twelve months were full of problems. First, Mrs Smith broke her leg. Then, Mr Smith fell downstairs and broke his arm.And then, Mrs Smith lost a toe, in an accident, which needed treatment in hospital for ten days. Things have gone better since then, and Mr and Mrs Smith are still living in the cottage in 1998.

COMMON END FARM

Of all the farms in the parish, Common End Farm possesses evidence of the oldest occupation. Ancient Britons lived, hunted, made their own pottery, tools and weapons and farmed on Common End over three thousand years ago. In the fields behind Common End Farm are the remains of Top Low Ancient Burial Mound. Top Low was opened up in 1849. It was found to contain the skeletons of thirteen people plus the burnt remains of a wild boar buried during the Bronze Age one thousand years before Christ. The boar had been killed by an arrow, or spear, tipped with the tine of stag's horn. The antiquarian Mr Bateman found an ancient axe and flint chips which were used for making tools and weapons. Similar items have been found by other farmers of Common End. A vase and various pieces of pottery were found, together with some bone implements which were probably the potter's tools.

John Dale occupied the farmhouse at Common End in 1802, but was farming only the twenty six acres of land surrounding the house. In 1829, William Howson was farming Common End. This was the time of the slump, which started in 1815 at the end of the War with France. William was having financial problems so he appealed to the landowners. In 1829, he was paying a half yearly rental of £115. The rental was reduced to £110 in 1830, £104 in 1831, and remained steady until 1839. The rent was reduced again to £97.10s.0d, and a certain part of his land was laid to someone else. In 1840, the rental was reduced once again to £92.10s.0d. Land Tax had been charged since the 1700s; it was based on ancient valuations. Between 1826 and 1831, the Rental for Land Tax purposes, was £87.12s.0d, against which a charge of £3.13s.0d. was levied.

According to the accounts of the carpenter Anthony Stubbs, a coffin was made in 1838 for an infant who had died at Common End, the child of Hanah Haryson/Rushton but no trace of this family has been found. The coffin was the most expensive one in the Stubbs account book, being charged at £3.0s.0d. William Hewson was still farming the land with his wife, Ann, and six children: John (25), Ann (20), Thomas (20), Henry (15), Maria (13), and Prisilla (11). According to the 1841 Census, the farm comprised of 154 acres.

The farm was put up for sale by the Hodgson Estate in 1844, and was bought along with considerable other property by the Okeovers. With the Sale, the property was consolidated into one holding including the farmhouse built of stone. It consisted of parlour, kitchen, dairy, scullery, 3 bed chambers, cheese room, cellar and garden. In addition, there was a stable, cowhouse, foddering house, piggery, cart house and barns and the farm comprised 171a.0r.15p. By 1851, William had died and his sons, John and Thomas, were farming the land and employed three servants: Mary Richardson, Wm. Stubbs (18) and Joseph (13).

The Howson (sometimes spelled Hewson) family were the next tenants. In 1861, Thomas Hewson was farming the 145 acres with his wife and three children, Fanny, Elizabeth and David. They employed three servants: Elizabeth Chadwick, William Smith and George Brent. In 1866, Elizabeth and David Howson started at Swinscoe School, for the first time. Around 1880, William and Hannah Harrison moved to Common End Farm from Onecote. They employed a farm servant called Charles Wood. The two eldest of their six children, Alice and Sampson, helped on the farm. The two youngest, Adam and

John, were at home, and the middle children went to Swinscoe School. In 1886, Sam Clowes was living at Common End Farm. He is one of the signatories who attended Swinscoe School to choose the Overseers of the Poor.

Mr Brassington and his wife Sarah, were farming at Common End Farm in 1918. Sadly, their baby daughter Clarice Sarah Brassington, age 9 months, died on the 20th July 1919. Her brother, Charles, was born on 3rd March 1914, and died on the 25th May 1989 at the age of 75; he was buried in the same grave as his long remembered sister. Another Brassington daughter died in 1993.

With an ancient burial mound on his property, Mr Brassington became interested in the ancient history of the area. In 1926, Mr Brassington found a perforated stone hammer, which is deposited in the Natural History Museum at Hanley. In March 1927, he told Mr Pape, the teacher and archaeologist, that quite a number of flint flakes and chips had been found in the garden and fields. His two sons picked up two Neolithic flint arrow heads, one of a sharply pointed pear shape $1^{1}/_{4}$ inch long.

Before the War the Morris family became the tenants and farmed Common End Farm. In 1953, George William Morris had the chance to buy. He and his wife bought the 144 acre farm, and The Croft next door with 12 acres of land, from the Okeover Estate. George William continued to live at Common End Farm until 1988. His son Bert Morris, and his wife, Ruth, moved into The Croft and renamed it Little Moor Farm. In 1988 Mr Alan Hewitt, bought the 144 acre farm. He and his wife, Denise, and two children, Louise and Christopher, continue to live there in 1998

CORNER COTTAGE
Mrs Polly Hardy lived in the cottage for thirty years. She was a regular attender at the chapel in Town End Lane. One of the local lads, Sam Salt, used to sit on the back row of the chapel during services. He was good at drawing and drew a picture of Polly Hardy inside the cover of one of the hymn books. A number of the local folk remember this hymn book which lasted till the chapel closed. Joan Hayes and Lindon MacIntyre live in Corner Cottage next door to Joan's parents, Mr and Mrs Major.

THE CROFT - *Island Cottage.*
According to the 1844 map, Samuel Harrison and Elizabeth Stubbs lived at the cottage on this site. The cottage was tied to Blore Hall, and farm labourers from the Hall were allowed to live there.

The Grindey family lived at the Croft in the 1930s and moved to Little Moor Cottage. Reg & Grace Bailey lived at the Croft from 1938 until 1940. John Feeley and Mabel Allen were married in 1940. They asked permission to move into the schoolhouse but as John was a Catholic the request was refused. Reg and Grace Bailey moved to the schoolhouse instead and John and Mabel took the Croft. John continued to work at Blore Hall with Reg Bailey. Both the Feeley children, Jennifer and Michael, were born in the cottage and later attended Swinscoe School. The Feeley family stayed until the 1950s.

An Italian farm labourer, Angelo Colombo, who worked at Blore Hall, moved into the cottage with his wife Naomi and brother Lupino. They did not stay long because of problems at Blore Hall, and they moved to Cubley. Around 1960, Tom Allcock from Calton bought the cottage from the Okeover Estate. He married Joan Briddon and they lived at The Croft. They moved on in the 1970s to Calton. Jeremy and Susan Campagnac, a French family, were staying in the cottage in 1984. After the Campagnacs left the cottage was empty for a long time. According to a Sale Notice in 1996, it is a stone built cottage with two reception rooms, fitted kitchen, three bedrooms, bathroom, and a garage and workshop.

ELLIS HILL
Ellis Hill Farm in the Parish of Blore-with-Swinscoe is remarkable for the richness of its soil and the fine South aspect, commanding views of great extent and beauty.

The earliest mention of Ellis Hill was during the 14th Century. The name is probably derived from Erles Hill. It may have had a similar derivation to that of Erles Way, the road used by the Earl of Chester's men to collect taxes. Earls Way still exists as far as Calton, but heading in the direction of Rocester. There is a road (referred to in some documents, as Rice Lane) up from Rocester, through Calwich towards Ellis Hill.

In November 1541, Francis the Earl of Shrewsbury was granted a pasture called Elieshil, in Swinscoe, which had belonged to the Monastery of Rocester.

According to some ancient agreement, Ellis Hill Farm paid no tithes. The land belonged to Rocester Abbey from the 13th to the 16th century and the freedom from tithes probably related to this. Instead, the Rector of Blore was allowed to have use of grassland for two beasts from May till Michaelmas. As the distance from Blore to Ellis Hill is a couple of miles, this must have been a doubtful benefit. The non-payment of tithes was certainly a matter of great contention. From 1612 through to 1844, when all tithes were commuted, the Glebe Terriers show the constant running battle between the Occupants of Ellis Hill and the Rectors of Blore.

The battle with the Rectors of Blore may have been a contributory factor to the move away from the Established Church in Swinscoe. The Primitive Methodist Religion was very strong in Swinscoe and the Phillips family who lived at Ellis Hill up to 1960, still adhered to Primitive Methodist beliefs.

Before 1605, Ellis Hill was owned by Edward Pegg. His daughter, Anne Pegg, married Thomas Southeby. For the next two hundred years the title to the property remained with their descendants - direct or through marriage. In 1690, Robt Belt and his wife, Goodeth, held the Farm under a lease for one thousand years.

Up to 1744 the farm was held by the descendants of the Willoughby family. One of the four daughters, Emma, married a member of the Hodgson family and in a share out of the property among the daughters, Emma received Ellis Hill. As a result the farm became part of the extensive estates of the Hodgson family for the next hundred years.

Samuel Goodwin tenanted Ellis Hill till around 1768 when he died. At the time, Ellis Hill and Ellis Hill Tars comprised 120 acres, including Swinscoe Wood of 14 acres. On the 7th July 1768, John, the son of Joseph and Anne Fletcher of Ellis Hill, was baptised at Blore Church. Between 1768 and 1780 a John Gallimore was the tenant of Ellis Hill Farm.

In 1802, Brian Hodgson offered Ellis Hill for sale by auction and it was bought by Lewis Teissier of London. However the sale fell through because defects in part of Hodgson's title to it. The defects related to missing documents of title, one hundred years previously: *"between 1685 and 1744 there is a chasm of 59 years unaccounted for"*. In addition there was also the vexed question of non-payment of tithes. There was no written evidence that Ellis Hill was free of the tithe payment and the church, who had been arguing the case for centuries, were certainly not going to support any assumption of non-payment. Mr Hodgson's Solicitor obtained sworn statements from three men who had lived in the Parish for many years. These men, John Gallimore, Philip Peach and William Braddock, affirmed that Ellis Hill was free of tithe. The auctioneer found himself in a very awkward situation. He had received £3980, the 20% deposit of the bid of £19,900 made by Mr Tessier. Tessier was claiming the deposit back. Mr Hodgson was claiming that the deposit was his rightful due. All parties sought legal counsel and, finally it was decided in Mr Tessier's favour. As a result, Brian Hodgson withdrew the estate from sale, and the Hodgson Family continued to hold Ellis Hill for another forty years.

Thomas Gallimore and his family farmed Ellis Hill in 1802. He paid £160 a year rent for the 126 Acre Farm. The field to the east of the farm buildings was called Colliers Ley and the two neighbouring fields on New House Farm were also called Colliers Ley. There was a lease agreement in 1804, allowing Michael Saxelby to search for coal. In 1829, Thomas Gallimore was paying a half-yearly rental of £110. Times had been very hard ever since the War with France which ended in 1815. There had been a post-war slump. In common with the other farms on the Hodgson Estate, the rental was reduced in 1831. In the case of Ellis Hill it was reduced to £102.10s.0d per half year.

Like many other local farmers, Mr Gallimore employed Anthony Stubbs of Saw Pit Farm, now the Old Post Office, to carry out a variety of minor repairs and improvements, and in February 1837 a new barn floor was laid at a cost of £9.17.11d. On 27th January 1838, following the death of his wife, Mr Gallimore ordered from Anthony Stubbs a fully furnished oak coffin lined with flannel and a wood mattress at a cost of £2.0s.0d. In 1841, Thomas Gallimore aged 80, and his family, Thomas, William, Mary and Sarah, still farmed Ellis Hill. Their 14 year old niece, Mary Leese, was working as a maid. Ellis Hill was described as a stone built farm house containing a parlour, kitchen, three bedrooms, dairy, cheese room, coal house, garden in front. The Farm Yard contained Cart Lodge, Poultry, Sheep and Calf

Swinscoe, Blore and the Bassetts   *91*

Houses, three-stall stable, two Cow Houses, Foddering House, Loft over. In Barn Field there was a stone-built Barn, two other Cow Houses, and a stack Yard. At that time, Ellis Hill consisted of 126 acres, including 16 acres of woodland. The Gallimores had a herd of thirty milking cows. Thomas Gallimore died on the 2nd October 1842, and left £16.0s.0d to his daughter Ellen, the wife of Mr Leese. His son John had already received his share when he got married. He left the rest of his estate, valued at up to £450, to be shared among his two sons, Thomas and William, and two daughters, Mary and Sarah.

In 1844, the farm was again offered for sale. By this time, all tithes in the Parish has been commuted, under the Tythe Commutation Act. Ellis Hill was charged an Annual Rental of £6.6s.0d so that one of the particular hindrances to the previous sale no longer applied. Ellis Hill was sold to the Rev Augustus Duncombe. The cottage in the woods housed the 15 year old son William and a farm labourer called Thomas Harrison.

The land was then farmed by the son Thomas Gallimore, as tenant from year to year, as follows:

Ellis Hill Meadow	Old Pasture	2-0- 0
Upper Meadow	Meadow	7-2-14
Calf Paddock	Ditto	0-3-32
Ellis Hill Farm House,	Outbuildings, Yards, Garden and Orchard	0-3-1
Colliers Ley	Old Pasture	3-2-13
Little Croft	Old Meadow	0-2-28
Near side of Ellis Hill	Old Pasture	14-0-21
Far side of Ellis Hill	Old Pasture	15-3-17
Ellis Hill Tors	Wood	5-3- 2
Plantation		0-0-11
Little or New Meadow	Old Meadow	4-3- 5
Baddaley Meadow	Old Pasture	12-1- 2
Briery Piece	Wood	1-3-18
Swinscoe Wood	Wood	9-0-12
Bigwood Piece	Old Turf	5-3-32
Little Wood Piece	Arable	2-1-14
Lime Tree Piece	Arable	3-2-21
Greaves	Old Meadow	4-3-11
Rise Redding	Old Meadow & Arable	7-2-21
Ellis Hill Barn & Yard		0-0-15
Barn Piece	Old Pasture	1-2-14
Piece below the Barn	Arable	2-1-34
Swinscoe Hill	Turf Pasture	3-3-14
Hill Side	Pasture	5-1-28
Slang	Turf	1-2-28
Narrow strip lying to Rise Wood and between Fence and Brook		0-0-34
Buckston's Close in the Parish of Mayfield, called Bucksome Close		7-2-28
		126-2-31

It is interesting to account for the field names given in the above, extracted from the Notice of Sale 1844. The majority of names describe the type of land or their proximity to a feature: Upper and Little and New Meadow, Near and Far Side of Ellis Hill, Lime Tree Piece, Briery Piece and Greaves (brushwood thicket), Slang (a small field). Baddaley Meadow is probably related to a previous tenant of the land. There were Cottagers by the name of Baggaley living on Ellis Farm from 1609 to 1638 - spelling used to be more a matter of how a name sounds! Rise Redding is unsolved; it may be related to Rice just south of Ellis Hill Farm as shown on Yates Map of 1775. Ellis Hill, surprisingly, is not shown. In the will of John Hood, of Swinscoe, 1623, he refers to his lands in Matherfield Ryse (Mayfield Rice?) bought from Mr Nicholas Hurt. John Hood farmed either Ellis Hill or New House Farm; he mentions Sir John Offley as his landlord, and at his death, left a sizeable inventory of goods. As mentioned previously, Colliers Ley was related to the miners search for coal; there are depressions in the field which are the old mine shafts. The actual meaning of Tars is unsolved.

On the 9th June 1857, son Thomas Gallimore died and left all his estate, valued at less than £300, to his brother William and sister Mary. His brother and sister continued to farm the 109 acres for a couple of years until 1859. They retired to Rose Cottage alongside the Main Road at the top of Swinscoe Hill.

Ellis Hill was rebuilt around 1860. The Finney family, Thomas and Ellen with their sons Thomas, Benjamin and Samuel moved in. The butter trade was thriving and Thomas Finney employed Henry Lovatt and Samuel Waring as carters and general labourers. In 1871, only two sons were at home: Thomas and Benjamin, and a young girl, Mary Allcock, who was employed as general servant.

There was a temporary hut called the Keepers House on the property, used by the gamekeeper for those people who leased the shooting rights on the property. Back in 1829/30, D. Smith paid £10 for the shooting rights and from 1831 until 1838, Court Granville also paid £10, but the rental was increased in 1839 to £20.

Around 1874, Luke Mellor began farming at Ellis Hill. In 1881, he and his wife Maria were living there with five children: Polly, Harriet, Elizabeth, John and Florence. Maria's father had died, and her mother, Mary Oakden, aged 75, and sister, Elizabeth, were living with them. They employed George Robinson as farm servant and Mary Berrisford as general domestic servant.

Ellis Hill was not shown on Yates Map, 1775, and there is no trace of Ellis Hill Farm in the census of 1891. Further search has been made within all neighbouring parishes to no avail. It was somehow omitted from the census; either it was empty at the time or it was just not recorded. No likely alternative has been identified. For a brief spell around the turn of the century, Beresford Wilson occupied Ellis Hill.

Charles Phillips and his wife Annie were married at Blore Church in April 1899. According to Kelly's Directory 1900, Charles Phillips is named as a farmer in Swinscoe, but Ellis Hill is not mentioned. He was definitely at Ellis Hill in 1902. Charles and Annie Phillips were lifelong members of the Swinscoe Methodist Chapel. In 1917, when new trustees were elected and Charles Phillips of Ellis Hill was nominated as one of the sixteen trustees. On the 6th February 1937, Ethel Phillips of Ellis Hill married her cousin, Stanley John Phillips, at the Swinscoe Methodist Chapel. Three years later, in 1940, her sister, Mabel Annie Phillips, married Arthur Naylor of Rose Cottage, also at the chapel. Mabel and her husband went to live at Ellis Hill. Mr Phillips was elected as one of the Managers of Swinscoe School in 1910, and he continued to hold that position for more than thirty five years. In 1946, a letter of appreciation was sent to Mr Phillips in recognition of his long term service to the school. According to the Electoral Registers, from 1945 to 1949, Charles, Annie and their three children John, Lizzie and Mabel Annie were living at Ellis Hill. His wife Annie died in 1953.

In 1954, at a meeting of the trustees of the chapel, the chairman Rev J.E. Bolitho *"wished to record his appreciation of the generosity of Mr Charles Phillips who throughout the years has been a most loyal supporter and devoted worker for the Methodist Society at Swinscoe."* Charles died on 2nd January 1955. Their children and members of the chapel placed a plaque in commemoration of his service on the wall inside the chapel. The Phillips continued to farm Ellis Hill until 1975. In 1975, Mr Philip Binder and his wife, Winifred, took up residence, and stayed at Ellis Hill until 1997.

FAIRBROOK COTTAGE - *Cabaret Cottage. Diana Dors Cottage. (Sometimes as Meadowside Cottage).*
It has been suggested that this cottage was originally built, like a number of other stone cottages in the village, in the 17th/18th century. On the 1844 map of Swinscoe, it is number 228, and appears to show one building, comprising two cottages. The two cottages must have been very small because the undivided cottage was small, before the extensions were carried out. Since the War, one of the tenants installed a spiral staircase to allow easier access to the bedrooms, and provided a removable floor to the bedroom, for getting the furniture upstairs. Confusingly, this cottage was sometimes known by local residents as Meadowside Cottage. This is now the name of the cottage on the other side of the pub, on the corner of Chapel Lane.

Fairbrook Cottage was owned by the Dog & Partridge. Mr Charles Clewes and his wife, Louisa, lived for a time in the school house. When a new teacher came along, the family moved across the road into Fairbrook Cottage. There were three children, Arthur, Ernest and Phyllis. On 12th August 1938, Arthur Clewes married Margaret Herron of Calwich. The bride wore a dress of ivory satin, with a head-dress of lilies of the valley, and a bouquet of red carnations. Ernest Clewes was the best man and his sister, Phyllis, was a bridesmaid. Phyllis Clewes married Harry Ratcliffe, and moved into the Peak View

Cottage near the end of Blore Lane. Later they moved to Mayfield, where they still live. Ernest Clewes continued to live in Fairbrook Cottage until 1948; his name appears in the electoral registers.

The Dog & Partridge at one time used to have a cabaret, and famous artists used to give performances at the pub. Jimmy Edwards, Tommy Trinder and Diana Dors were among the artists who visited Swinscoe. Diana Dors came to Swinscoe a number of times and the cottage became known as Diana Dors Cottage. After one of her visits, she told a local newspaper that she had seen a wild-looking ghost in the cottage. She thought that the ghost was possibly one of the Scottish soldiers who was killed in Swinscoe during the retreat of Bonnie Prince Charlie in 1745. The cottage has changed hands a number of times since then.

In 1984, Mr Peter Sullivan is shown in the Electoral Registers as resident in the cottage. In 1984, Fairbrook was offered for sale as a stone and tile cottage of great character, with beamed sitting-room, open tread staircase and three bedrooms. Mr and Mrs Burgess, and their children, moved into the cottage in 1987 and have remained there ever since

FLEECE HOUSE - *Golden Ram. Spotted Cow. Golden Fleece. The Fleece.*
With the increase in passing travellers through Swinscoe in the mid 1800s, another public house besides the Dog & Partridge was opened in the village. Unlike the Dog and Partridge, it has changed its name on three occasions. First, it was called the Golden Ram, then the Spotted Cow and then the Golden Fleece. The building is still locally called the Fleece.

According to Anthony Stubbs' account book, John Smith was at the Ram from 1834 to 1851, and was charged with a number of minor items. The publican needed to protect his property and his ale so Anthony Stubbs had installed guard windows. Like many others in the village, John Smith made his own cheese, and he was charged eight pence for repairing a cheese ladder. Frederick Thompson was at the Golden Fleece in 1884 and 1885. In 1886, he was elected as one of the Overseers of the Poor for the parish. In 1888, Benjamin Salt was licensee. He recognised that the local and passing trade was not sufficient to support two public houses. In 1892, he moved to the Dog & Partridge, and took over from Sarah Yates. The Dog & Partridge is the public house that has survived.

John and Sarah Howson moved to the Fleece in 1918 and their names are recorded in the Electoral Registers. When John died in 1936, his wife Sarah went to live with her son and daughter at the Dog & Partridge. Laura Ditchfield, from the Leasowes, worked for the Howsons as a housekeeper, and acted as Nanny to Eileen Howson. Grandmother Sarah was a staunch Methodist and participated in all the activities of the chapel. She is remembered as wearing floor-length black dresses, with black boots peeping out from underneath. An inveterate card-player, she loved to play cards with anyone that she could persuade to join her. Sheila Allen recalls that she and her best friend Mabel Howson were regularly invited to play cards with Grandma. Sarah's son, John William, sometimes used to walk down to the pub for a pint and the inevitable game of cards. Sarah continued to live at the Dog & Partridge until her death in 1953. Her daughter Mabel Blore was running the pub and John William was living at the Fleece

The Fleece was surrounded by a large area where a fleet of up to eleven green and yellow lorries were based. Among the local men who drove the J.W. Howson lorries, were Wilfred Allen, Bill, George and Tom Grindey, Percy Hill, Bill Jackson, and Alfred Wallis. Mr Howson worked alongside his men, and carried out much of the maintenance himself. He was often found lying underneath his beloved lorries with a grease gun in his hand. He had a very good reputation as an employer - he paid good wages and looked after his men. One of his drivers, Mr Brunt from Mayfield, shot his girl-friend's mother, and was arrested and put on trial at Stafford. Mr Howson went to Stafford to act as a character witness, but in spite of his good report, the jury found Mr Brunt guilty. The judge sentenced Brunt to death, and he was hanged at Manchester Gaol - the last execution ever to be carried out at Manchester.

In 1949, the Labour Government nationalised the road transport industry. At the Fleece the lorries were lined up for the last time, and driven off to the British Road Services Depot at Hilton. Mr Howson retired and bought Dove Cottage, by the river at Clifton. The Fleece had no electricity, no water and an old fashioned closet at the bottom of the garden. Each morning before school, the children went to fetch the milk from a nearby farm and the water from the well in Chapel Lane. The washing was boiled in an old boiler in the stable, agitated with a dolly peg, and squeezed part-dry through the mangle, ready for hanging on the washing line. John and Gladys continued to live there until their mother's death in 1953. Mr Howson sold the property to Mr Lewis Hill who occupied it with his wife and three boys, Lewis, Gordon and David, until 1984.

The Fleece was bought by Mr Wood. The electoral register for 1984 lists Austin Wood, Elsie, Mark, Samantha. The Wood family could not get used to the quietness, and the bleeting of the sheep, so they sold the property ten months later to Mr Tom Clowes of Green Farm. Mr Clowes' daughter, Marylin, and her husband, Roy Sandal, moved into the cottage, and Mr Clowes added the land to his holding at Green Farm. In 1996, the names of Roy Sandal, Marylin, Mark, and Claire were recorded in the Electoral Register as eligible to vote.

FOREST FARM - *Forest Side Farm. South Side. Side House.*
This Farm has changed its name during the past 150 years from South Side Farm, to Side House Farm, to Forest Farm and to Forest Side Farm. The reasons for these changes of name is unknown, but the present name could easily relate to centuries ago when Swinscoe was covered by forest (the name Swinscoe means Forest or Wood of Swine). In 1829, Richard Harris was living at a small cottage and farming a plot of five acres at a rental of £7.19s.0d. This rent was reduced to £6.10s.0d. in 1830. In 1830, Charles Smith farmed a small plot for which he paid £5.0s.0d rental per half year. In 1838, William Howson of Common End was having problems and the Hodgson Estate agreed to let Charles Smith extend his holding to eleven acres, at a total rental of £11.0s.0d.

Around the beginning of the 1830s, John Ford and his wife Mary with their daughter Sarah and two young servants, Elizabeth Stannah, aged 14, and James Warrington, aged 15, lived at South Side. The stone-built Farm House contained a Parlour, Kitchen, Scullery, Three Bed Chambers, Threshing Barn, stable for four horses; Cow Houses Two Foddering Houses, Cart Lodge; Calf Pen, Coal House, and Piggery. They farmed one hundred acres of land. Two other fields, comprising 9a.0r.26p, were farmed by Charles Smith. Samuel Archer of New House Farm was farming 20a.1r.26p. The land belonged to the Hodgson family and, along with most of the rest of their estate in Swinscoe, was put up for sale in 1844. In 1844 it was in the occupation of Mr John Ford, Mr Charles Smith, and Mr S. Archer:

		Acreage	
Clay Pit Piece	Pasture	4.0. 0.	Smith
Rye Grass Piece	Pasture	5.0.26.	Smith
Horse Pasture	Pasture	6.3.23.	Ford
Croft	Old Pasture	0.1. 9.	Ford
South side Farm House etc		0.2.26.	Ford
Plantation & Garden Ground		0.2.39	Ford
Hurd's Common Piece	Turf	5.3.12.	Ford
Near Common Piece	Arable	5.3.19.	Archer
Hurd's Meadow	Old Turf	8.3.10.	Ford
Far Common Piece	Arable	5.3. 1.	Archer
Plantation		0.0.26.	In Hand
Big Common Piece	Pasture	8.3. 6.	Archer
Spring Close	Pasture	5.0. 0.	Ford
Three Acre Piece	Arable	3.1. 0.	Ford
Lime Kiln Piece	Pasture	9.2.18	Ford
Clover Piece	Pasture	4.2. 4.	Ford
Long Piece	Old Pasture	4.0.18.	Ford
Lane		0.2. 6.	Ford
Near Meadow	Arable & Turf	5.2.17.	Ford
Little Meadow	Arable	3.3.25.	Ford
Dry Knobs	Old Pasture	8.2.20.	Ford
Smithy Piece	Turf	8.3.31.	Ford
Well Piece	Old Pasture	5.3.28.	Ford
Upper Coal Piece	Old Pasture	6.1.30.	Ford
Lower Coal Pit Piece	Turf 1	0.1.15.	Ford
	Total Acreage	129.3. 9.	

The two pieces called Upper Coal Piece and Lower Coal Pit Piece, probably relate to the search for coal which took place in Swinscoe in the early 19th century. According to the census in 1851, William Slater, a farm labourer, his wife Sarah and two babies, Joseph and Emma, were living at Side House. In 1861, the Lees family were farming Forest farm. Francis Leese had taken over the farm with children Thomas and Frances. Francis died at the age of 74 on 29th June 1868. They had two servants: Alice Coxon and Elija Hampson, and a cow boy John Hampson aged 13. Thomas worked the farm and hired the labour. In 1868, he hired Henry Smith as a farm labourer, but Henry absconded from service. Thomas Lees summoned him to court in Ashbourne, where Henry was ordered to return to work and to pay costs.

In 1871, William and Sarah Mountford were living at Forest Farm, along with Sarah's son by her previous marriage, George Titterton. They employed two farm servants, James Birch and Rupert Charlesworth, and a dairymaid Eliza Stannah.

Around 1875, William Stannah and his wife, Hannah, moved from Calton, where their eldest two children Mary and Francis had been born. By 1881, another three children, Alice, Martha and William, had arrived. William's 84 year old father and 82 year old mother, William and Fanny Stannah were living with them. They employed Elizabeth Chadwick as a domestic and James Chadwick and George Mathews as farm servants. The Stannahs moved to New House Farm.

The tenancy was taken by Joseph Moss. From 1888 to 1892, Joseph and his wife, Lousia, and three children, George (22), Lizzie (18) and Anne (16), were living at the farm. They continued to live there until Joseph Moss died on 27th November 1903 age 73. Louisa, his wife, died on the 5th February 1908 age 67. They are both buried at Blore.

Mr William Charles Twemlow along with his wife Lizzie and son, also William Charles, took the tenancy in 1908. In 1913, Mr Twemlow was appointed as one of the Managers of Swinscoe School. In 1917, he was elected as one the sixteen trustees of Swinscoe Methodist Chapel. William Charles moved from Forest Farm in 1915. His son died on 27th April 1930, and William Charles died two weeks later on 13th May 1930. His widow Lizzie died on the 11th July 1937 at the age of 65. According to the Electoral Registers, James Harrison was at Forest Farm in 1939.

The Cottons moved from Cauldon and Mr Jack Cotton stayed at Forest Farm until 1945. He was involved in a serious accident; his arm was caught in a threshing machine and had to be amputated. His daughter, Enid Cotton, went to Swinscoe School and in his retirement Mr Cotton lived with her in Waterhouses until he died in his 80s. The farmhouse contained two sitting rooms, a living room and scullery, and two small pantries, one of which was used as a cellar. Upstairs there were five bedrooms.

From 1945 until 1959, John and Alice Oakes were at Forest Farm. Their daughter, Margaret, was married to Margaret and joined him at Ox Close Farm, Offcote. Two brothers, Geoff and George Prime, bought Forest Farm in 1959, and moved from Bull Gap. Their widowed mother kept house for them until her death. Their sister, Mrs Mary Salt, lived at the Mire, which Geoff and George had also acquired. In 1998, Geoff and George are still farming at Forest Farm with 138 acres, but have reduced their cattle herd, from seventy five to forty cows.

GILMAN HOUSE - *Caurus*

In 1951 Mr Reginal Bailey of the school house in Swinscoe, bought five acres of land down Town End Lane from Peter Gregory, the owner of the Dog & Partridge. In 1979, he sold two thirds of an acre to Don Derbyshire, a master builder from Long Lane in Derbyshire. Mr Derbyshire built two houses on the site: Oakfields and Caurus. Caurus, which is Latin for North West Wind, was built in 1986. It was sold to Mr and Mrs Peter Holiday, who lived in the house until 1990. In May, 1990, the house was bought by Mr Graham Trevarthen and his wife Lindsay, who live there with their two children, Hannah and Howard. They changed the name of the house from Caurus to Gilman House. Since her arrival, Lindsay has taken a vital interest in the parish, and made a major contribution to its activities and has been a significant contributor to this book.

GREEN FARM

Around 1700 Green Farm was built with walls a yard thick. Ever since 1840, there has been some confusion in the records between Green Farm and The Green. Chapel Farm used to be known as The Green but this farm has always been known as Green Farm.

In 1844, Mr Porter and Mr Samuel Birch are recorded as tenants of the stone-built Farm House containing Parlour, Dairy, Kitchen, Scullery, Cellar, Two Sleeping Rooms, Landing, Lumber Room, Coal Shed, Farm Yard, Two Cow Houses, Foddering Houses, Barn, Calf Pen, Cart Hovel, Stable, Piggery, etc and comprised sixty four acres. In the sale notice in 1844, Green Farm was Lot 6. Lot 6 included the present land holding, and land that subsequently became known as Hill End.

Back of the Hill	Pasture	6.1. 2
Plantation		1. 1
Short Rakes	Arable	2.3.30
Hill End	Old Turf	6.1. 6
Near Hill	Arable	3.2. 7
Middle Hill	Pasture	3.1.21
Plantation		0.0.19
Far Hill	Pasture	3.1.21
Lime Kiln Hill	Old Ditto	2.0.35
Back of the Hill	Pasture	5.2.30
Lime Kiln Plantation		1.1.12
Croft	Old Meadow	0.1.29
House Outbuildings Yard and Garden		0.2.00
Part of Lane		0.1. 5
Crofts	Old Pasture	8.1.38
Two Dwellings, Gardens and Croft		0.2.19
Little Well Croft	Old Meadow	1.1.31
Corn Croft (incl 6 perches from Road)	Old Pasture	3.2.25
Far Croft (incl 16 perches from Rd)	Old Meadow	5.2.27
Croft	Old Meadow	0.1.28
Green	Old Pasture	2.0.36
Green Meadow	Old Meadow	0.2.37
Hodge Croft	Old Meadow	2.0.34
Lane Nursery Plantation		0.1.29
		63.1.39

Either when the sale took place, or subsequently, the land was divided into the two different farms, Green Farm and Hill End. In 1892, the name of Jas Alcock is recorded as resident at Green Farm. In 1928, Mr Clowes senior took the tenancy of Green Farm and a year later his son, Tom Clowes, was born at Green Farm. Tom has remained in residence ever since. In 1955, Mr Clowes bought the farm from Mr Charles Phillips. On 21st July 1963 Elaine, daughter of Thomas Frederick and Joan Irene Clowes, was baptised at Swinscoe Primitive Methodist Chapel. In 1964, the farm was thirty one acres in size. When the Chapel was closed in 1981, Mr Clowes bought it and since then has used it as a store for his business. Around the same time the old Post Office closed and Mr Clowes applied to open a new one at Green Farm. This was approved and the new Post Office at Green Farm now serves the residents of Swinscoe.

HALL FLATTS

There have been people farming the lands at Hall Flatts for centuries. The signs of ancient ridge and furrow probably date back to the 12th and 13th Centuries when the monks of Rocester Abbey set up a chapel and farmed the land. The site of the chapel "surrounded by ditches" was, most likely down in the marshy ground at the bottom of the fields. According to Dr Alan Rogers of Leicester University it was very common for monks to build their monasteries on marshy land. The site, just outside the remote Township of Swinscoe, was an ideal place for the monks of the abbey to establish themselves.

The name Hall Flatts means "Flatts belonging to the Hall". Among the Okeovers papers is the Rocester Abbey Chartulary which refers to Vecc-le-Hall. The probable site of the Hall, belonging to the Beck family, is nearby New House Farm. According to the Glebe Terriers for Blore Church, prior to 1755 Philip Peach was due to pay seven pence to the Rector, in lieu of Tithe Hay for Hall Flatts.

The cottage, now known as Hall Flatts, was built sometime in the early 1800s and by 1841 it was occupied by Edward Leese and Judy his wife, with their son, John, and a female servant, Georgiana

Stubbs. When Swinscoe School was opened in 1865, Ellen Leese was one of the first pupils.

In 1850, a small amount of work was carried out at Hall Flatts by the local carpenter, at a cost of 5s.7d. This was charged to Mr Samuel Archer of New House Farm, who owned the land. By 1851, the Leese family had moved on. Edward Leese died at the age of 71 on 27th May 1860 and his wife Judith died 2nd March 1873 aged 73. They were both buried in Blore Churchyard.

George Bott left his brother at Town End Farm, and took the tenancy of Hall Flatts where he and his wife, Mary Ann, with their four children, Hannah, Mary, Alice and Sarah lived. Ten years later, in 1861, George and his wife were still living there, but the elder three daughter had moved away and two more children had been added to the family, George aged 9 and Ellen aged 4. According to Kelly's Directory in 1880, George is recorded as a cowkeeper, and according to the census, his wife, Mary Ann, was a school mistress. George Bott had a long and close association with Blore Church. As a young man, he was Sexton and Gravedigger, and in 1860 he was appointed Churchwarden and Clerk of the Parish. He occupied the position of Clerk of the Parish for over thirty years until the 1890s.

In 1881, Joseph Renshaw and his wife, and five children, were living at Hall Flatts. The eldest daughter was working at home, the three middle ones, Agnes, George and Emily, were attending Swinscoe School, and Sarah was only 11 months old. From 1884 until 1896, John Rowe and his wife Sarah, and daughter Nelly, lived at Hall Flatts. At the beginning of the century, Thomas Coxon occupied Hall Flatts.

In 1918, William Twemlow and his wife Catherine were living here. Catherine died 22nd April 1921 age 81, and her husband William died just over a year later on the 18th September 1922 at the age of 77. Their son William Charles Twemlow and his wife, Lizzie, continued to farm Hall Flatts. Their son, also called William Charles, tragically died on the 27th April 1930 at the age of 25. William Charles Twemlow died in May 1933 at the age of 62 and his wife, Lizzie, died 11th July 1937 at the age of 65.

In 1939, Jim Mycock and his wife Ellen were farming at Hall Flatts and they stayed through the 1940s. After the War, Mr and Mrs Hardy lived at Hall Flatts and the farm was recorded as twelve acres in size. In 1978, Mr Bertram White and his wife Doreen, retired from New House Farm and handed over the farming to their son Kevin, and his wife, Sheila. Mr and Mrs White modernised the cottage and took up residence at Hall Flatts. In 1994, Mrs Doreen White died, and sadly three years later her husband Bertram died.

HILLCREST - *Netlows Woodcock Abbey? The Old Chapel?*

On the eastern side of the main road through Swinscoe just at the top of the hill there used to be an ancient burial mound. The field in which it was situated was called Net Low; the word "low" is an old gothic word meaning burial place. The name was sometimes corrupted to Nettles or Nettlows. The name was used not only for the field containing the mound, but also for the upper part of the hill and the cottages on either side of the road. Hillcrest was originally two cottages. Close by there is one of the four springs and wells in Swinscoe, which provided water for the residents.

According to one of the older residents, Hillcrest was, once upon a time, called Woodcock Abbey but so far this has not been substantiated from any records. One of the buildings at the crest of hill was used as a chapel, before the chapel in Town End Lane was built. It may have been Hillcrest or Rose Cottage, or the barn.

In the census for 1861, the Allen family were living at Nettles House. William Allen and his wife, Hannah, had five children: Mary, Sarah, David, James and Hannah. William was a farm worker, but his eldest children Mary (20), Sarah (16) and David (14), were working at the factory at Mayfield. James and Hannah Allen, both 8 years old, were still at Swinscoe School. Mrs Hannah Allen had another baby called George in 1863. After her husband died, she stayed on at Nettles House for a few years. In 1871, her son David was still working at the mill and her 8 year old son, George, was a scholar at Swinscoe School. Another family of Allens, Frank and Ellen Allen, occupied the cottage at the beginning of the War and in 1930, Mr and Mrs Bagnall lived here. Sadly, after the birth of her baby, Mrs Bagnall, in what must have been a fit of post-natal depression, drowned the child in a nearby stream.

Another Allen family lived here, Frank Allen and his wife Ellen, who lived here with Ellen's mother, Mrs Bailey. They changed the name of the cottage to Hillcrest. In 1941/2, Mr William Jackson, and his wife, Mary, moved from Stanton to the cottage. A year later, in 1943, their son Neil was born. He went to Swinscoe School and appears on three of the school photographs during the early fifties when Mrs Smith was the teacher. In 1948, Bill Jackson's brother Sidney was living with them. When his uncle Tom Stannah died, Sid moved to Mitre Farm, at the other end of Swinscoe, and lived in a Countess Caravan on the site for many years. William Jackson died in 1982, at the age of 71, and his wife, Mary, continued to live at Hillcrest until 1996 when she moved to Ashbourne.

HILLEND FARM

Swinscoe Hill climbs up from Mayfield to almost 1000 feet above sea level, and at the end of the long climb is the farm now called Hill End Farm. In 1800, Philip Peach was farming part of the land that now forms Hill End Farm. He kept ten milking cows and a few sheep and ploughed about eight acres of his one hundred and eight acre holding. He paid a rental of £130.0s.0d and Land Tax of £3.17s.6d. Around 1845, the land East of the Main Road and South of Field Lane, was owned by the Hodgson Estate, but was divided into a number of parts and farmed by various individuals. Excluding Cliff Top Farm and the Netlows, the land comprised:

In the occupation of Robert Yates and Joseph Bott as year to year tenants

Little Flat	3-0- 4
Big Flat	6-3-18
Lime Kiln and Quarry	2-0- 9
Little Upper Flat	1-3- 3
Big Upper Flat	5-3-38
Greaves Land	5-1-25
Field Meadows	6-2- 8
Upper Close	10-0-20
Lower Close	16-2- 2
Ferney Lee Plantation	0-2-31
Long Rakes	4-2-38
Ferney Leys	7-1-24
	71-0-26

In the occupation of W. Swettenham and Samuel Archer on a year to year basis

Near Gorse Lane	3-1-10
Far Gorse Lane	4-0-16
Long Croft	3-1-23
Near Long Croft	4-0-10
The Hill	12-0-16
Hill Plantation	0-3-23
	7-3- 8

and a number of other closes:

Back of the Hill	6-1- 2
Plantation	0-1- 1
Short Rakes	2-3-30
Hill End	6-1- 6
Near Hill	3-2- 7
Middle Hill	3-1-21
Plantation	0-0-19
Far Hill	4-1-17
Limekiln Hill	2-0-35
Back of the Hill	5-2-30
Limekiln Plantation	1-1-12
	36-1-26

In 1845, the Trustees of the Okeover Estate bought this land from Rev Hodgson. In 1847, the Okeover Estate made a tenancy agreement with John Chadwick of Mappleton, for eighty nine acres of the land, excluding Long Croft, New Long Croft, The Hill and Plantation. The rent was £120 per year but the agreement only lasted three years. Samuel Archer, of New House Farm, acquired the tenancy of the land in 1850. On that piece of land called Hill End, the Okeovers built a new farmhouse and it became known as Hill End Farm. Mr Archer installed his 17 year old son, Samuel, at the new farm along with his brother, Thomas, and sisters, Mary and Elizabeth. In 1861, young Samuel had reached the age of 26. He was still farming the one hundred and ten acres of Hill End Farm, and his sisters, Elizabeth and Fanny, were with him. His sister Mary had married, and gone to live elsewhere. He had a young boy as a servant, Samuel Chadwick, aged 12.

At the census of 1871, John Fielding is recorded as farming 126 acres which, although not named, was undoubtedly Hill End Farm. In 1881, Thomas Stannah aged 40 was farming 127 acres and his uncle Thomas Stannah aged 75 was living with him. A sister Ellen and a niece and nephew, Lilian Stannah and Thomas Barker Stannah, were also living at the farm. They employed George Buxton as a farm servant. Thomas was one of the signatories at a public meeting held in Swinscoe School, to choose Overseers of the Poor for the parish. Mr Ralph Webster of The Waterings and Mr Frederick Thompson of the Fleece were elected. In 1891, Thomas was still at the farm and his sister Ellen was acting as his housekeeper, but her two children were only there as temporary visitors. Their farm servant was George Poyser, from Stanton. Thomas continued to farm Hill End until around 1908, when there was some kind of swap with Mr Warrington who was then living at The Mire. Mr Warrington took over the tenancy.

According to the parish registers, a family of Robothams lived at Hill End, but this was probably in a part of the house or one of the buildings - they were not farmers. This family may have been remotely related to the Robothams of Town End Farm. Mr Samuel Lowe Robotham and his wife were schoolteachers at Waterfall School for a number of years. They had a son, Archibald William who died at the age of 28 in 1908. Mr Samuel Lowe Robotham died 2 October 1912 age 75. Another tragedy befell the Robotham family when, in 1917, Mrs Robotham's son Herman was called up for military service and went to Brocton Camp. He contracted pneumonia and died at the age of 35 years within three weeks of joining. His funeral was held at Blore Church on 11th February, attended by his widowed mother, his uncles and aunts, Mr G. Bott, Mr and Mrs Braddock of Calton, Mr and Mrs Robotham of Chesterfield and his sister Miss Robotham together with many local residents, Mr J. Phillips JP, Mr C. Phillips, D.Green, J.Brassington, W.C.Twemlow, J.Hall and P. Lees. The bearers were J.Howson, J.Salt, C.Grindey and T. Wooliscroft. Mary Ann Robotham, mother of Herman, died 20 March 1919, age 74.

Like his grandfather before him, Thomas Stannah farmed Hill End and his wife, Ellen, and two daughters, Nelly and Ethel, lived with him. Sadly, his wife had a terrible fear of thunder and lightning. One day when Mr Stannah was out on the farm, a tremendous storm broke out. He hurried back to the farm but when he got there, his wife did not answer, when he called. He searched the house and found her body, lying behind an armchair, having had a heart attack, probably brought on by fear of the thunder and lightning. This shocking event appears to have had a sad effect upon his two daughters, who ever after were rarely seen out of doors. Gladys Jackson lived with Mr Stannah and looked after the girls. Ever after that, the mirrors were always turned to the wall and all bright objects covered, when a storm threatened. There had been a previous case of death as a result of lightning, in the village, when Mr Guilfoyle was struck whilst standing on his own doorstep at Little Moor Farm.

Mr Warrington who was living at Clough House did a swap with Tom Stannah. He took over Hill End, and Tom Stannah and his two daughters moved into Clough House, along with Gladys Jackson, who continued to act as housekeeper. Mr Stannah was one of the trustees elected by Swinscoe Methodist Chapel in 1954.

George and James Warrington, and Lizzie Twemlow, George Warrington's sister, were at Hill End Farm from 1935 to 1954. Ken Twemlow, who was to take over the farm many years later, first moved to the farm in 1935, at the age of six. When George Warrington retired in 1954 and moved to Chapel House, Ken Twemlow took over the farm. Ken saved the life of a young girl who had fallen into a water trough at Cliff Top. He dragged her out, threw her over his shoulder, and ran to the farm. His prompt action and the running and jogging, which brought up all the water, started her breathing again. Ken also confesses to a brush with the law. He was cycling home one night, without lights when a policeman spotted him and shouted at him. Ken, knowing it was too dark to be identified, sped off with the policeman in hot pursuit. Ken hid behind a wall at the Fleece, and after the policeman had passed, went off across the fields home to Hill Top Farm. His eldest son, Charles, was married in 1983 so Ken temporarily moved to Chapel Farm, before going to his new bungalow - Weaver Cottage. He left his son to continue farming Hill End, and now they are farming three hundred acres, including Cliff Top, Woodhouses and part of Blore Hall.

LEASOWES FARM - *Ox Leisure.*

Leasow is the Anglo Saxon word for pasture. It is therefore quite apt that Leasowes Farm, with it extensive pasture, should be so-called. The name Leasow or Leesow has often been corrupted to Leisure, just like Ox Leasow Farm, in Blore, became Ox Leisure. There is plenty of evidence that the land was farmed in the 12th and 13th centuries and almost certainly for centuries before that. In spite of Swinscoe being bleak and remote, Leasowes Farm occupied a prime position in the Township. The first probable mention of the Leasowes is in the will of Nicholas Cowper, of Swinscoe, who died in 1639. *"I give unto Humfrey Millington my said daughter Elizabeth's sonne one kowe which is in the custodie of Willm Peach OF THE LEESHOUSE."*

The house has been considerably altered over the years; little of the original building remains. At the back of the house there is an old stone mullioned windows with drip mould above it. If this is an original window, it could date that part of the house back to the 17th century and make it one of the oldest houses in the village. Examination of the Land Tax Records, shows that Mr B.Hodgson was the landowner in 1783 and his tenant, Samuel Smith, was paying 5s.3d per quarter Land Tax. Samuel Smith continued as tenant through 1800, when Land Tax recording was changed to an annual basis of £1.1.3d, and on to 1801. According to the Land Tax Records, Thomas Finney took over as tenant, from 1802 until 1818, when the property reverted to Brian Hodgson, for a year.

In 1820, Robert Archer was the tenant, for one year. He was followed by Joseph Ely, 1821 to 1823, who also held some other land from Mr Hodgson. In 1824, Samuel Felthouse and his wife were farming thirty acres of land at The Leasowes at a half-year rental of £37.0s.0d. Although the War with France had been over since 1815, the post-war slump continued. Like the rest of the farms in Swinscoe, in 1831 they received a reduction in rental to £32 per half year. In 1840, Samuel Felthouse and his wife Elizabeth, together with their two sons, William and Charles, and daughter Ann, were living at The Leasowes. The stone built farmhouse with its garden comprised a Parlour, Dairy, Scullery and four chambers with two stall stable with loft over, Calf pen, Cart Lodge, stockyard and piggery.

In 1845/6, the Hodgson Estate put up their land in Swinscoe for sale. The Church of England derived much of its income from land holding and the Ecclesiastical Commissioners for England bought The Leasowes, New House Farm and Common End Farm. The Leasowes included:

Ox Leasow (incl 15 perches from Road) Old Turf Pasture		16.0.27.
Ox Leasow Field	Arable	2.2. 6
Calves Croft	Old Pasture	6.0.12
Rough in Calves Croft		0.2.13
Big Day Meadow	Old Meadow	4.2. 0
Lees Head Lane		0.2. 1.
House, Outbuildings, Yard & Garden		0.1.31
Little Day Meadow	Old Meadow	2.3.33
		33.3. 3.

Nursery Piece 2a.2r.35p. which had been part of the holding in 1844 at the time of the Tithe Award, was not included in the sale.

By 1851, Mr Felthouse's son William had left The Leasowes and another son, Thomas, was helping to run the farm. A grand-daughter, Caroline, was staying with the family. Ten years later, Thomas was running the farm but Samuel, now in his eighties, and his wife were still living there along with their grand-daughter Caroline. In 1871, Thomas, his wife and Caroline, along with 94 year old Samuel, were still at the farm. Samuel died in 1872 at the fine old age of 95 and was buried with his wife Elizabeth in Blore churchyard.

From 1884 to 1892, John Harrison, cowkeeper, and his wife Mary and two sons, William and Herman, were tenants at The Leasowes. William got married and he and his wife, Mary, continued to farm there until 1895. Their daughter, Elizabeth, and a niece, Emily Key, both attended Swinscoe School. Robert Richardson succeeded the Harrisons at The Leasowes for a brief period around 1896. On 9th April 1897, Thomas Hayes, the eldest son of William Hayes of Snelsdale Farm, Okeover, married Alice Seals, the second daughter of Richard Seals, of Ox Leisure Farm Blore. The young couple took up residence at The Leasowes. Frank Briddon was the tenant in 1919, when the Commissioners sold the property to Charles William Clowes of Weaver Farm, Oakamoor for the sum of £1200. There had been some changes to The Leasowes because, according to the schedule, the land now comprised:

Farm House etc.	1.29
Turf	4.2.23
Turf	5.3.37
Plantation	2. 2.
Turf	2.3.31
Lane	1.14
Turf	12.0. 1
Turf	1.2.27
Turf	2.3. 2
Arable	2.1.32
Turf (detached)	1.2.15
Turf (detached)	1.0.15
Part of Plantation	12
	36.2. 0

In 1933, the Mr and Mrs Ditchfield moved from Calton. They had fifteen children and those who were of school age moved from Calton to Swinscoe School. Mr and Mrs Ditchfield, with Mr Ditchfield's mother, Mrs Alice Ditchfield and seven of the children were actually living at The Leasowes: May, Laura, Arthur, Ernest, Stephen, Tom, Peter, Michael and Robert, the baby. There was no gas or electricity, and Grandma and the children used to go down the 152 steps to Cuckoo Cliff to gather sticks for the fire each day. They played for many happy hours in the three old pigsties and yard at the back of the house. Like other local families, the children attended Sunday School at Swinscoe Methodist Chapel, and on special occasions, such as St George's Day, went to Blore Church as well. The Ditchfields moved on to Calwich, where three more children were born. Members of the family now farm at Ellastone.

In the 1940s, Thomas and Beryl Clowes, with their family, Charles, Sylvia, Cynthia and John, were living at The Leasowes. This is the house where Mr Charles W. Clowes of Brailsford Hall was born. Sadly, brother John died in a motorcycle accident. Tom and Beryl Clowes' family moved from The Leasowes to New House Farm. Tom's brother, Samuel, and his wife Edith, moved into the cottage.

After their marriage in 1945, Bill and Linda Thompson came to The Leasowes and all three of their children were born here. A daughter, Kathleen, was involved in a serious accident when her leg was cut off by a mowing machine which her father was driving. Luckily, the hospital were able to stitch the leg back on. The Thompsons moved from Swinscoe to the Rose & Crown at Middle Mayfield.

On the 18th April 1951, Linda Thompson conveyed the property to Mr David Shaw. Mr Shaw was a Methodist preacher and a member of the trustees of Swinscoe Primitive Methodist Chapel. His wife Lilian May Shaw was a staunch supporter of the chapel. They had three children, Edwin, Geoffrey and Philip who were born at The Leasowes. In cooperation with Mr Graham White, the headmaster of Swinscoe School, Mr Shaw helped to form the Swinscoe Youth Club in 1956, with a wide range of activities including a dancing class, which was instructed by Miss Dale of Trentham.

On the 28th April 1976, there was an agreement between C.W. Clowes (Investments) Ltd and Peter Magee, and his wife Brenda. Three years later, it was sold through a local solicitor, Mr Dawson to John Hanson and his wife, Barbara Eileen, with their two children, Richard John and Emma Jane. In 1982 it was bought by the present tenants, Mr Roger Dear and his wife Susan, with their two children, Steven and Katie, who still occupy The Leasowes in 1998.

LEYRAIN

Tom Clowes of Green Farm built this bungalow in 1976. His son Adrian, and wife, Elizabeth, have lived here since then. Their names appear in the electoral registers, from 1984 to 1996.

LITTLE MOOR COTTAGE

According to the map drawn up in 1844, the cottage was occupied by a man called Thomas Mould. In 1891, the census shows that Little Moor Cottage was unoccupied.

Mr George Bott, brother of Annie and Marian Morris's mother, lived in a number of places around the village. He lived at Chapel Farm, Yew Cottage and moved to Little Moor Cottage with his wife and children. He was a very familiar figure at local markets. He died at Turnditch near Wirksworth, on 11th March 1938 at the age of 85. Many of his family and friends attended the funeral at Mayfield Parish Church. Mr John William Prime met his wife-to-be, Annie Warrington, whilst working together at Calton Moor House. On 26th August 1918 they were married and moved into Little Moor Cottage. Mr Prime is described as a Private in the Army and William Anson and Nellie Warrington were the witnesses. Although John William was a successful small farmer, he never owned a cheque book, or drove a car. There is a photograph of Mr Prime proudly holding the horse and cart that won first prize at Ashbourne Show in 1913. Mr Eric Smith used to live at Little Moor Cottage. Mr and Mrs Sutton, from Manchester, lived here for a short period in the 1930s.

Charles Grindey, his wife Elsie and family, lived at Little Moor Cottage in the late 1930s. The Grindeys were quite lucky because just outside their house was a spring which supplied all the water needs. Mr Grindey worked, with Sid Jackson, as one of the roadmen, who each maintained a given stretch of road, in the parish. During the War, three members of the Grindey family served with the armed forces, George, Thomas and William, whilst the two daughters, Elsie and Violet, stayed at home.

Bill and George Grindey worked at Mr Howson's haulage company, which operated from the Fleece. Tommy Grindey is seen on one of the school photographs and he, too, went to work at Howson's. June Rowlinson was living with her grandmother in 1946 and attended Swinscoe School. When Mr Grindey died, Thomas, Elsie and Charles were living at Little Moor Cottage. A local man broke into the cottage in the middle of the night, but was caught, found guilty, and sent to jail for two years. In 1977, Mr R.J. Lumbard lived in the cottage. In 1984, David and Carol Latham were living here and carried out a lot of alterations to the cottage.

LITTLE MOOR FARM - *The Croft. Common End. Common End Cottage.*

Around 1928, George Smith a baker, and his wife Mabel, occupied The Croft, Common End. They were followed by Mabel's brother, Bill Howson and his wife Gladys. Mrs Eliza Salt, the widow of Ben Salt moved into the cottage and later moved to an old people's home in Cheadle. Mr William Guilfoyle, and his newly-wedded wife Elizabeth, lived at The Croft, Common End. William Guilfoyle worked on the railway. One day in 1936, he was standing at the front door to the cottage, watching a lightning storm. Lightning struck the handle bars of his bicycle and injured him very seriously. His wife Elizabeth was already at the hospital for minor treatment, and received a terrible shock when her husband was brought in dying. He died in the hospital of his injuries. His wife quit The Croft, and returned to The Cottage where her family, the Mellors, lived. At the beginning of the War, Matthew Redfern, a farm labourer, and his wife Lucy, moved from Calton.

Alfred and Nellie Wallis, with their children, moved into The Croft. Alfred worked as a lorry driver for the J.W. Howson haulage company at the Fleece. The children went to Swinscoe School and they appear on the school photographs. Mr Wallis stayed at The Croft until 1953. In 1953, the Morris Family bought The Croft from the Okeover Estates, and changed its name to Little Moor Farm. They also bought twelve acres of land, to go with it. In 1956, Bert and Ruth Morris were married, and moved into Little Moor Farm. They stayed there, until 1975, when Annie and Marian Morris took over. As the oldest resident of the village of Swinscoe in 1998, Annie, and her sister, Marian, have been very helpful in supplying a lot of information for this book.

MEADOWSIDE COTTAGE

On a map of Swinscoe dated 1844 is shown a small building (numbered 233), consisting of two cottages, occupied by Mary Birch. This is the first evidence of the cottage now called Meadowside.

Rupert Hill and his wife Ada Mary, lived here after the Great War, in 1918. Rupert worked at Blore

Rectory. Ada used to work for Rev Young at Blore Rectory for 9d per day, and was cleaner at the school. The schoolteacher, Miss Prince, was very angry when Mrs Hill used the schoolteacher's cane to poke the stove - and burnt the end. An earlier schoolteacher, Mrs Beard, used to use the small croft by the cottage to pasture her donkey called Barbara. Mrs Beard tried to harness the animal to a small cart, without success - its loud bray could be heard all over the parish. The donkey was a great favourite of the local children. In 1939, Ada Hill was still living in Chapel Lane, and continued to do so until 1945. Her son Percy, who worked for the Howson haulage firm at The Fleece, was living with his mother in 1939.

The cottage deteriorated badly and was almost derelict. In 1984, Mr Gordon Constable bought it. Over the last fourteen years, Mr Constable has carried out extensive restoration to make it the attractive cottage of today.

NEW HOUSE FARM

In the 13th Century, Swinscoe was a bleak and remote place covered by extensive woodland. Nevertheless, there were a few families living here and farming the land. The Okeovers held a large part of Swinscoe but gave, or sold, half to the Abbey of Rocester. With the exception of the Okeovers, the family with the largest holding was the Bec(k) family. The Bec family were very devout and they too gave land in Swinscoe to Rocester Abbey. It is impossible to identify the specific pieces of land. From available descriptions, "the chapel surrounded by ditches" may have been situated on Hall Flatts. If Hall Flatts means "the flats belonging to the Hall," the site of the Hall, belonging to the Becs, must have been close by. Vecclehall is mentioned in the Rocester Chartulary, and this may be a mis-spelling of BECC le Hall - spelling was very much a matter of pronunciation. One spot suitable for the building of a Hall is that rocky outcrop on which New House Farm stands, and which has been the site for other buildings since then.

The Bassetts of Blore had held land in the Parish of Blore, and many parts of Staffordshire, for centuries. This passed from the last of the Bassetts, to his daughter Elizabeth. Elizabeth married William Cavendish, later Duke of Newcastle, and the lands were inherited by their descendants - the Cavendishes, Holles and Harleys. In 1719-20, a large part of the Bassett lands was sold to Penistone Lamb, a wealthy landowner and he in turn sold parts of that land. He sold a house and farm in Swinscoe to Daniel Lowndes, of Grindon, for £270. The Lowndes family had been in Grindon for years, and continued there well into the 1800s.

Daniel Lowndes leased the house and land in Blackshaw Fields and land in Town Meadow, to Joseph Millington. When Daniel died, in 1737, Joseph Millington and his wife, Elizabeth, continued to occupy this land, under a lease with Daniel's son Richard Lowndes. Their son Richard Millington took over the lease in 1744 and continued to occupy the land until 1747. The Millingtons sold their interest in the land back to Richard Lowndes.

Richard Lowndes himself held the twenty three acres of land including the Withy Beds, Back of the Hill, Blackshaw field Top and Mean Land in Town Meadows. The farmhouse in which he lived is described as a House, Barn, Kitchen, Cow House, stable, Cart House and outbuildings. He and his wife slept in "the chamber over the Houseplace." Richard, prior to 1755, was paying 3s.6d per year, in lieu of Tithe Hay, to the Rector of Blore Church. Richard also farmed a number of other pieces of land owned by Mr Meanell and Mr Bill. Mr Meanell was probably Meynell of Meynell Langley; Mr Bill was a landowner, with very large holdings in North East Staffordshire. When Richard died, he left his twenty three acres to his son Daniel. He requested in his will that his son should be allowed to continue to farm the rest of New House Farm.

In 1781, the twenty three acres of land was sold by Daniel Lowndes and his wife Hannah, to J.Allcock, of Martins Hill, for the sum of £500. John Allcock installed his sister's son, William Waterfall, as his tenant. William was the local Assessor for the Land Tax and was himself paying 5s.1d. for the twenty three acres. Land Tax was calculated at four shillings in the pound per year, based on the Valuation. In 1797, when John Allcock died, his sister and co-heir, Mrs Elizabeth Waterfall, gave to her son William Waterfall, the land that her brother had owned.

According to the will of Thomas Smith, in 1790, he lived in the old house and farmed Big Croft, Blackshaw Field. He owned the new house with Little Croft, Heem Croft and the Pinfold and Wetpiece.

He left the Barn, Cowhouse, Stable and Carthouse, to share between to his sons Thomas and John. The land belonging to Mr Meanell was sold to Mr Hodgson.

Up to the Enclosure Award, Swinscoe had 360 Acres of common land. One part of this lay between New House Farm and Ellis Hill Farm. The landowner, Mr Brian Hodgson, held both these farms, and exercised his right to use the land between. He leased the land to Michael Saxelby, of Mayfield, for the purpose of mining for coal. The land was named Colliers Lea and evidence of three shafts still exist.

During 1824, some major work was carried out on the stable at New House Farm, which involved 303 feet of Board, 2 Pieces of Oake Scantling, 5 Joists, 7 Long Flags and one oak reel at a cost of £5.8.1d. The cost was split, Mr Charles Archer paid £2.15.0d. and the Hodgson Estate paid the balance. Mr.William Archer farmed New House from 1829 until 1840. For the first two years, he was paying a rent of £132.10.0d per half year, but in 1831 he received a reduction in rental to £120.0.0d. He was eligible to vote, and his name appears in the electoral registers, from 1832 to 1837.

Mr W. Swettenham (Swetnam) farmed nine acres including Barn Close and Top of Blackshaw Field. He paid a half yearly rental in 1829 of £8.17s.6d, which was reduced in 1831 to £7.10s.0d. In 1834, in White's Almanac, Mr Swetnam is recorded as a Nailer. 1840 was a tragic year for Mr George Swetnam, first his daughter Emmilie died, and then his wife died. The coffins were made by the local carpenter and cost 10s.0d for the child, and £1.10s.0d for his wife. They both were buried in Blore Churchyard. Walter Swetnam was the one of the leading lights in the local Primitive Methodist movement. Walter registered his own home as a place of worship before the chapel was built in Town End Lane. The cottage was one of three buildings alongside the Main Road: Hillcrest, Rose Cottage and the barn.

In 1844, the whole of the Swinscoe Estate belonging to the Hodgson family, comprising 835 Acres, was put up for sale in thirteen lots. New House Farm was bought by Representatives of The Ecclesiastical Commission and comprised: Stone-built Farm House containing Four Bed Rooms, Parlour, Kitchen, Dairy, Scullery, Cheese Room, Cellar, etc. Garden, Farm Yard, Stable, Cow Houses, Calf House and Piggery:

Withy Meadow	Plantation	0.1. 0
Withy Meadow	Pasture	4.1.28
Corn Field	Arable	4.2.19
Corn Field	Plantation	0.0.23
New Piece	Old Pasture	4.2.26
Croft (incl. 8 perches from Road)		0.3.27
Plantation (inc. 16 perches from Rd)		0.1. 0
Pasture	Old Pasture	12.2. 5
Newhouse buildings, Yards etc		0.2. 2
Plantation		0.0. 5
Croft	Old Meadow	1.0.26
Little Town Meadow	Arable	1.2.19
Rushy Piece	Plantation	0.1.19
Rushy Piece	Old Pasture	16.0. 0
Town Meadow	Plantation	0.1.23
Lower Town Meadow	Pasture	6.0.21
Big Town Meadow	Old Mead.	11.0.25
Upper Town Meadow	Turf Past	6.1. 5
Pingle	Old Mead.	0.3.34
Collier's Ley)	Old Pasture	7.2.30
Collier's Ley	Old Pasture	4.0. 5
Lower Blackshaw's Field "		4.1.25
Upper Blackshaw's	Pasture	3.1. 2
Barn Close	Old Pasture	6.3.13
Top of Blackshaw's Field "		2.2. 1
Blackshaw Field	Plantation	0.0.17

Samuel Archer and his wife Hannah, lived at New House Farm and had six children, Mary, Samuel, John, Thomas, Elizabeth and five months old Charles. There were two servants, Mary Hampson and Eden Hampson. In addition to farming the ninety two acres, Samuel Archer continued to farm a number of other pieces of land. He rented nineteen acres, including Long Croft, New Long Croft, the Hill and Plantation, at an annual rent of £40 from the new Owners - the Okeover Estate. In 1847, when the Okeover Estate bought the land east of the main road up to Field Lane, they made a tenancy agreement with John Chadwick of Mappleton, on a year to year basis, for eighty nine acres at an annual rent of £120. This agreement with John Chadwick only lasted three years. In 1850, Samuel Archer obtained the tenancy and installed his eldest son, Samuel, and his sister, Mary, at the newly built Hill End Farm. They took with them their younger brother and sister, Thomas (12) and Elizabeth (10). It must have been a very proud young man who told the Census Taker, in 1851, that he was 17 years old - and the Head of the Household

By 1851, Hannah Archer had been busily producing three more children, Ann, David and Fanny, making a total of nine. Hannah was twenty years younger than Samuel. Samuel Archer died on 12th February 1857, and his will survives in Lichfield Joint Record Office. He left his estate, valued at £1660, to two trustees in Ashbourne, George and William Woolley, drapers, in trust for his wife and children: Mary, Samuel, John, Thomas, Elizabeth, Charles, Ann, David and Fanny. His widow Hannah continued to farm New House Farm for a number of years with the help of her sons John, Charles and David and daughters Sarah and Ann. Hannah sold the estate, without consulting the trustees, and as a result, in 1866, it was necessary to execute a release of trust, with the agreement of all the family. She moved to Wichnor Grange, near Burton upon Trent, with her son Samuel, and continued in the farming business. According to the Index of Owners of Land, in 1873, Hannah still held seventeen acres in Swinscoe, and was renting it out at 32s.11d per year.

Mary Archer, the daughter of Samuel, married Thomas Howson, of Swinscoe. She lived until she was 86 and used to tell her family of the building of the farmhouse. The three storey stone-built farm house had four bedrooms, parlour, kitchen, dairy, scullery, cheese room and cellar. Although there have been a number of internal changes, all the old rooms can still be identified - but where is the cellar? The main chimney is so large that when some alterations were carried out in recent years, two men climbed up it, side by side. There was a garden and the farm yard contained a stable, cowhouses, calf house and piggery.

Charles Archer, farmer of Swinscoe, married Fanny Smith of Northwood in January 1868 and Elizabeth Archer married Richard Fowler of Cauldon. Briefly, between 1870 and 1874, Luke Mellor and his sister, Hannah, were living at New House Farm. They had a farm servant and farm hand, and George Gaily, a gamekeeper, was living with them. Luke got married, in 1874, and moved to the farm next door - Ellis Hill

In 1881, 72 year old William Phillips, retired farmer, was living at New House with his son's wife and her four children, Ernest, George, Charles and Thomas. The three eldest children were at school, but Thomas was only 2 years old. In the mid 1880s, William and Harriet Stannah moved from Forrest Farm to New House Farm. William attended the meeting in 1886 at Swinscoe School to choose Overseers of the Poor for the parish. Mr Ralph Webster of the Waterings and Mr Frederick Thompson of the Golden Fleece were selected. Just around the time of their move, their young eight year old son died. In 1887, William's mother, Fanny Stannah, died at the fine old age of 90, and was buried at Blore church. In 1891, they were living at New House, with their four daughters Mary, Frances, Alice and Martha. Martha, the youngest, aged 14, was still at school but the other three girls were working around the farm. They employed one farm servant, George Baring. Mr William was appointed as Guardian in 1893 and continued to farm New House until 1900. In 1903, John William, son of Joseph and Martha Ann Stannah, was baptised at Blore Church

The barn was built around 1900 and on its beams are old prize certificates awarded for Shire Horses which competed in local Horse Shows. Mr James Salt was the tenant from 1904 until after the Great War in 1918. The farm had been owned by the Ecclesiastical Commissioners since 1844. However, in April 1919, Rev Percy Gordon, Rector of Sheldon, Stoke on Trent, with the approval of the Commissioners, sold New House Farm to James Salt, the existing tenant. Mr Salt did not stay at New House Farm very long. It was announced, in the Ashbourne Telegraph, 18th March 1921, that Messrs. Bagshaws had received instructions from Mr J. Salt (who is leaving) to sell by auction: 2 cows, 3 horses, a portion of household furniture, outdoor effects and 15 couples of fowls.

1921 was a bad year for farmers; there was a drought from March until October. Charles Clowes, who was then living in Weaver, bought New House Farm, and he and his wife Sarah, and son Tom, moved into the Farm. In 1932, Frances Elizabeth Clowes married Frederick Harold Cotton, of Hurst Farm, Cauldon, at Swinscoe Methodist Chapel and the witnesses were Marian Clowes and Doris Clowes. In 1938, her sister Doris Sarah Clowes married John Thomas Salt, of Throwley Moor, Ilam, also at Swinscoe Methodist Chapel.

In 1939, Samuel and Sarah Clowes were living at New House Farm. They were both included in the Electoral Registers as eligible to vote in the local elections. After the War, Tom and Beryl Clowes lived at New House for a number of years. In 1949, Arthur Ditchfield from Leasowes, was one of the farm workers who worked for them. Mr Charles William Clowes was a trustee and lifelong member of the Swinscoe Primitive Methodist Chapel and his wife was a keen supporter and always attended the meetings and services at the chapel. A photograph of the ladies, in front of a marquee at the chapel, shows Mrs Frances Clowes and Mrs Doris Salt. Charles' son, Thomas Clowes, got himself into a lot of bother. In the days before different categories of milk and reprocessing, it was forbidden to sell watered milk and Thomas Clowes was found guilty of watering milk and sent to jail.

On Good Friday, 1963, Mr Bertram White was looking for a suitable farm and someone happened to mention that New House Farm was going to become available. He quickly made up his mind, rang the agents, and started the process of acquiring the farm. It was a long job, there was a lot to do. Even after he had taken possession in August 1963, there was still more than eighteen weeks of work on the house. It was not until 1964 that he moved in. The farm then comprised 101a.2r.8p. Bertram White retired to Hall Flatts and in 1978 left his son, Kevin White, and wife, Sheila, to farm New House Farm. Since their occupation they have acquired some additional land, formerly part of The Leasowes, which now provides access via Town End Land and Hall Flatts. Mr and Mrs White still live at New House Farm and contribute to the activities of the church and the parish.

OAKFIELDS

In September 1979, Mr Reginald Bailey sold two thirds of an acre of land in Town End Lane to a master builder, Don Derbyshire. In 1985/6, Mr Derbyshire built the first of two houses on the site and sold it to Mr and Mrs John Bancroft. In April 1988, Mr Bancroft sold Oakfields to Mr Ken Bainbridge and his wife, Jill, who have lived there since that time.

OLD POST OFFICE - *The Cobbler's Shop. Sawpits Farm.*

The old Post office was originally built as three cottages - it has two staircases. Originally, it had a clay floor and the remains of a coal house still exist. In 1840, these cottages were occupied by members of the same family. In one half, old Mrs Hannah Stubbs lived, whilst in the larger part, her son Anthony Stubbs and his wife Mary lived with their son, George. George Stubbs was at Swinscoe School in 1864.

Anthony Stubbs was the local joiner and builder who carried out a lot of work in the halls, churches, farms and houses in the area. His account book for the period 1830 to 1850 was found hidden inside a wall cavity in a bedroom of the cottage. From the book has come much information about Anthony Stubb's work in the district.

In the early part of the 20th century, the cottage was known as Sawpits Farm. Obviously a similar kind of business to that which Anthony Stubbs had developed was being carried on. The saw pit was in the cowshed, which is now the garage, at the end of the house. The beams, where the trees and logs were pulled through, can be seen inside the building. When the pit was no longer of any use Tom Allen and Reg Bailey filled it in. At the other end of the building there was a dairy and an enormous water tank for cooling butter and keeping eggs and milk.

Thomas Allen, boot maker, married Hannah Slater on the 2nd May 1895 and they went to live in the cottage. Mr Allen used part of the cottage as a cobbler's shop where he used to sit with tacks in his mouth, working on the boots and shoes. It became a centre for local residents to call for a chat, and sometimes to play darts and dominoes or rings. It was very cosy with its central stove and the children used to play in the room above where it was kept warm by the stove chimney. The same year Miss Shei!a Allen was born, 1929, in response to local requests Mrs Hannah Allen opened a post office was opened at the lane end of the cottage. Grace Bailey lived here, and went to work at Bond's Mill at Hanging Bridge, Mayfield, cycling up and down Swinscoe Hill each day. Four fields belonged to the cottage and the Allen family kept four cows. As two of the fields were across the main road, Sheila Allen used to have to take the cows over the road each day - the main road was less busy, in those days. When Mr Allen died on 13th December 1940 at the age of 67, the cobbler's shop was closed and the leather and machines were sold off. He was parish clerk for forty years and is buried in the churchyard at Blore.

Tom Allen, schoolmaster and local historian, lived here. He was Clerk to the Parish Council for eleven years. During the war, he was a sergeant in the Army Education Corps and spent some time in the Falklands as a lecturer to the sailors stationed there. In 1948 the Okeover Estate offered for sale many of the smaller properties int Swinscoe, including The Old Post office. Grandma Allen was very worried about the possibility of being turned out by the new landlord, so Tom Allen bought the cottage. Tom died in July 1981, and his niece, Sheila Allen, stayed on in the cottage. Mrs Veronica Drugan and her husband Kevin and daughter Penelope occupied part of it. In 1981, Sheila moved to Derby, and the Post Office was closed. Mr T. Clowes applied to run a new Post Office at Green Farm and permission was granted.

Mr Ronald Woodley and his wife Margaret bought the cottage and have carried out a number of alterations and improvements. The old cobbler's shop and the dairy have been converted into a kitchen. It was Mr Woodley who found the accounts book of a previous tenant, Mr Anthony Stubbs, who lived there in the mid 19th century.

PEAK VIEW COTTAGE - *Common End.*
Peak Cottage used to be three separate cottages. The cottage in the corner was occupied by Henry Harrison, known as Donkey Harrison. Henry owned a dozen donkeys which he used to take down to Dove Dale every day during season and ply his trade, giving rides to the visiting tourists. The middle cottage was occupied by the Wallis family. It must have been very crowded because there were nine children in the family and the cottage was only tiny. Mr Wallis worked for a time at Howson's haulage, across the road at the Fleece. Most of the children attended Swinscoe School. The end cottage, closest to Field Lane, was occupied by Mrs Bott.

When Joyce Austin married Joseph Robotham at Mayfield Church in June 1941 they moved into the cottage which is next to Field Lane. When the other families moved out, Joseph Robotham knocked the three cottages into one and called it Peak View Cottage. Joseph and his father did a swap and Joseph moved to Town End Farm, the family holding. His mother Jane moved into Peak View Cottage.

Joseph Robotham, with his wife Joyce, farmed Town End Farm for a number of years, until his death in 1990. John Robotham, the son of Joseph and Joyce, took over Town End Farm, and his mother Joyce moved back to Peak View Cottage. She is still living there in her eighty first year, in 1998.

A Smith family lived at Common End until the early 1920s. Arthur Smith died on 30th September 1920 age 62 and was buried on 4th October. His wife Annie Maria died five years later on 20th April 1925 aged 71.

In 1891, Robert Webster, cattle dealer, his wife Fanny, and their six young children moved to Common End Farm. Four of the children, John, Clifford, Henry and even 3 year old Frank went to Swinscoe School. Nelly age 2 was at home and a new baby Bertha was born shortly after the family arrived at the farm.

ROSE COTTAGE - *Netlows*
According to the 1841 census, Michael Rose occupied Rose Cottage, and this may be the reason why the name Rose Cottage was adopted. However, Michael Rose is not mentioned in the electoral registers for that year, because the land he farmed did not meet the minimum requirements. When he was farming the larger Cliff Top Farm, in 1835, he had been eligible to vote. In 1859, William Gallimore and his sister Mary, left Ellis Hill Farm and retired to Rose Cottage. In 1939, according to the Electoral Register, the cottage is referred to as Netlows not as Rose Cottage. Mr Richard Naylor and his wife, Frances, moved

from Chapel House to Rose Cottage, with their sons, Percy, Arthur and Denis and daughters, Minnie and Elsie. Mr Naylor is described as a cowkeeper and worked for New House Farm. Arthur Naylor married Mabel Annie Phillips of Ellis Hill, on 6th April 1940 at Swinscoe Methodist Chapel. His brother, Percy Naylor, was one of the witnesses. During the War, Alec and Dennis Naylor served with the armed forces. Mrs Naylor and Dennis moved to a pub at Wetley Rocks when Mr Naylor died.

John and Alice Harrison moved in. John died in 1992 but his wife remained in the cottage until 1996. Daughter Margaret married David Froggatt of Thorpe and Deborah married Christopher White, the youngest son of Bert White of Hall Flatts.

SONLEY

After one hundred years without any new building in Swinscoe, Mr Reg Bailey built a bungalow on a part of his land in Town End Lane. He called it Sonley. His son, Maxwell Bailey, occupies the bungalow with his wife Margaret. The names of Maxwell and Margaret have appeared in the Electoral Registers since before 1985 as eligible to vote in the local elections. His son and family now live at the school house, where Max's father and mother used to live.

THE COTTAGE - *Mellors' Place.*

Around 1840 The Cottage was built of red brick, instead of stone like all previous buildings in the village. The internal doorways were originally 6'6" in height, but for some unaccountable reason were reduced to 5'3". They have been returned to the original 6'6" in height by the present owner Mr Alan Large.

Many of the records do not always give specific house names. It has been difficult to identify those people who lived in The Cottage during the late 19th century. The first resident of The Cottage was probably Mr Robert Smith in 1844.

Mr John Ollerenshaw and his wife, Harriett, lived at The Cottage in 1917. On Wednesday 10th January 1917, their only daughter was married to Fred Phillips of Waterhouses. The bride wore a dress of cream silk, with wreath and veil, and was given away by her father. The bridesmaids were Alice Phillips and Jennie Allsop, and the best man was William Burton, a cousin of the groom. The Rev T.J.S. Roberts officiated. Mr Phillip's fellow workers on the North Staffs Railway, gave the bride and groom a beautiful clock. In 1918, William Hand was living with the Ollerenshaws. From time to time it has been used as a shop and sold toffee, ice cream and drinks to the local residents and passing travellers.

The Mellor family originally lived in an old miner's cottage at Thorswood. They moved to Rectory Cottage, at Blore. At neighbouring Blore Hall, wedding receptions and other events were catered for, and Mrs Mellor used to "wait on" for these events.

The Mellors moved from Blore to The Cottage in Swinscoe, where they lived for fifty years. The names of Blanche and Clifford Mellor appear in the Electoral Registers from 1939 to 1945. The name of Elizabeth Guilfoyle also appears in the registers. After Elizabeth's husband was killed by lightning in 1936, Elizabeth returned home to live with her family.

Mr Clifford Mellor was a road man and labourer and worked all over the parish. There is a photograph of Mr Mellor wearing his waistcoat and wielding a scythe. One of his sons, Keith Mellor, was a pupil at Swinscoe School and appears on a number of the school photographs. He recalls that, each morning before school, he used to fetch water in a churn mounted on large wheels from the well near the Caravan.

Most members of the family worked at one time or another at the Dog & Partridge. This experience may well have been valuable to Keith and his wife, Christine, who now run the Lichfield Guest House at Hanging Bridge.

At The Cottage one of the sons died and within the following two years, the rest of the family living there, also died. The Cottage was empty for a couple of years and was bought by Mr and Mrs Robinson but although they owned it for two years, they only occupied the house for a few months. In 1989, the present owner, Alan Large, acquired The Cottage and lives there with his wife and children.

TOWN END

The Township of Swinscoe in the Parish of Blore is centred around the top of the hill. The original road up the hill ran in front of the Dog & Partridge and left along the lane, to the end of town, near to a small farmhouse. It is not surprising to find the lane called Town End Lane, although it was sometimes called Chapel Lane. Nor is it surprising that the farm on the edge of town is called Town End Farm. This farm has been standing in this place for almost 300 years, confirmed by the lintel over the front door bearing the date 1703. From a sketch map of the land for sale in 1802, Philip Peach farmed the following:

Woolleys Croft	9.0.14.
Little Hay (which was divided into two fields)	2.3.34.
The Hay Wood	3.2.17.
Well Croft	4.0.38.
Upper Croft	3.1.25.
Little Croft	1.1.13.
Round Croft	2.2.37.
Yards	3.2. 1.

plus other unidentified pieces of land.

Philip Peach was paying £3.17.6d land tax in 1802, which is the same as he had been paying since 1793.

In 1829, Joseph Bott was farming Town End Farm and paying a half yearly rental of £100. Like the rest of the farms in Swinscoe, the rent was reduced by 10% in 1831. He continued to pay this reduced rental of £90 through to 1840. His name appears in the Electoral Registers from 1832 to 1843, as eligible to vote in the local elections. Like many of his neighbours, Joseph Bott made use of the services of the local joiner/builder, Anthony Stubbs, to carry out minor repairs and maintenance. In April 1838, he paid Mr Stubbs 7s.2d for two days work.

By 1841 Joseph Bott and his wife Mary had a grown up family living at the farm. They had a daughter Hannah, George age 35, Joseph age 30, Samuel age 20 and young Charles age 15. Their son, John, was not at Town End when the census was taken. They had a young girl, Dorothy Carver working as maidservant.

Son George, besides working on the farm, was also sexton and gravedigger at Blore Church. In 1844 a young woman who had wandered about disguised as a man for many years, died at Calton Moor House, and was buried at Blore. The grave sank, and it was suspected that her friends may have stolen the body. George re-opened the grave, and although the coffin was burst, he reckoned that he saw the hand of the corpse. However, two other villagers who were reputed to be present, believed that the body was gone.

In 1844, the stone-built farmhouse with garden in front comprised: parlour, kitchen, dairy, scullery, two bedrooms, landing, cheese room, cellar, cow house, stable, two other cow houses, threshing barn, calf house, and cart shed. The Executors of the Brian Hodgson estate offered sixty eight acres of land for sale, of which forty eight acres were being farmed by Joseph Bott, twelve acres by William Smith, five acres by Isaac Smith and two and a half acres by Samuel Felthouse. When Joseph died, on the 23rd June 1849, his estate was valued at less than £200. He left everything to his sons and daughters "share and share alike". His son, John, continued to farm Town End Farm, but George moved to Hall Flatts.

In 1849, the Farm was owned by Edward Jackson, yeoman, of Marton Hill, Mayfield. When he died in November 1849, the property passed to his two brothers Joseph and George Jackson. They held the farm until 1870, and on their death it was sold to William Smith of Stanton. He later held it jointly with Joseph Beeston and John Harding.

John Bott continued to hold the tenancy after his father's death and married his wife, Mary Ann, in 1850. They had a baby called Mary Elizabeth. A year later, John's brother Charles was still at Town End, together with a nephew, Henry, aged 14. They employed 15 year old Louisa Poyser as their house servant. His wife, Mary Ann, died on 23rd February 1863, aged 37, and John died ten years later, in 1873. He was buried with his wife in the churchyard at Blore.

In 1878, Town End Farm was owned jointly by Joseph Beeston, of Muggington, and William Smith, of Pethills. They sold the farm to Robert William Hanbury of Ilam. The land then comprised:

Site of farmhouse outbuildings and garden and orchard	1.0.35
Woolley Croft	9.0.14
Part of Lane	0.0.15
Little Hay	2.3.34
The Hay Wood	3.2.17
Yards	3.2. 1
Upper Croft	3.1.25
Well Croft	4.0.38
Little Croft	1.1.13
Near Croft	3.3.12
Far Croft	3.0.22
The little common piece	1.2. 2
The Middle common piece	3.2. 5
Salts Nursery	0.0.35
Clough Nursery	2.3.34
Plantation adjoining	1.2.??
Clough Meadow	2.0.19
Clough Hollow	10.1. 9
Hearn Croft	1.3.10
	60.2. 7

For a brief period around 1878, Mr F. Pigott, reputably related to the famous jockey Lester Pigott, was farming the land on a year-to-year basis at a rent of £85 per year. Thomas Phillips took over the tenancy. In 1881, Thomas and his wife, Barbara, had five children. William, Sarah, Charles aged 7, 6 and 4 went to Swinscoe School, but Jane, aged 3, and Annie, only one year old, were at home.

For a brief period, Mr Twigg lived at Town End Farm. In 1896, he was one of those chosen as Overseers of the Poor for the parish. The Robotham family has lived in the area for centuries and they moved to Town End Farm. In 1891, Joseph Robotham and his wife Sarah (née Smith) with their children, William, Henry and Mary, were living at the farm. The Robothams have lived there ever since.

Mr Joseph Robotham was an important member of the local community, who in 1891 was elected Overseer to the Poor. A year later he was nominated by the Rector of Blore Church as his warden, and held the post of churchwarden for many years. He audited the church accounts and attended local meetings and conferences. His wife and daughter were involved in many of the activities of the church. On 30th September 1896 Winifred Sarah Robotham was born, but only lived for two years. She died on 16th July 1898 and was buried in Blore churchyard.

On Thursday, February 12th 1903, at the Blore Church, Mr James Blood, son of Mr John Blood farmer of Stanton, married Miss Mary Florence Robotham. The wedding was of a simple unostentatious nature, though the party drove up in the usual carriage and pair. The churchwarden gave his daughter away, and Miss Young, daughter of the rector, played the "Wedding March". An auspicious omen marked the event: the morning was dull, but whilst the ceremony was taking place, the sun broke out in brilliant splendour. After the wedding breakfast, the happy pair set off for London to spend their honeymoon.

In August 1903, Mr Joseph Robotham was appointed by the County Council to serve as a Manager of Swinscoe School. The first meeting of the school committee under the new act was held at Blore rectory, on Thursday 24th October. The following managers were present: H.E. Okeover, Rev Young, Mr Howson, Mr Hayes, Mr Jos Robotham. Joseph Robotham died, 24th February 1905, age 75. Sarah his wife died, 16th April 1907, age 72. They were both buried in Blore churchyard.

One of Joseph's sons, Arthur Robotham, born 20th June 1861, became a colour-sergeant in the Royal Marine Light Infantry. He served his country in several overseas engagements including Egypt, The Sudan, and West Africa (The Benin Expedition) and the taking of Coomassie. Finally he retired to Greendale, Oakamoor, and where he lived until his death on the 2nd May 1913. He was buried at Blore.

Another son, William, married Jane Mellor and they went to Oakamoor where they ran the Cricketers Pub for a while. They were not there for long before William bought Little Bull Gap Farm. In 1913, William hurt his finger on blackthorn and, leaving it untreated, it turned septic. This gradually got worse, which caused damage to his kidneys. He was taken into Derby Royal Infirmary and one kidney was removed, only to discover that the other was damaged. William died, on 13th December 1913, at the age of 54. A large contingent of friends and relatives, including members of the Oddfellow's Club of which he was a member, attended the funeral at Blore Church.

His poor wife Jane was left to look after three small children. The newly born baby, Enid Sarah Mellor, was only thirteen days old. Jane had a two year old son, Joseph William, born 26th December 1911, and a daughter, Mabel Mary, born 30th November 1912. The task of this courageous lady, in bringing up a family of such small children, and running a farm at the same time, is a wonderful example of strength and fortitude. The story goes that, when going about her farm business, she kept each child in a separate room, while she did the milking. When they were old enough, they were placed in a hayrack in one the cowsheds while she carried on with her work. This too had its problems. One of the children threw a toy at a cow, which caused the startled cow to kick Mrs Robotham. The kick damaged her leg, as a result of which she limped for the rest of her life.

In 1911, the property was owned by Mrs Bowring Hanbury of Ilam Hall. It was put up for sale with a lot of other properties. Town End Farm was bought by Mr James Morton, of 7 Hugo street, Leek, and he owned it for nine years. The rent paid by Mrs Robothams was £80 per annum. In June 1920, Jane Robotham, widow of William Robotham, was offered the chance to buy the farm, which the family had tenanted for over thirty years. The prudent Jane wisely chose to do so, and managed to scrape together sufficient money to complete the purchase. Her name appears in the Electoral Registers as eligible to vote in the local elections.

After a hard working life, Jane died on the 14th March 1956 at the age of 85. Her son, Joseph, named after his grandfather, inherited the farm and married Joyce Hannah Austin at Mayfield Church in June 1941. Joseph Robotham died at the age of 78, on the 22nd July 1990, and was buried at Blore. His wife moved to Peak View Cottage, leaving son John to continue at Town End Farm. In spite of a recent operation for cataract in one eye, Joyce is still going strong at the wonderful age of eighty. Joyce has contributed a lot to this book. In 1998, John is still farming Town End.

TOWN END HOUSE - *Town End Lane*
Mr and Mrs Stelfox, proprietors of the Dog & Partridge at Swinscoe, built this house in 1991.

WEAVER COTTAGE
After many years at HIll Top Farm Mr and Mrs Kenneth Twemlow moved to Chapel Cottage, with their family. In 1985, they decided to build a new house, just across the lane from Chapel Cottage. With the magnificent views of the Weaver Hills, they called it Weaver Cottage.

YEW TREE HOUSE
Mr George Bott moved from Chapel Cottage to Yew Tree. In the 1891 census, he is recorded as living at The Yew with his wife and six children, and his 76 year old mother. According to Mr Major, the cottage was used as a bakers but, so far, it is not possible to say who was living there at the time.

In 1939, George and Sarah Hodge lived there with two children Derek and Freda. Both children went to Swinscoe School. The Yew had the emblem of the Cycling Tourist Club over its front door, and offered teas and a repair service, to passing cyclists. Derek worked at the munitions factory at Froghall during the war, but also provided other services to the residents of Swinscoe. He was the local chimney sweep and offered a hair cutting service to the men, at a cost of an old threepenny piece. He was a familiar figure on his BSA Bantam motorbike as he delivered the newspapers across the fields. Derek died, but an old pal of his, John Howson, found his BSA Bantam in the late 1990s, and has restored it to its former glory. Freda, who still lives in Ashbourne, was the organist at Blore Church and Derek used to work the organ blower. Local children used to buy their sweets from the cottage, and recall that one of the rooms was dark and filled with stuffed animals and birds.

According to the electoral registers in 1984, Mr Kenneth Major and his wife, Christine, were living at The Yew. They and two of their family, Shane and Tracy, continue to live there, and another sister Jane lives next door, in Corner Cottage.

Derelict and Disappeared

Over the centuries a number of houses and buildings, have disappeared, or become derelict, and although this cannot be an exhaustive list, the following buildings still need to be recorded.

HOME GUARD HUT, Swinscoe

During the 1939-1945 War, men from Swinscoe, Stanton and Ellastone formed a local battalion of the Volunteer Regiment - the Home Guard. The Swinscoe men held their meetings in a hut across the road from Rose Cottage and Hillcrest, just at the brow of the Hill. The hut was on Mr Twemlow's land and Mr Twemlow was himself a corporal in the Territorial Army Home Guard Unit. Among the residents who were members of the local unit, were, Reg Bailey, Arthur Hayes, John Phillips and Reg Twigg. They used the school playground in the evenings for their drill and practice. Fire-watching was carried out from the vantage point of Bonfire Hill, behind the school, which was the site of a huge bonfire to celebrate the end of the War in 1945.

BRIDDON'S COTTAGE *(HAWTHORN?)*

During extensions to the Dog & Partridge this cottage was incorporated into the structure and became the garage of the public house. The cottage originally had a tiny porch at the front which contained the staircase to the bedrooms. There was a flower border with hedge and a wall towards Chapel Lane, ending at the barn belonging to Mrs Hill. Frank and Jessie Briddon and their three children lived here from 1939 to 1949, and their children went across the road to Swinscoe School. Two children, Joan and Mary, appear on the school photograph around 1941.

HEARN CROFT

Close to Town End Farm used to be a small cottage called Hearn Croft. It was occupied by John Ratcliffe prior to 1876. In 1878, Thomas Smith erected a new house on the site which he occupied, along with Mr Bott. In 1878 it was occupied by Thomas Phillips.

COTTAGES ON MAIN ROAD (South of Dog and Partridge)

The 1844 Map shows at least four cottages between the Dog and Partridge and Hall Flatts. The nearest to the pub is Fairbrook (Cabaret) Cottage which still stands, but the others have disappeared. In 1844 a cottage, probably Fairbrook, with map number 228, was occupied by Mathew Fernihough; number 227 was occupied by Robert Smith; number 226 by Robert Smith; and number 225 by Benjamin Yates.

PETTS COTTAGE (Opposite Field Lane)

According to the 1844 Map, across the main road opposite Field Lane was a cottage, belonging to the Okeover Estate and occupied by Hannah Petts. There is a badly damaged gravestone in Blore churchyard which is dedicated to Archibald Petts, Anna Petts and their son William Petts, who all died in 1846. There is no trace of the cottage, although Mr Ken Twemlow recalls a building on the site which was used as garage by a local nurse - Nurse Stevenson.

RECTORY COTTAGE

Originally, the Rector lived in a cottage behind Blore Church. In 1909 there was a mysterious fire which burned down the cottage.

THURMAN'S COTTAGE (Near Town End)

According to a plan of Town End Farm there was a piece of land just outside the farm boundary which was occupied by Richard Thurman. In the 1891 census, Mr Wigley was living at Thurman's Cottage.

COTTAGE IN WOODS AT ELLIS HILL This was probably the gamekeeper's cottage.

Calton Moor Cottage

Calton Moor House

Chapel Cottage

Cliff Top farm

Clough House

Corner Cottage

Common End Farm

Ellis Hill

The Croft

The Stables, Ellis Hill

Forest Farm

Mr Prime of Forest Farm, proudly displays his first prize from Ashbourne Show.

Howsons Transport - the Fleece

The Fleece

Fairbrook

Green Farm

Gilman House

Hillcrest

Hall Flatts

Hill End Farm

The Ditchfield family
Above, left to right: Mr Ditchfield, Laura, with baby Robert, May, Violet,
Arthur. Ernest, Leonard, Steven, Thomas, Peter, Michael.

Right:
Back row: Laura, Violet, May
Middle: Ernest, Mrs Ditchfield, Arthur
Front: Leonard, baby Stephen

Leasowes

Little Moor Farm

Little Moor Cottage

Leyrain

Meadowside Cottage

New House Farm c1910

New House farm from the rear

New House Farm today, front view.

Oakfields

The Old Post Office

Peak View Cottage

Rose Cottage

Sonley

The barn at Town End Farm, dilapidated to the point of ruin

Town End Farm

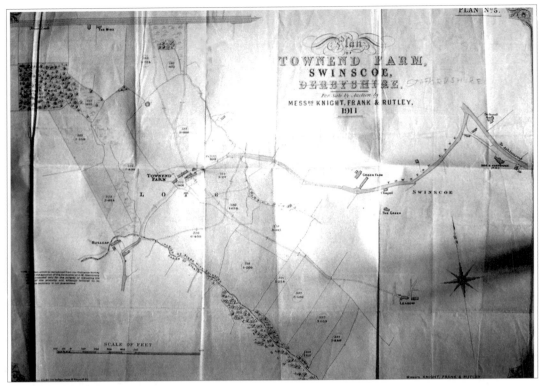

1911 Estate plan of Townend farm

Town End House

Weaver Cottage

Yew Tree Cottage c1910 and
left, as it looks today

The Waterings - snowscape

The Waterings

Waterings - the yard and the byre

THREE
BLORE

BLORE VILLAGE

All that remains of the village of Blore are Blore Hall, St Bartholomew's church, the rectory and one cottage. In spite of its importance as the home of the Bassetts, the village of Blore was never of any significant size. At most there were a few more houses around the Hall and the church.

Opposite the Hall, across the road, there is the site of another building. On the 1631 map, there is a pencilled outline drawing which suggests that it may have been a large barn. Some maps show house sites around the Hall, and church, and there were one or two cottages along the road towards Coldwall.

In the field beyond the old barn and pond, on the Okeover side, there are traces of humps and bumps where some kind of buildings stood. Their position in relation to the Hall, and the ridge and furrow where the villagers cultivated their strips of land, suggests possible remains of the original village. The earthworks are indistinct, which make them difficult to interpret. The longer shape of one of the "humps" probably indicates the site of a barn, shown on the 1631 map. In the walls alongside the present main road can be seen a number of mediaeval roof tiles, possibly from these old buildings.

Close to the earthworks ran the original road which then turned right around the south side of the moat and up the slope towards the church. It went past the cottage at the entrance to Church Green, where the Phillips lived in 1630, and past the church down Blore Dale. Just before entering Blore Dale there was a small cottage on the left, called Rushon Croft.

In 1666, there were twelve households chargeable with Hearth Tax, plus other households shown as exempt, in a joint list for Blore and Swinscoe. Up to the middle of the 17th century, the village of Blore provided service to the Bassett Family and their descendants at Blore Hall. The last descendants to occupy the Hall were the daughters of Lord Newcastle and his wife, Elizabeth, née Bassett, around 1652. After that the Hall was occupied by tenant farmers, or the rectors of the parish. This meant that the followers and servants drifted to other places, leaving only essential farm labourers to work the land. Never large, Blore got even smaller and became the virtually deserted village of today.

BLORE HALL

The first written mention of a manor house at Blore was in 1331, when the Lady of the Manor, Joan de Hastang, was robbed and raped. The moat around the site, was probably excavated in the 13th century but no evidence of an earlier house has been found. It is assumed that it would probably be situated at the other end of the courtyard from the present hall. In 1449 the Hall is mentioned when it was attacked and laid to siege.

Sampson Erdeswick, the Elizabethan historian, says *"A little southward of the meeting of the rivers Manifold and Hans, is Blore, a goodly antient house and a parke, now the seate of the Bassetts, of Staffordshire."* This appears to confirm an older house; the goodly appearance can hardly be ascribed to the present building. The older house was probably the source of the old mullion windows, which have been added to the present Blore Hall.

The 1631 Map by William Senior, shows the central courtyard surrounded by buildings. At the southern end of the inner court is the outline of a three-bay building, with crosses at the apex of each gable. Beyond the pencilled outline of this building is Diall Yard. The word dial was normally used in the 16th century to mean a clock or sundial. Could there have been a clock on the older building? It is assumed that the building was the original home of the Bassetts before it was destroyed. The destruction must have taken place between 1631, as shown by Senior's Map, and 1666, when Ashmole described the present building. The conclusion is that a previous building was destroyed during the Civil War.

On William Senior's Map, the Great Hall, the present Blore Hall, is shown at the northern end of the inner court yard.

On the west side of the site there are remains of the causeway across the moat. This runs to the probable site of an earlier gate house, where the older stone building now stands. Sir William Bassett's brother, Frances Bassett, bought a "lytle gate house" from Croxden Abbey, when the abbey was dissolved,

A sketch from a 16th century map of old Blore.

in 1538. It may be that the gate house was erected here. He also bought the roof of the dormitory at Croxden. This is one possible explanation for the 14th century re-used timbers in the roof of Blore Hall. In 1631 the moat had been filled in and was being used as gardens. By the side of the causeway an ancient bottle and rubbish dump has been located. During a brief examination by the Staffordshire and Peak District Archaeologists, some evidence of a possible entrance roadway was observed, just outside the south east corner of the moat.

The moat, at 700 feet, is the second highest recorded moat in Staffordshire. It was dug, at great expense, as a kind of status symbol, copying the moated castles of the powerful overlords. It was used for keeping fish and watering cattle. Next to the moat, between the pond and the old barns, there is an oval shaped pit surrounded by stonework, which was first thought to be an ancient midden. Although it was later used for refuse, it was more probably a keep for fish taken from the moat or the fishpond down by the river.

The moat was useful as a form of defence. The defence could only be limited, because the timber buildings would be vulnerable to attack by fire from burning arrows or other projectiles. It possibly provided some security in 1449, when Blore was laid to siege by the *"grete nombre of riotes people"*, led by the Vernons and Cockaynes. The Bassetts were able to withstand the attack, until help arrived. One stack containing forty cart loads of hay, and another of twenty cart loads of peas, were burned. The following week, the same mob, of whom more than seventy were named, attacked neighbouring Okeover and extensive damage was done to Okeover Hall.

The south side of the moat is a hollow in the field on the Woodhouses Road side, outside the boundary of Blore Hall Farm. The pond on the Okeover side of the property has been found to be paved. Between the farmhouse and the main road, the hollow was part of the north side of the moat. The west side ran in a curve, across the lane, to the edge of the graveyard near the east end of the church. The shape of the moat can be seen curving back to cross the road again, near the entrance road to the church green.

The moat is approximately 500 metres in circumference, 10 metres at its widest and probably 4 metres deep which represents 20,000 cubic metres of soil and rock. It must have taken years to dig out, remove and redistribute 20,000 tons of earth with the primitive tools then available. The excavated soil was dumped on the south side of the church. The low Norman doorway, built before the excavation of the moat, is three feet below surface level, as a result of the dumping of the soil. The number of men available for such labour in a remote place like Blore was very small. Conservatively, it has been estimated that it would take a minimum of four years for fifty men to excavate such a moat. The Moated Site Research Group (now part of the Mediaeval Settlement Research Group) has identified hundreds of moats, most probably originating in the 12th and 14th centuries. Is it possible that during this "Digging Period" of mediaeval history, gangs of men were employed and moved from site to site? It is doubtful if there were sufficient local men to perform such a large task. The other major excavation task would have been the leat for the watermill, down by the river. As the watermill is recorded in Domesday, the digging for the leat must have taken place much earlier than the 13th century, assumed for the moat.

The water supply was fed from a spring up on higher ground in Waterings Wood, by a system of natural gullies and channels down to Blore.

Like many old houses, in Staffordshire/Derbyshire, there are stories of a tunnel, connecting the house and the church. There are underground passages in the neighbouring parish of Mayfield, under Mayfield Hall. It is difficult to see how this could be achieved at Blore. The church is on higher ground and the moat would be a serious obstacle. If there were a tunnel, it would probably end in the church, in the vault below the Bassett Tomb. When the vault was opened in 1996, there were no signs of a tunnel entrance. The only known "tunnel" is the old drain from the centre of the courtyard out to the smaller of the two ponds, now merged into one, on the Okeover side. As the exit to this "tunnel" would be within the bounds of the moat, it would negate the purpose as an escape tunnel.

Sir William Bassett is referred to as "Kinge of the Moreland" by Leland. As the Lord of the Manor, he would administer his justice at his Manorial Court, held in the Great Hall.

Originally, the Great Hall was a single building, with no upstairs floor. The smoke from the central fireplace would billow up to the high ceiling and escape through ventilation slots. This hall is the nucleus which, over the centuries, became incorporated within the present structure as other buildings and rooms were attached. The Great Hall is the large room on the north side of the present building. The wall of the present main staircase was one of the external walls; an original supporting buttress juts into the staircase. This external wall is more easily seen in the loft space above the stairs where original ventilation slots still exist in the brickwork.

A floor was inserted into the Great Hall at bedroom level, and fireplaces and chimneys built at either end of the building. Access to the upper floor was originally via stairs on the outside the building. The external doorway is now an internal entrance to a bedroom off the upstairs corridor. Within the bedroom, on what was then the external wall, can be seen the block of wood that supported the banister rail. There are three "foreign" bricks, inserted over the doorway, which held the supports for an inverted 'V' shaped porch, erected as protection from the weather. When the room to the left of the present entrance was added to the Hall, the staircase was enclosed within the building, inside that room. It was removed several years ago, and the staircase opening was boarded over.

The fireplace has always been the centrepiece of an Englishman's home, with its cheerful warming blaze and welcoming smells of good food cooking in the hanging pots. Meat was skewered on a spit, supported on firebars or gratebars in front of the fire; the fat was caught in a dripping pan standing under the spit. Meat was smoked and cured on the hooks inside the ceiling beam, in front of the fire. In the ceiling space, between the fireplace and the beam, there are examples of Elizabethan wooden beams.

In 1904, the large old chimney, presumably the one at the west end of the Hall, was supported only by a single wooden beam, and had become a serious hazard. It was necessary to demolish it, together with the massive fireplace. During the demolition a hidden "closet with a niche" was found and this was assumed to have been a "small prayer closet" dating before the Reformation. It was probably the beehive oven, which has been boarded up, and wallpapered over. Mrs Burton who lived at Blore Hall for thirty years, was never aware of this oven hidden by multiple layers of wallpaper. It is also probable that the story of a tunnel originated from the Burtons. They knew about the hollow area above the oven, and the external shape of its walls, and assumed that this was a possible entrance to a tunnel.

The beehive baking oven is built of handmade bricks. The handmade brick, like the rest of the bricks of which the hall was built, probably came from a brick kiln in the fields on either side of the road to Ilam, opposite the Hall. Brickkilne Close is identified on the 1631 map. The oven has the appearance of being built of solid brick up to the ceiling. From the cupboard space in the room above, a hollow space can be seen in the top of the oven brickwork, measuring approximately 5ft x 4ft x 3ft. This is similar to, but not as deep as, the priest-hole above an old oven at Harvington Hall, which is boarded with three thicknesses of planks to eliminate the hollow sound. This possible priest-hole at Blore Hall further supports the accumulating evidence that the Bassetts were Catholics.

The beehive oven used to be filled with wood, or furze. This was burned until the inside brickwork of the oven was hot. The hot ashes were removed and dumped into the ash space below. Dough was placed into the oven, using a long handled wooden spade called a peel, the oven was resealed and the bread baked.

The Will of Sir William (III) Bassett (died 1553) mentions a *"hangynge arysse for the grate hall of Bloore"*. This tapestry is mentioned again in 1662, as *"an old hanging in the chamber"*. Tapestry, of this kind was of the type woven in Arras, in France, and therefore acquired the name "arysse". This tapestry was a very important family heirloom, passed from generation to generation. According to Sir William's will, it was used for worship and would therefore depict scenes or symbols of religious significance. It was not unusual for the Arras to be carried from place to place as the Lord of the Manor went on his travels. It would be useful too - it would help keep out the draughts, in the cold places he visited.

In 1593, a Catholic priest, Robt Gray, was interrogated by the notorious Catholic-hater and torturer Topcliffe. The priest admitted, probably under torture, that he had visited William Bassett's house at sundry times. It is not clear however, whether it was Langley or Blore.

While Sir William Cavendish, later Duke of Newcastle, was in exile, he was found guilty of treason by the Parliamentarians and all his lands were confiscated. On the 16th June 1652, the Manor of Blore was purchased by Colonel John Goring and Richard Mellor for a sum of £1978.2.4d. In September 1652, the actual grant was made to John Goring of Kingston, and Richard Mellor of Blore, for one life, of the "Manor of Bloore, manor house called Bloore Hall, 2 courts, 1 brewhouse, 3 gardens, 1 barn, 1 stable plus "2 lead cauldrons" and most of the land in Blore. Colonel Goring got the "Manor House and Parke" and Richard Mellor the rest of the lands farmed from Blore Hall. So far, there is no record, or indication, that Goring ever used or occupied the Manor House. Richard Mellor continued to farm the land until his death in 1679.

The brew house referred to in 1652, is the room to the right of the entrance to the Hall. At one time, this had been a separate building, keeping away the smells, and close enough to safeguard the cauldrons and their contents. This was incorporated into the structure of the Hall.

Blore Hall was visited by Elias Ashmole. In his heraldic notes he describes the coats of arms in the great chamber, the lodging chamber, the kitchen and the pantry. The Hall had two floors, and the great chamber was the bedroom above the Great Hall. The lodging chamber was the place where personal servants and senior members of the household lived and slept, and where visitors were accommodated. It was probably the bedroom overlooking the road down to Okeover. At the time of Ashmole's visit, the kitchen would be the Great Hall, where all the household activity took place. The pantry was the room just across the foot of the stairs from the kitchen. Next to it, down the steps, was the larder for keeping meat and perishables.

According to the Staffordshire Hearth Tax Assessment of 1666, Blore Hall had sixteen hearths. This ranks it, in size, as one of the sixty largest houses in Staffordshire at that time.

After many years of living in the old rectory behind the church, William Yates, the Parson of Blore, moved into Blore Hall. In 1689, his will gives the contents of the various rooms. On the upper floor, the "chamber over the house" was obviously used as the sitting room, with its cupboard, chest, table and five chairs and a low bed on wheels suitable for overnight visitors. His study was off the main room, where he kept his books and prepared his sermons. The "over chamber", looking down the road to Okeover, was the bedroom. It was used by the parson and his wife and contained two beds, a chest and a desk. The "nether chamber" was the other bedroom, for his children, with a bed, 2 tables and 2 chairs. The room off the middle landing was called the buttery, but it was being used as a "junk room", with odd bits and pieces of household stuff.

Downstairs, the Great Hall was used as the kitchen, but also contained two beds for the kitchen staff. To avoid the constant stream of visitors and interruptions, the parson had moved his study, at the left of the front door, to the room above. His old study was being used to store the wool due to him as tithes, and from his own flock of eighty three sheep. The brew house had become the milk house and contained all the churns, tubs, vats and equipment associated with milk, cheese and butter making. The kitchen parlour was next door, and the cool larder was used as a cheese chamber and a place to store the bacon. According to his will, he also owned eight horses, referred to as eight pieces of horse flesh; horse flesh was one of the terms used for riding horses, as distinct from working horses.

The porch facing the main road on the north side of the building, had not yet been built in 1689.

When William Yates died in 1689, the Reverend Samuel Smalley succeeded him as rector of the parish. Samuel Smalley moved into Blore Hall. He lived there for twenty years, until his death in 1708. The inventory of his worldly goods lists the contents of each room in Blore Hall, although the rooms bear different names from those given at the death of his predecessor. The brew house of the Bassett era, which became the milk house with William Yates, returned to its original purpose, and contained a copper and other brewing vessels and an arke. As a scholar, the most valuable item in his inventory were the books and papers in the library, valued at twenty pounds.

A layout of the buildings surrounding the courtyard, is shown on the 1631 map. Of the original buildings, the old barn facing down the road to Okeover remained unchanged from the 16th century. This barn was restored with dedication and craftsmanship by a previous owner of Blore Hall Farm, Mr John Massey and subsequently further changed to suit its new purpose as holiday cottages, by Kevin Ellis.

When it was used as a barn, the high doorway allowed access for the loaded haywains. The corn was off-loaded to the upper floor, on the left, from which it was later tossed down on to the floor of the central bay. Threshing, to separate the grain from the corn, was carried out on the central floor using a flail. The small door in the rear wall allowed a through draught to carry away the chaff and the dust. The straw was temporarily stored in the right hand bay, for use as litter for cattle and horses and conversion to manure. The central bay was used at sheep shearing time, a very busy time in the farmer's life.

Around 1718, Thomas (III) Rivett acquired Blore Hall, and it passed to his son, Thomas (IV), in 1724. The property was leased to Richard Taylor, yeoman, of Blore, whose name often appears in business dealings associated with Thomas Rivett. In 1727, Richard Taylor was accused of fathering the child of Anne Rylet (probably Ryley of Woodhouses). He was sent to jail until "good sureties" arranged his release. The unfortunate lady was adjudged a lewd disorderly person and mother of a female bastard child. She was committed to the House of Correction, severely punished, and kept to hard labour for twelve months.

Samuel Shore, of Norton, near Sheffield, bought Blore Hall Farm from the Rivetts in 1758, and it stayed with the Shore family for one hundred years. The principal part of Blore was farmed from Blore Hall, although the glebeland was held by the rector Rev Bayliffe, John Port of Ilam held Hinckley Wood and the small Lodge among the trees on the Blore side of the River Manifold.

From the early 1780s until 1792 John Sutton and his family lived at Blore Hall. In 1784 John Sutton is named, along with Thomas Dennis and John Smith, as eligible to serve on a Jury. John Sutton's son, also John, continued as joint tenant of Blore Hall with his mother. In 1798/9, The Waterings was split off from Blore Hall, and John Heath was given the tenancy. Grandson Benjamin Sutton continued to farm at Blore Hall for another twenty years.

Mechanization came to Blore around the beginning of the 19th century, when an unusual polygon shaped building was added to the back of the old barn. This building housed a horse-wheel, known locally as a ginny ring, which provided a covered space for horses to walk round and round, attached to a revolving shaft. The original half-height of the walls allowed ventilation, to cool the horses as they plodded round. This horse power was transmitted via the revolving shaft and a system of cogs and wheels, to another machine inside the old barn. The machine in the barn was one of the early mechanical threshing machines, which replaced the hard monotonous labour of the flail. According to John Weller in his "History of the Farmstead", a horse-wheel driven by two horses, could thresh and dress one hundred and twenty bushels of oats. The use of a flail would only produce seven bushels of oats in a day.

Between 1833 and 1835, Thomas Smith moved from Mayfield, and was farming all 743 acres of Blore. He lived in Blore Hall with his wife, Elizabeth, and four children, William, Thomas, John, Sidney and his mother, Margaret Smith, aged 60. They had three manservants, Joseph Phillips, David Pegg and John Radcliffe, and four maidservants, Lydia Taylor, Mary Mycock, Mary Rushton and Emma Brown. His son, Thomas, suffered a serious accident, and had to have his leg amputated. He was educated at Ashbourne Grammar School and although his father offered him the chance to go to Oxford, he refused. He later became a farmer at Admaston, like other members of the family and wrote a pamphlet "The Story of a Staffordshire Farm" - a copy is held in the William Salt Library at Stafford.

In 1843, Thomas Smith Senior had a severe shock when his landlords' bank, Parker & Shores of Sheffield, were declared bankrupt. It took eighteen years to settle the affairs of the bank. The failure of the bank meant that the improvements he made to the farm were of benefit to the creditors, not to Mr Smith himself.

Thomas Smith was still farming the whole of Blore in 1851, and another two children, Arthur and Mary Jane, had been added to his brood. His mother was no longer with them but his mother-in-law, Elizabeth Carrington, had come to stay. Thomas employed ten farm labourers to help him around the farm. He died at the age of 56 in March 1855, and was buried in Blore churchyard. This was an opportune moment for the landlords to split Blore once again into two farms, Blore Hall Farm and The Waterings.

Thomas's son William Carrington Smith was allowed to retain the tenancy of Blore Hall Farm with 495 acres. His young brother, Arthur, and sister, Mary Jane, stayed on with him at Blore Hall. William employed a carter, three farm labourers, a dairy maid and a house servant.

After years wrangling over the Shore Estate, in 1868 the Okeover family bought both Blore Hall Farm and The Waterings. They retained the split, and allowed William Smith to continue as tenant. He stayed there for only a couple more years and then moved to Alton, where he married Louisa Maulton.

The Oldfields came to Blore around 1870. John Oldfield and his wife, Ellen, had twelve children and lived at Blore Hall for twenty years. At the 1871 census, John and Ellen and three small children were living at Blore Hall. They had a nursemaid, a general servant, a dairy maid and five farm servants.

The genial, grizzled old John was one the local characters renowned for his "home brewed", carrying on the tradition of producing good ale at Blore Hall. He also told a good tale and is reputed to have told the following with great relish: *"One of his great great grandmothers who had high instincts and a bit of family pride, being, as she was, the wife of a descendant of the learned scholar and divine Dr John Oldfield, a non-juror, determined to outdo her neighbours by introducing at a family christening a "dish" of tea, then an expensive beverage lately introduced from China. And this is how she did it. She boiled the leaves in a pot and SERVED THEM UP DRY. The result was not satisfactory. The guests all tasted but failed to appreciate the compliment paid to them. The parson who was present said with courteous simplicity, 'If you please Ma'am, I will also take a sup of the brew'. Whereupon the old lady threw up her arms in unfeigned amazement and exclaimed, 'Why, God Bless you mon - it was as black as ink and as bitter as gall and there was never a pig in the parish would have tasted of it.' The worthy old dame had poured the "broth" down the sink!"*

John Oldfield was the churchwarden at Blore Church, one daughter Ellen was the organist and Louisa was a member of the choir, but all the family attended the services when they were at home. John died in 1890 and his family stayed on a little while but then moved away from Blore. When one of his daughters Alice Oldfield married George Gillott in 1914 at Brassington, their old friend the Rector of Blore, Rev John Young, officiated at the wedding.

David Howson had lived with his father on Common End Farm, Swinscoe and been educated at Swinscoe school. He worked for his father until his marriage to Lucy Wheldon of Wootton. The young couple moved to Worcestershire, where the first two of their daughters, Florence and Hilda, were born; they had a total of ten children. In 1890, Blore Hall Farm became available and the Okeovers agreed that David Howson should be given the tenancy. David and his family were well known to the Okeovers; his father and grandfather had farmed Common End Farm from 1826 to around 1870.

Mr Howson, like a number of tenants of Blore Hall before him, was a Churchwarden. Local youths took advantage of his strict churchgoing. A Mr Hill who lived at The Fleece in Swinscoe used to relate how, as a young lad, he went scrumping in the large apple orchard opposite Blore Hall, while Mr Howson was in church. A few very old apple and pear trees remain as the only evidence of the orchard.

David and Lucy Howson moved to Yoxall where they lived for many years into their 80s; they are buried in a double grave in Yoxall churchyard.

In 1926, Richard Lewis Torr and his wife Amy left Stydd Farm in Yeaveley and moved to Blore Hall Farm. They brought with them eight of their children: Thomas, Richard, William Ernest, Annie, George, Patricia Amy, Constance and Stanley Arthur. Their eldest daughter Mary Elizabeth was already married.

Mr Torr died in 1929, but his wife continued farming at Blore for ten more years. By 1937, five more children had married and left the fold so Mrs Torr moved to a smaller farm at Foxt, accompanied by two sons and a daughter. Mrs Torr died in 1947 and was buried close to her husband in Blore churchyard.

For a very brief spell, Mr Fred Thompson took over the tenancy of Blore Hall, just before the War, but his sudden death left the property empty once again.

Mr James Arthur Burton and his wife Edith took the tenancy at Blore Hall and stayed there for a number of years. In 1939, they had three farm labourers, John Campbell, John Feeley and John Mark, living with them. Reg Bailey, who was then living at the Croft in Swinscoe, also worked there. Other farmers in the area expressed doubts about the unprecedented luxury of installing a bath on the premises for the benefit of the farm workers. Mr Burton died in August 1975 at the age of 74, and his wife moved from Blore Hall to Ashbourne where she lived until her death in 1991 at the age of 86 years.

In 1975, Blore Hall was bought by John Massey for £40,500. He set about the enormous task of restoring the buildings with the patience and dedication of one who had fallen in love with the old hall. For eight years, in his spare time and with the assistance of local craftsmen, he re-roofed the whole complex including the ginny ring, rebuilt the wall and arch of the old barn, and restored many of the features within the house.

Unfortunately, in 1986 John Massey felt that he had to sell the property. His regret was tempered by the knowledge that the new owner, Kevin Ellis, appreciated its historic associations and had the enthusiasm and the resources to complete the work of restoration started eleven years previously, the conversion, of the outbuildings into holiday cottages, and Blore Hall into a guest house.

Cherry and Ivan Cope are the present owners. Cherry Cope tells their story:

"It was a dark cold night in October 1986 when four friends ended up for a drink at "The Bowling Green" Pub in Ashbourne. They had just come from a near derelict property known as "Blore Hall Farm" just 3 miles away. Our friends, Kevin Ellis and his wife Sharon, had driven us (yet again!) to look at the property that we had all first seen on another cold dark winter night. It was seven years previously that Kevin's bid at the auction for Blore was beaten by that of John Massey; both of them had had similar ideas for the development of the old hall and outbuildings.

Kevin explained to us the current situation. Blore Hall was still owned by John Massey - structurally John Massey had carried out a lot of external work but he had other business commitments and was willing to negotiate to sell Blore privately. Kevin wanted to know if we were interested in a joint purchase.

Kevin proposed that we should purchase the Old Hall and develop the business of bed & breakfast, a bar, a small food operation for residents and the "changeover" management of the Cottages - Kevin would form a limited company to buy and convert the old farm buildings into holiday cottage accommodation. But we had to move quickly.- and make a decision within one week.

We owned a small two bed roomed bungalow ten miles away. Our daughter Rebecca was two years old. Ivan was in full time employment and I was self-employed with a small shop in Derby. It was a big decision. Within one month our bungalow and my business were up for sale and in the middle of winter the purchase of Blore was going through. Each Sunday we would drive out and wander round the buildings, with Rebecca in her snow suit, making plans for the future.

Contracts were exchanged in February 1987; the sale of our bungalow was complete. So with heating, lighting, chemical loo and microwave, our family moved into Blore Hall on 9th April - sharing with twelve tradesmen who were already there. Those early days before we were open to the public are hazy now, but I remember making 20 pairs of curtains and endless pots of tea for all those workmen. I started up the accounts and other systems.

For our financial survival, Ivan remained in his full time job for the first eighteen months. The money I sold my business for furnished the Hall and kept us going until the first guests arrived. In late June 1987 we first let the "Mahogany En-Suite" for bed & breakfast. Then on August 1st the first of the eighteen cottages was ready to let: Alstonfield, Butterton, Callow, Dove and Edale. That week we saw a family in Edale and a family in Alstonfield. In those early days Ivan would come home from work and open the bar at 7.00 pm and I would run the kitchen with Ivan waiting on, and Rebecca, now three year old, putting herself to bed. It wasn't long after that, when eight months pregnant, I came out of the kitchen permanently.

The cottage renovations continued in phases over the next eighteen months. After the first five, came Mappleton, Norbury, Farwell, Carpenters; then Hartington, Ilam, Jodrell, Kinder, and finally the Old Tythe Barn was converted. Since that first year many things have changed! Just the "changeover" of the cottages involves 14+ staff. The bar is now open from midday onwards. The food service has grown to include take-aways and a full restaurant licence. As for what the future holds.....?"

BLORE PARK

Blore Park was created before 1227 so that the Lord of the Manor could indulge in his passion for hunting, and copy the style of the King and the Barons. Venison was a very popular meat - for those who could afford to eat it. The Park was most probably stocked with fallow deer, although in some parks in Staffordshire red deer were common. The park was not solely used for the hunt. It was a source of timber for building and firewood, and pasturage of animals such as dairy cows, oxen, goats, and of course the ubiquitous rabbit. Sheep were kept away from the park, because they would have destroyed the pasture for the deer. Blore Park was one of ninety-four parks in Staffordshire which were created for food supply and pleasure.

This two hundred acre park existed for over 500 years. Mr F.J. Johnson in his "Settlement Patterns of North East Staffordshire" suggests that Blore was deserted in the Middle Ages as a result of the creation of Blore Park. The Park was in existence prior to 1227, when Clemence de Blore and William Audley were married, which seems a little early for desertion or displacement. So far no evidence of an alternative village site has been found.

In 1248, Hugh de Okeover gave up his claim to free chase in the park in return for one buck and one doe in fawn, each year. The extent of the herd of deer is not known. In 1449, in neighbouring Okeover Park, there were 120 deer, 115 of which were slaughtered in an attack on Okeover Hall. In 1577, William Bamford was the Keeper of Bloore Park. The deer still roamed the park in 1652, together with goats and wild sheep. The deer of Blore Park are mentioned in the biography of the Duke of Newcastle, in 1660. The park has always been used as pasture, and local farmers who pastured their animals in the park were charged agistment rents. A list of rents for Blore Park during the 1690s is to be found among the Portland Papers deposited at Nottingham Archives. The rents started low but then rose very quickly:

       1691 £18. 0. 0.
       1692 £19. 0. 0.
       1693 £26. 0. 0.

1694 £34. 2. 6.
1695 £40. 5. 0.
1696 £47. 6. 0.
1697 £46. 8. 0.

This probably reflects the demand for pasture based on rising prices during the period. However, in 1762 a glebe terrier reports that Blore Park had been disparked and leased out to pasture.

On most early maps of Staffordshire, and some of Derbyshire, Blore Park is shown, and the large scale map of 1631 clearly shows the boundaries. The boundary of the old park can be traced along field boundaries which still exist; some of the area is still thickly wooded. The watering place of the deer is easily identified, with limited but easy access to the edge of the river. The high opposite river bank and the fast flowing confluence of the River Dove and River Manifold acted as a barrier to prevent escape. Some form of barrier was erected upstream, across the River Manifold, similar to the palings around the boundaries of the park mentioned in 1490. In 1656, a list of Bloare Rents shows *The Parke in my Lords Hand £50.0s.0d.* and provision for repairing the pale in the park, at a cost of £1.11s.6d. In 1701, an indenture was drawn up between John, Duke of Newcastle and Rich. Brown of Shelton, Wm Allison of Paulterton and Sam Wyld of Hucknall, for the trees in Bloore Parke, with a licence to fell until 1707. In addition to the payment of £1800 by instalments, the agreement also called for the supply of timber to repair the park fencing: 700 stoopes, 800 rayles, 700 pales. One of the residents of Blore, James Kent, was paid £5 for fencing and looking after the Parke Pale, at Bloore, in 1714. In 1718, William Leese rented the park with the Lee at £80.0s.0d.

A clear view of the parkland hillside can be obtained from the opposite bank of the river, on the road down from Thorpe, or from the Izaac Walton Hotel.

WOOD LODGE - *Blore Lodge. Ilam Lodge. Wood Cottage.*
Wood Lodge is hidden away among the trees on the Blore side of the River Manifold, by the old bridge from Ilam Hall. It was built at the same time as other property in Ilam. In 1939 Stanley Dawbarn lived there with Henry Herbert Mellor. Stanley was schoolteacher but unfortunately died of meningitis. The Hayes family moved into Wood Lodge in 1954 and remained there until 1972. One of the Hayes family worked at Ilam Meadows and lived on the farm. Mr Hayes still works with Mr Ian Smith at Ilam Meadows.

BLORE RECTORY
The first mention of a rectory or parsonage was in a glebe terrier dated 1612. The parsonage in the field on the north side behind Blore Church, is described as having three bays. It had a barn of four bays and another little house of two bays. A bay was the distance between the main timbers and measured about sixteen feet, so the parsonage was quite substantial in size, and the barn even bigger. The barn was for the storage of the tithe, which was paid in kind - one tenth of the crop. The parsonage is shown on the Map of Blore drawn by William Senior for the Duke of Newcastle in 1631. In two paintings, one by the artist L.J.Wood c1830, and one by J. Buckler c1847, part of a cottage can be seen behind the church.

In 1830, the cottage was reported to be totally unsuitable for the rector of Blore. It was occupied for some time by Mr Lees, who actually farmed the glebelands on behalf of the Rector. In 1861, a rector's gardener William Bennet, his wife Sarah and daughter Charlotte, lived in the cottage. In 1903 it was burned down in a mysterious fire and not a trace now remains.

Under the auspices of the Lord of the Manor and Patron Samuel Shore, a new rectory was built around 1837/8. During the building, a young boy, John Barnett, accidentally fell from the new rectory house and died. The new rectory with Coach house, Stable, Barn, Cow house and Cart Shed was built in the field called Terrace Croft, facing the entrance to the church. Rev Hugh Wood was the first rector to live in the new rectory with his wife, Jane (née Marshall), with their twin daughters, Ellin and Catherine. The local joiner and builder, Anthony Stubbs, carried out a lot of internal work on the new rectory for the Rev Wood. In 1858, Rev Hugh Wood succeeded his father as Squire of Swanwick, and two years later, he moved from Blore to Swanwick. He introduced two curates in succession, to look after the parish of

Blore. The first curate in 1861, was the Rev Joseph Dun Miller, who lived at Blore rectory for less than two years. In 1862 the Rev John David Glennie moved into the rectory and remained for six years. In late 1866 the Rev Glennie employed a new cook, Margaret Humphreys, who was a stranger to the area. At the beginning of January 1867, whilst Rev and Mrs Glennie were away in London, she gave birth to a stillborn child and tried to hide the body. The body was found by a manservant, Edward Cheavin who informed the local policeman, PC Wood of Mayfield. Margaret Humphreys was accused of concealment of birth and sent for trial at Stafford Assizes where further evidence was given by a domestic servant Elizabeth Yeomans and Dr Hall of Waterfall. Margaret Humphreys was found guilty and sentenced to two months imprisonment. She was lucky not to be charged with murder, as a similar case elsewhere, a little earlier in the century, resulted in a verdict of guilty and in the poor mother being hanged.

Rev Glennie left the parish in 1869, following problems which arose from confrontations with the Primitive Methodists of Swinscoe chapel. There followed a period of six years when there was no incumbent in the parish. The Rev J.H. Young moved into the rectory in 1875 and served the parish faithfully and well for forty years. In 1916 a soft-voiced Welshman, Rev T.J.S. Roberts, moved to Blore. He was a bachelor and doted on his nephew Clifford John, who acted as a kind of handyman and chauffeur to the rector.

In 1952, an agreement was made between the Rev R.W.D. Peck and Mr G.C. Kirkham for the occupation of Blore Rectory House with his wife and children only, and specifically excluded lodgers.

Around 1955, the Diocese of Lichfield put Blore Rectory on the market at the modest price of £600 or near offer. The Revd Smith, a retired clergyman, descendant of Thomas Smith who farmed Blore Hall in the mid 19th century, came to look at the house. He was very attracted by the size and splendour of the rooms. His wife recalled the difficulties of the Smith family, one hundred years before, and was relieved when her husband's offer was not accepted.

In 1977, Stuart G. Worthington and his wife, and three daughters came to the Old Rectory. Since those days, Mr Worthington has taken a lively and loving interest in St Bartholomew's Church, which faces his house. In 1977, he became a member of the Parochial Church Council. In 1983, he was elected as a churchwarden and took on the additional responsibility of Treasurer in 1992. The old church badly needed restoration, and Stuart volunteered to carry out the necessary fund raising and manage the whole project. Within three years of the start of his work, Mr Worthington had successfully raised £125,000 and supervised the complete restoration of the church. A supreme effort by one dedicated man.

BLORE COTTAGE

Blore Cottage, sometimes referred to as Rectory Cottage, was originally a barn belonging to the Rectory. There had been a previous Rectory Cottage situated behind the church, but that was burned down in 1909. Although there was a tap in the cottage, there was a lot of difficulty in obtaining more than just a trickle of water.

In 1940 the tenancy was taken over by Mr Charles Mellor. The Mellor family lived at Blore Cottage. Mr Mellor worked at the Copper Works at Froghall and Mrs Mellor used to do general housework for the rector. When Blore Hall held a function or wedding in the large room upstairs, Mrs Mellor used to "wait on". The Mellors moved to The Cottage in Swinscoe.

Mr Clifford John lived with Rev T.J.S. Roberts at the Rectory and drove an American Oldsmobile car - acting as chauffeur to the Rector. When he got married, he and his wife Kate moved across the church green to Blore Cottage, and lived there till 1948/9. They had two children, Ann and John.

When Mr Oulsnam came out of the army he went into partnership with his grandfather Mr William Redfern, delivering goods to farms in the area. He learned from Clifford John that the cottage was vacant He moved there from The Grange, Cauldon Low, together with his grandparents. As Blore Hall had a large herd of dairy cattle, the Oulsnams fetched their milk from Blore Hall each day. During the time that they lived at Blore, Mrs Oulsnam's brother, Roy Redfern, attended Ilam School. One daughter, Shirley Ann, was christened at Blore Church in 1947 and another daughter, Ivy, was born at the cottage in April 1948. Shortly afterwards, the family moved to Nook Cottage, Wootton. .

Mr Michael Griffin and his wife Dorothy, occupied the cottage in 1984.

In 1996, Alexandra Carr was living at the cottage.

ILAM MEADOWS - *Ox Leasowe. Ox Leisure. Blore Hollow. Blore Lea.*
By the river there used to be a mill, not far from where the stepping stones crossed the river to Ilam. Around 1600, the Austen family lived at the Mill and farmed the land by the river. In 1609 the miller, Thomas Austen, died, and the inventory of his estate states that the rent of the mill was £3.6s.8d per year. The Austen family were not only millers and farmers but also made buckets and tubs and pewter and copperware. Thomas' son William took over as Miller. In 1612 it is recorded that the Parson of Blore collected 3s.4d in tithes for the mill called Ilam Mill in Blore Parish.

In 1656, the Bagnalls were tenants of the mill, and mill meadow, at a rental of £12. They continued as millers until 1689. According to a list of rentals, from 1670 to 1686 James Yattes was paying a yearly rent of £18.6s.8d for land which included Ox Leasow.

In the early 19th century, there was a cottage called Ilam Steps, probably on the site of the ancient watermill. At the 1841 census, Ilam Steps was occupied by Edward Thompson and his wife Ann and their daughter Mary.

In 1861, Richard Berresford and his wife Rebecca and their daughter, Mary, were living at Ilam Steps. Ten years later four more children had been added to the family, Annie, Lucy, Hannah and Richard.

Ox Leasow Farm was built by the Okeovers in 1881. Over the door to the house there is a lintel showing the date 1881 with the initials H.C.O. - Haughton Charles Okeover. The farm has changed its name a number of times: Steps Farm, Ox Leasow, Ox Leisure, Blore Hollow, Blore Lea and now Ilam Meadows.

Richard Seals began life as a farm servant at Brassington. By steady plodding and conservation of his money, he was eventually able to rent a farm for himself. His name appears in the Electoral Register for 1885. He had no real interest in politics and left such matters to "all them ranting chaps" and, although he was not a member of the church, he usually drove with the parson to record his vote.

At the census of 1891 Richard Seals and his wife, Alice, were living at the farm, then called Blore Hollow Farm, with their daughters, Emma, Alice, Mary, and grandson, John Wigley. Richard went about the farm in honeycomb smock frock. When he went to market with his wife, he drove in the old fashioned way, seated on the cart bottom. On 20th January 1900, Richard Seals age 73 of Ilam Meadows died. When he died his wife Alice moved to The Poplars, Hognaston, and lived there until her death in June 1917. When the Seals left the farm, the Shilcock family moved. Unfortunately, their fifteen month old son, Archibald Shilcock died here.

Walter Joseph Moor, farm labourer, and Jane Watson, both of whom worked at Ilam Meadows, were married at Blore Church on 27th August 1906.

According to the electoral registers Thomas Deaville was at Ox Leasow Farm in 1908.

Bertie Cecil Kidger and his wife Agnes moved from Ilam to the farm and lived there for twenty five years. In 1940 Mabel Kidger contracted meningitis and because of the heavy February snow had to be carried by sledge to Ilam. She was taken to hospital but sadly died and was buried in Ilam churchyard. Sydney Allen, age 23, was working as a farm labourer on the farm. He also contracted meningitis and died. Local opinion says that the illness was contracted by infection from one of the horses. There appears to have been an epidemic of meningitis around this time, as Vera Smith from a cottage opposite the school in Swinscoe also died of the disease.

The Smiths have lived in the area for over one hundred and fifty years. One branch of the family farmed at Cliff Top Farm in Swinscoe, from 1845 until 1875. In 1941 one of their descendants, Mr Frank Smith, moved from Ilam with his family, to Ox Leisure. He remained there until his death on the 9th July 1949, at the age of 71. His wife Ellen Smith lived on for thirteen years until, at the age of 80, she died on 13th May 1962. She was buried beside her husband in Blore Churchyard.

Cyril Smith married his wife, Sylvia, in 1948, and moved into the farm in 1949, following the death of Frank Smith. After his death, Sylvia Smith took over the farm. In 1984, Mr Ian Smith took over the farm and Sylvia and her sister Joan moved to Ilam, and then to Thorpe. Mr Ian Smith and his wife Yvonne have been living at the farm since, which comprises 150 acres, and have kindly loaned some of the photographs. Sadly, Mrs Yvonne Smith died shortly before the publication of this book.

THE WATERINGS

Five miles from Ashbourne, a mile from the A52 Calton Moor Crossroads towards Blore, is a farm whose history can be traced for hundreds, and possibly thousands, of years. The Waterings Farm stands at the foot of Hazelton Clump, whose tree-covered summit has been a landmark for travellers for centuries.

Water has always been vital not only to local inhabitants, but also to the traveller, and the cattle drover and the shepherd on the way to market. It is not surprising that The Waterings, with its own natural water supply close to one of the principal local roads, has always been an important settlement.

People lived in this spot more than one thousand years ago, which is confirmed by the burial mound called Dun Low behind The Waterings. In 1849 one of the early barrow diggers, Samuel Carrington, attempted to excavate Dun Low barrow but was deterred by the trees and the tree roots on the mound. Although he mentions a hollow, which might have lead to an interment, nothing of any significance was found. He was more successful when digging two other ancient burial mounds on the top of Hazelton. These two mounds produced evidence of ancient burials of the Anglo Saxon period.

From Anglo Saxon times through the Middle Ages, ploughing was done by teams of oxen, pulling a wooden plough around long strips of land. The characteristic signs of ridge and furrow ploughing can still be seen on the lower slopes between the farmhouse and Hazelton.

In 1087 the Domesday Survey states that four Saxon Thegns had holdings in Blore before Robert de Stafford gave it to Edric. From the evidence of previous settlement, ridge and furrow ploughing, its water supply and location, it is reasonable to assume that The Waterings was one of those four Saxon Holdings. The name ending "inga" is of recognised Anglo Saxon derivation.

In 1630 William Senior, Professor of The Mathematics, was commissioned to survey and produce a map of all the lands in Blore belonging to the Duke of Newcastle, second husband of Elizabeth Bassett of Blore. The map still exists in the Portland Collection at Welbeck. It shows Waterings, Waterings Meadow and Waterings Pasture, a total of ninety five acres.

According to the Blore Rentals for 1656, The Waterings was farmed by John Hanson and Millington. The previous tenants had been Ralph Philips, John Millington and Alice Broadbotham. The rental was £21.0s.0d and the tax abated £4.4s.0d.

Ten years later, in the Hearth Tax Returns, three households in Blore had two hearths: The Rector William Yates, Richard Mellor, who was farming Blore Hall Farm, and Mathew Stone. It is reasonable to assume that Mathew Stone was farming The Waterings, which was the only other residence of significance in Blore.

The old road from Ashbourne passed through Thorpe and forded the River Dove near Coldwall. It went through Blore between the church and the present rectory, and up Blore Dale, more or less parallel with the present road. It forked right where the cattle grid used to stand, and along the track behind The Waterings. A little way along the track, known as Waterings Gate, stood a house belonging to the Austen family who, father and son, were coopers by trade. They provided buckets and barrels to the local community, and passing travellers. The Austen family were millers at the watermill from 1600 to 1640. In 1666, Philip Austen and his wife lived at Waterings Gate. Their son Timothy was born that year and was baptised at Blore Church. In 1679, Philip paid ten shillings rent for his part of Waterings land. The Austens lived at Waterings Gate until 1740, when Elizabeth Austen, widow, died.

His Grace, the Right Honourable the Lord Harley, installed a Bailiff, Mr Thomas Millward, to farm The Waterings on his behalf. In 1679, the rent was £10 per half year. In 1685/6, the rent had reduced by £1 to £19. In 1686/7, John Alcock took the tenancy and the rental was reduced again, to £18 per year. As frequently happened, the farm was shared by the whole family; John's brother Richard and his wife, Dorothy, were also living on the farm.

In 1745, The Waterings was farmed by a "great, strong, desperate mon" called Robert Smith. Some Scottish soldiers, part of Bonnie Prince Charlie's Army, raided The Waterings and stole some horses. Robert Smith followed the raiders on their way down to Derby and eventually found his horses in a very sad state. He vowed revenge. On the retreat of the Scottish Troops, Robert Smith killed three of them and their bodies were buried on Swinscoe Flatts, near a limekiln. Many years later the remains of one of the soldiers was discovered whilst quarrying. Diana Dors, who often stayed at Fairbrook Cottage in Swinscoe, reckoned that she had seen the ghost of one of the soldiers.

An Act of Parliament was passed, in 1762, giving authority for a turnpike road from Thorpe, over Coldwall Bridge, through Blore, Calton Moor, Cheadle and Oakamoor to Blythe Bridge. On the section between Blore and Calton Moor, the new road followed the more direct route, in front of The Waterings, rather than the old track around the back. To pay for the building and maintenance of the turnpike, toll gates were erected at various places along the route. A chain was placed at the junction of the old track and the new turnpike near the cattle grid. So that the toolkeeper could see in all directions, a wooden shed was erected on top of a small hillock. This shed was maintained up to 1822, when the tollkeeper asked for a house to be built on the spot. In the accounts of Anthony Stubbs, 1833 to 1836, there is an item that reads "paid for tool bar £2.16s.10d"; this probably relates to work on the toll gate. There are tales of the tollkeeper running down to the gate to collect the fees, but no physical trace has been found of the place where the tollkeeper would carry out his duties.

Not far along the road, towards Calton Moor Crossroads, opposite the old track from behind The Waterings, there was a windmill. It is shown on the map of sale of 1844. In 1894, the remains of the mill were being used as a cowhouse and barn in 1894, and a barn still stands on the site.

From 1768, Samuel Shore of Norton Sheffield, owned the whole of Blore, including The Waterings, and rented it out to Mr John Sutton, at a rental of £32.11s.6d.

John Heath farmed The Waterings from 1799 to 1823, and paid £2.19s.0d Land Tax. He died on 23rd March 1823, at the age of 52, and was buried in Blore churchyard. He left his estate to his wife, Mary, and son, Thomas, and they continued to farm the land. John also left small bequests to his other sons, John, Ralph, William and Gilbert and daughter, Dorothy. John and his son Thomas could both write but Mary, his wife, put a cross as her mark on the Probate Document.

Edward Leese took over the tenancy from 1824, and remained at the Waterings until 1839. He and his wife Judith moved to Hall Flatts.

The Waterings was again consolidated with Blore Hall Farm. Thomas Smith, who lived at Blore Hall farmed the whole of Blore including The Waterings, a total of 743 Acres.

According to the accounts of Anthony Stubbs of Swinscoe, he was involved in *"Building Certain Buildings as per Contract at Waterings Farm as per contract with Sam'l Shore Esq of Norton Hall."* The cost of this building was £425.12s.6d. There was *"sundry extra work in Cowshed and Gooshouse and dividing a Chamber as may be seen by plan,"* at an additional cost of £21.0s.0d. This occurred between 1833 to 1836 and obviously describes building the present farmhouse. The building, which is now the stable and barn, was probably the previous farmhouse.

In 1841 the farmhouse was occupied by the foreman, George Swift, and his wife, Elizabeth, and small son, Charles, along with their manservant, Thomas Snape. After Thomas Smith died on the 13th March 1855 at the age of 55, his son William continued to hold Blore. In 1865, it was again split into two farms, Blore Hall Farm and The Waterings, and sold to the Okeover family.

The last entry in the Calton Baptismal Register, kept by the Clerk of the Parish, William Rowbotham, is *"John, son of Benjamin and Mary Mellor Bap'd Sep'r the 16th 1792."* In 1861, John Mellor was farming the 230 acres and his wife, Hannah, and two sons, Charles and Luke, were living at The Waterings. They had a young sixteen year old house servant called Elizabeth Finney and a carter, John Rushton. Ten years later, in 1871, son Charles was still living with his parents along with a daughter, Barbara. The Mellors employed two girls, Sarah Tideswell and Jane Alcock, as general servants, Arthur Sellers as cowman, and Walter Gould, as waggoner. In October 1875, Charles Mellor, farmer, was charged with drunkenness whilst in the parish of Ilam and he was fined 10s.0d plus 13s.6d costs, with the alternative of seven days in Stafford Jail if he did not pay.

Barry Robbins of Cauldon Low, a descendant of the Mellors, tells a story of the time when John Mellor was called for jury service in the case of a young woman charged with murder. After much deliberation, eleven members of the jury gave a verdict of "Guilty", but John steadfastly refused to agree. After the trial was over he was asked the reason for disagreeing with the rest, and he said: *"a good looking young woman like that couldna do such a thing"!!* In the twilight of their lives, John Mellor and his wife Hannah retired. Still active at the age of 90 in December 1883, John decided he would visit Calton, the place of his birth. He set out through the winter snows but his family went after him, and persuaded him to return home. That afternoon he dozed by the fire and after tea went upstairs. He sat on the side of the bed, put his head on the pillow, and peacefully passed away. He was laid to rest in Blore Churchyard, by the side of his mother, who had died 83 years previously. Hannah, his wife, lived for another ten years, until 6th February 1892. At the equally fine old age of 87; she was laid to rest with her husband at Blore.

Sometime during the ensuing period, the farm was extended from 230 acres to 278 acres. By 1881, John Heathcote and his wife, Mary, and their eight children were living at The Waterings, but did not stay long. From around 1885, Ralph Webster and his wife, Elizabeth, and son, Ralph, were tenants. In 1896, Ralph was elected as one of the Overseers of the Poor for the parish. The Websters subsequently moved to Common Farm in Cubley.

Joseph Hayes was farming The Waterings in 1900. His daughter, Mary Elizabeth, married Samuel Shirley of Coldwall Farm, a mile down the road towards Okeover. Joseph continued to farm at The Waterings until the middle of the Great World War. One of his farmhands, George Hickton, was killed in action around 1917. Joseph Hayes was the Churchwarden at Blore Church for many years. His wife died on 15th May 1915, and he died the following 6th February. After many years of faithful service to Blore Church, it is there that he and his wife Sarah were laid to rest. His son Joseph Hayes, with his wife Martha Ann, continued with the tenancy but the job was too much for him. In February 1921, he was declared under distress for rent. His seven cows, implements and 20 tons of new hay were put up for sale. Joseph Hayes, Junior died in 1938, and was buried in Blore churchyard. His wife, Martha Ann, died in 1961 and was buried beside her husband at Blore.

In the early 1920s Daniel Bradbury became the tenant. On the 3rd November 1926 Lilian Gertrude Bradbury, aged 24, was married to Frank Harrison of Calton Moor House. The wedding took place at Swinscoe Primitive Methodist Chapel and her father, Daniel, was one of the witnesses. One of two brothers, James Bradbury, took over the tenancy and the second brother, Bert, moved to Ashbourne. An uncle, Owen, lived with James and his wife and family of six children. In 1948, three of the children were attending Swinscoe School: Jimmy, Enid and Nancy. The Bradburys employed a number of farm workers, some of whom lived on the farm. Mr Hodge and his wife and Arthur Robinson were there, in 1949. James William Bradbury held the tenancy until he died on the 6th January 1951, at the age of 51. His wife, Ivy Elizabeth, moved to Mayfield. In 1954 Ivy Elizabeth Bradbury was appointed as one of the trustees of Swinscoe Methodist Chapel. She moved to Mayfield and died at the age of 80, in 1981. She was buried by the side of her husband in Blore Churchyard. One of her grandsons, John Antony Bradbury, son of James David and Margaret Rose Bradbury, was baptised at Swinscoe Chapel on the 12th September 1965. Tony, his son, took over the tenancy, and continued to farm there until he retired from farming in 1967 and went to live in Perth, Australia. Daughter Enid Rosemary died on the 1st October 1992, aged 54.

When it became known that the Bradburys were leaving, the Okeover Estate decided to split The Waterings into two separate lots. George Mansfield was farming at Leese House Farm, down Yearley Hill, towards Okeover. He was offered one of these lots and went to have a look. Rather than split the farm, George proposed to the Estate that he should take over the whole of The Waterings and relinquish his tenancy of Leese House Farm.

In 1967, George Mansfield moved into The Waterings. During his tenancy, he extended the land holding, introduced improved methods and tried out a variety of new breeds of sheep. After a lifetime of farming George Mansfield and his wife Mo retired to Ashbourne, in 1996.

In three hundred years the acreage of Waterings has tripled from 95 acres to 300 acres. With modern methods and improved breeds the number of sheep per acre has increased, from one per acre to four or six per acre. The price of old sheep in 1630 was about ten shillings each, which by 1950 had risen to around £5, and by 1994, to around £50, and in 1996 to £80. The costs of farming have similarly increased. The rent per acre has increased more than one hundred-fold, and modern methods involve much greater financial commitment.

The Waterings has the unusual reputation of rearing the first sheep whose carcasses were burned by French Farmers in the 1990s. They were protesting against the import of English mutton to France. However, as the largest sheep farm in North East Staffordshire, The Waterings is still making a contribution to the local community, and to the requirements and needs of the greater European Economic Community. The new tenant, Mr Parry, who was previously the shepherd on the Devonshire Estate at Chatsworth, came to The Waterings, with his wife and children in 1996.

Map showing the field enclosures

The view from Ilam meadows

The Cottage

Blunder Cottage

Blore Lodge, Ilam

Ilam Meadows

Cyril Smith and Desmond Miller at Ilam Meadows Farm

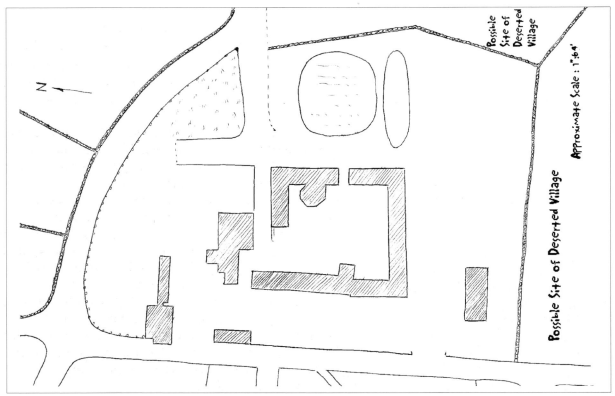

Plan of Blore Hall

FOUR
PEOPLE

DOMESDAY BLORE

After the Battle of Hastings, William the Conqueror rewarded his followers with positions of high office, and by sharing out the conquered land. Robert, the son of King William's personal standard bearer, Roger de Toeni, was given extensive lands throughout the Midlands. He adopted the name "de Stafford", and in one small corner of Staffordshire, one of his holdings was Blore.

Prior to the Conquest there had been four separate holdings of land in Blore, held by four Saxon Thegns in return for military service to the King. These four holdings were most probably Blore Hall Farm, with land down to the River, The Waterings, based on the vital water supply, land in Swinscoe, and possibly Calton.

Robert de Stafford nominated Edric as his tenant of Blore, encompassing all four previous holdings. Although in area there was sufficient land to occupy five plough teams, only about thirty acres were actually under cultivation. Edric had a plough, and there was one shared by a couple of local villagers. There were two furlongs of Spinney, most probably on the slopes down towards the River Dove, later to become Blore Park. Such sloping wooded land would be difficult to cultivate, but ideal for wood for fuel and building, and as a place where the pigs and the deer could forage for food.

The bleak upper moorland of Blore offered only a bare living, and was, therefore, valued at only five shillings. The Domesday Survey in 1086 described Blore more succinctly:

> THE SAME (Robert de Stafford) HOLDS ONE VIRGATE OF LAND AND EDRIC OF HIM. FOUR THEGNS HELD IT AND THEY WERE FREE MEN. THERE IS LAND FOR FIVE PLOUGHS. IN LORDSHIP IS ONE PLOUGH AND TWO VILLAGERS WITH ONE PLOUGH. THERE ARE TWO FURLONGS OF SPINNEY. IT IS WORTH FIVE SHILLINGS.

According to Domesday, Robert of Stafford also held one third part of one hide in Grindon which Wulfgeat had held before him in 1066.

DE BLORE FAMILY - *Or on a chevron between three pommes a crescent of the field*

There is no indication whether the De Blore Family was descended from Edric of Domesday fame but eighty years later, in 1166, Robert de Blore held Blore and Grindon, also of the honour of Stafford. Land was held in return for supplying Knights to the Overlord. This Knight Service was usually fixed at forty days per year. The estate which supplied a single Knight was called a Knight's Fee and worth about twenty shillings a year.

Robert de Blore held "One and one third knight's fees in the Manors of Blore and Grendon". About 1170, Robert gave Nicholas, his servant, use of two bovates of his land in Grendon at an annual rent of two pennies or a pair of spurs. Geoffrey de Blore, son of Robert, confirmed the gift of land for use by Nicholas at the same rental and Nicholas in gratitude gave his Lord a white horse for his Lady.

Robert's daughter married Ralph Fitzorm, forebear of the Okeovers and their son Hugh was the first to bear the ancient name of Okeover. When Geoffrey died, the estates were transferred to his younger brother, Ralph, who held Blore and Grendon until 1209. Ralph did not get along with his sister's son, Hugh de Okeover, and there was considerable quarrelling and litigation over ownership of land in Blore. In 1203, Radulfus de Blore accused Hugh de Acovere of wrongfully taking land in Swinscoe, and at the same Lichfield Assizes there were two further cases of disputes over land in Blore.

According to Tom Allen, a chapel was founded at Blore in the early 1100s. Around 1180, the Blore Family were responsible for building the church at Blore. In 1209, William the Abbot of Burton acknowledged that the advowsons of Blore Church belonged to Radulfus de Blore, in return for which Ralph agreed to pay an annual fee of one mark. The advowsons of the church allowed the Patron to nominate his own clergy and through the clergy, exercise influence over his tenants. No doubt he was also able to call for prayers for his own soul and plead his worthiness in heaven.

The Blore Family were also responsible for creating Blore Park and stocking it with deer for the hunt and meat for the table. William de Blore married Agnes, daughter of Peter Thornton, cleric, and had two daughters Clemence and Alianora. Their daughter Clemence was given in marriage to William Audley, son of Henry Audley, favourite of the Earl of Chester.

AUDLEYS AT BLORE
WILLIAM AND CLEMENCE DE AUDLEY
Henry, the father of William Audley, began his career as constable to Hugh de Lacy. He was highly esteemed by Ralph, Earl of Chester, who gave him large possessions in Cheshire and Staffordshire. In 1217 he married Bertha Mainwaring and had two sons, Jacob and William, and two daughters, Alice and Emma. Henry was Under-Sheriff of Staffordshire and Salop, from 1217 to 1221, and Sheriff from 1227 to 1232. He was Lord of the Marches from 1223 to his death in 1246.

The trade in arranged marriages was common, especially in cases where land and property was involved. Henry de Audley bought for his son, William, the right to marry Clemence, the eldest daughter of William de Blore. Henry paid sixty marks to Philip Orresby for the right to arrange the marriage. Philip de Orresby acquired the right from Milicent de Stafford. There is no record of where Milicent had obtained this right but it is probably related to the fact that Blore was held from the Barony of Stafford. According to the Testa de Nevill, in 1249, William de Audley held two knight's fees in Blore, and Grindon, of the Barony of Stafford. The marriage settlement provided that William and Clemence should jointly hold the Manor and Park of Blore, plus land in Grindon and Ellaston.

Soon after their marriage the young couple ran into trouble with one of their neighbours, John Mareschall, of the adjoining parish of Stanton. The clear definition of land boundaries, especially in undeveloped moorland, was very difficult, resulting in claims and counter claims. After a number of suits a jury was called to decide who held which part of the disputed land. The jury gave right of tenure of all land in a direct line from Hillsdale, in a south westerly direction to Deepdale, to John Mareschall. William and Clemence retained part of the land to the Northwest. They obviously got along well with their other neighbours, the Okeovers, because in 1248 a long standing dispute was brought to a close. William de Audley and his wife Clemence came to an agreement with Hugh Okeover regarding free chase of deer in Blore Park. Hugh gave up his claim to free chase in the Park in return for one buck and one doe in fawn each year. His annual rent of half a knight's fee, held in Swinscoe, was reduced by half a mark per year, so that he would not have to pay more than twenty shillings. William and Clemence also gave Hugh five marks. Everyone was happy. William and Clemence were able to claim the park for their sole use and Hugh Okeover was able to reduce his payments at a time when he was having financial problems. William and Clemence had two sons, Thomas and John. Thomas died before his father, and Blore was inherited by brother John.

JOHN DE AUDLEY
King Henry III is generally regarded as ineffectual and unable to manage the finances of the realm. Instead of selecting his advisers from among the English Barons, he chose his advisers from among his favourites in France, and Savoyard relatives of his wife. These factors, together with his demand for large sums of money to support a papal war in Sicily, resulted in a rebellion of the Barons, under Simon de Montfort, against the King. It was reported that the whole of the County of Stafford was against the King.

John de Audley of Blore is reported to have been one of those who took up arms against the king. There is no trace of John having been present at the Battle of Lewes, when Simon de Montfort captured and imprisoned the king. Nor is there any trace of his presence in 1265, when the Barons were defeated at Evesham. This was the year that John de Audley was named as Patron of Blore Church.

Among the Staffordshire men who remained loyal to the Crown was Sir Hugh de Okeover. This may have provoked John de Audley into carrying on his own feud with his neighbour. The good relations between the Audleys and the Okeovers became very bad. John de Audley was sued in the King's Court for having carried away goods and chattels from Okeover. John had three children, William, Hugh and Henry.

WILLIAM DE AUDLEY
William de Audley, son and heir of John, had two wives - Alianora and Constance. Each wife had a child; Alianora was the mother of Margery (Margaret) and Constance was the mother of Alan.

In 1266 and 1282, Edward I carried out a series of campaigns against the Welsh which ultimately resulted in the defeat of the Welsh Princes and capture of extensive lands in Gwynedd. In March 1282, William Audley and John Lestrange, together with Roger de Somery, were ordered by Royal Writ to take the field against the Welsh. William died in the same year but it is not clear whether his death was in connection with the military activity.

Constance, his second wife, remarried after William's death, to Roger, son of Jordan Pulesdon, but Roger died and she was a widow again, in 1333.

MARJORY DE AUDLEY AND LAURENCE OKEOVER

In 1300 a cousin of Sir Roger Okeover, called Laurence, married "a woman of quality - Marjory de Audley of Blore", the daughter of William's first wife Alianora. Perhaps the reference to "woman of quality" infers that Laurence was marrying above his station in life. From the number of law suits against them, following their marriage, it does seem that they had more than their fair share of harassment from their relatives and neighbours.

Although reputedly a distant cousin, Laurence was held hostage and maltreated by Sir Roger Okeover, who later pleaded in court that Laurence and his ancestors had always been serfs on the Okeover Estate. Laurence won his case against Sir Roger and was awarded £70 damages. This involved further legal action when the money was not paid, but no record has been found of the actual recovery of the damages. It is likely that Sir Roger avoided this and other obligations when he obtained a pardon from the King, in recognition of his service in Scotland and elsewhere.

In 1313/4, on the death of her half brother Alan, Marjory and her husband took Blore and Grindon. However, her uncle Hugh de Audley sued for the return of the estates to him as brother and heir of William, Alan's father. His claim that he was of full blood, whereas Marjory was only half blood, was upheld and Marjory and her husband lost their claim to Blore and Grindon.

ALAN DE AUDLEY

Alan de Audley, son of William by his second wife, Constance, was Lord of the Manor in 1303. In 1306, he and his wife Joan gave to John Tuk, the Vicar of Blore, the advowsons of Blore Church. Alan died in 1313 and his uncle Hugh retained the Manor of Blore. His wife, Joan was still living in 1337, when she sued for land in Skerington, Notts, due to her as her dower, from another marriage.

HUGH DE AUDLEY

Immediately following his successful suit against Marjory and Laurence Okeover, Hugh received £100 from Joan, former wife of John Le Estrange. In return for this payment, he acknowledged that the Manors of Blore and Grindon and the advowsons of the churches, except for a third of two parts, belonged to Joan.

The situation becomes very complicated because it is not obvious who Joan was. She was evidently related to the Audleys, although the specific relationship has not been established. The other third of two parts, including Blore Hall, was held by John de Hastang Junior, and subsequently by his widow Joan de Hastang. There is a possibility that these two Joans were one and the same person.

King Edward III revived much of the prestige of the monarchy, and reconciled the differences with the English Barons. With the support of the Barons, he was able to mount a long campaign against the French. Hugh de Audley is named as having joined a mission to France in 1330.

MID 14TH CENTURY BLORE
CONFUSING PERIOD BETWEEN AUDLEYS AND BASSETTS

The history of the Manors of Blore and Grindon is extremely obscure and confusing during the early and middle part of the 14th Century. It is unclear how two ladies - Joan, former wife of John Le Estrange and Joan, former wife of John de Hastang - came to hold parts of the Manors of Blore, and Grindon, and how those parts were again joined to be held by the Bassetts. Hugh de Audley successfully sued Marjory, the sister of Alan de Audley, for the return of the Manors of Blore, and Grindon, except for a third of two parts. On the death of her husband, a widow could claim one third of the estate as her right, until her death or remarriage. So, the other third belonged to Alan's widow.

In 1314, Joan, former wife of John le Estrange, paid Hugh the sum of £100 for the Manors of Blore, and Grindon, except for a third of two parts. Alan died before 1311/12 and his wife's name was Joan. Although no documentary evidence exists, Joan could have remarried John Le Estrange who died very soon afterwards. Joan, the widow of John Le Estrange, was suing in 1313/14.

In 1317, Joan Le Estrange was suing Laurence and Marjory for trespassing on her estates. In 1324, she was named with William Wodegryn in a suit by Constance, second wife of William de Audley, in respect of lands in Blore. Constance did not appear in court, and the case was dismissed.

The Subsidy Roll, 1327, lists major tenants for Blore but no mention is made of Joan Le Estrange whereas William Wodegryn is named. There is a "Joan daughter of John" named among the tenants of Grindon, but without other identification. Her name is linked with Ralph de Calton in 1336, in connection with the detention of eleven oxen, belonging to Thomas Meverell of Throwley. Joan alleged that she had acquired the rights of Throwley Manor from the father of Thomas Meverell.

At this point, all trace of Joan Le Estrange disappears and so do references to the Manor of Blore and Grindon, except for a third of two parts. G.D. Wedgwood suggests that it was the daughter of Joan Le Estrange who married Sir Henry Brailsford. Unless both Joans are the same person, this cannot be true. However, it demonstrates the confusion about this period of the history of Blore. It is of course possible that Joan could have married for a third time, to John de Hastang, and become a widow yet again.

At the time of his death in 1323/4, John de Hastang junior held the other third of two parts, including Blore Hall. This was acknowledged to be the right of his widow Joan de Hastang in 1332. William Wodegryn is named as the Bailiff of John, son of John, in 1323/4. Joan de Hastang, the lady of Blore Manor in 1331, accused Thomas de Whenlesbarwe of stealing 3 horses, a silver cup, 2 fold spoons, 2 buckles and 4 gold rings. She accused Thomas of coming to her room in the Manor House of Blore, and holding her firmly, while Robert de Whenlesbarwe ravished her. This is the earliest mention of the Manor House at Blore.

In 1333, a warrant was issued for the outlawry of Robert Whenlesbarwe, and others, on an appeal of robbery by Joan, late the wife of John Le Hastang. The law required that Joan should appear in person at the Appeal Court and because she did not do so the case against Thomas and his brother was dismissed. It is interesting to wonder whether these scoundrels prevented Joan from attending the Appeal Court, especially as Thomas received a Royal Pardon for rape and robbery. Major General Wrottesley, the Antiquarian (SHC XIV) suggests that this type of alleged rape was common. He suggests that it was used either to enforce a marriage, or to establish rights of tenancy in the eyes of the court.

In Final Concords 1335 Hugh Adam and Alice his wife granted to Joan, wife of John Hastang the third of two parts and the advowsons. This was on condition that if she died without issue the estate would descend to her son John, and his issue, or Thomas, brother of John, and his heirs, or to Joan, sister of Thomas.

In spite of the terms specified, in 1335, Joan's daughter Joan de Hastang inherited the Estates instead of her brother John. Daughter Joan de Hastang married Sir Henry Brailsford. In 1352/3, her brother John was suing Joan and Henry for the Manors of Blore and Grindon but John was unsuccessful in his suit. Joan and Henry recovered from Hugh, son of Laurence Okeover, fifteen acres of land in Grindon and in the following year eight acres in Slyndon. In 1361 Thomas, son of Hugh Adam, claimed from Joan and her husband, Sir Henry Brailsford, the third of the manor, but was unsuccessful in his suit. In 1375, Joan Brailsford, the daughter of Joan and Henry, married Sir John Bassett and took to him her inheritance of a third of two parts of Blore and Grindon. By this tortuous route of complex inheritance claim and counter-claim, and shadowy figures, the Bassetts acquired Blore.

THE BASSETTS

The name Bassett has appeared in a number of forms: Baseht, Baseth, Baset, Basset and Bassett. The most common earlier spelling was Basset but since the 16th century the form in most frequent use in Staffordshire has been Bassett. It is this form Bassett which is used in the account that follows.

P.H. Reaney, in his Dictionary of Surnames, suggests that the name Bassett is derived from the French "bas" meaning "low or of mean stature". This assumption is also based the chronicles of Orderic Vitalis, in which Orderic states that Richard Bassett was "raised from the very dust," by Henry I.

The late Dr. H.T. Betteridge, Senior Lecturer in North European Languages at Glasgow University, agreed that the name probably derives from a similar sounding name used by the Vikings. The few written examples of the viking name would be in Runic script and some letters have no equivalent in latin languages. The name in Old Norse probably sounded something like "Bathet" - the people of France and Mediterranean countries have difficulty in pronouncing "th" and thus the corruption of the name to Basset. The Norsemen (Normans), from whom the Bassetts probably descended, settled in Northern France during the 9th and 10th centuries.

The Bassetts of Blore claimed to descend from those who came over with the Conqueror from Normandy. On William (V) Bassett's tomb, in St Bartholomew's church, is the inscription:

"HERE LIES A COURTIER SOULDIER, HANDSOME, GOOD WITTY, WISE, VALIANT AND OF PURE BLOOD FROM WILLIAM'S CONQUEST AND HIS POTENT SWORD

The inscription uses poetic licence in lauding the praises of William (V) Bassett (died 1601). His descent may have been from a Bassett at the Conquest, but not Thurstan, commonly and erroneously named as of Drayton Bassett in Staffordshire. An error in Domesday has caused some historians and antiquarians concerned with Staffordshire to presume a Bassett descent which is incorrect. Erroneously, within Domesday for Staffordshire, there is an entry which reads:

THURSTAN HOLDS 5 HIDES IN DRAYTON Land for 5 ploughs in lordship 3 ploughs 2 slaves 12 villagers and 4 smallholders with 3 ploughs A Mill at 4s. The value was 100s. Now £8.

This entry was clearly demonstrated by Charlotte S. Burne, in 1880, to be in respect of Drayton in Oxfordshire and not Drayton (Bassett) in Staffordshire. The Bassetts subsequently held Drayton (Bassett) in Staffordshire, and it has been wrongly assumed that this Thurstan of Drayton, was one of their forebears. Thurstan, son of Rollo, standard bearer, accompanied William the Conqueror but no link can be established with the Bassetts of Staffordshire.

The Bassetts of Staffordshire descended from Normans who came to England after the conquerors were well established. They could have been related to the same family of Bassetts who are assumed to have arrived in the company of Hugh de Grandmesnil, in William the Conqueror's army. There is no evidence to support this conjecture, except that they all came from Normandy.

The First Bassett of any repute in the County of Stafford from whom an acceptable line of descent can be traced is Richard Bassett, a chief justice of England. He was the son of Ralph Bassett, who was also a justice, under Henry I. Richard Bassett built a castle of great strength and magnificence, in Montreuil-au-Houlme, in the Canton of Briouze, 35 km North West of Domfront. When Geoffrey, Count of Anjou, invaded Normandy, in 1136, he captured Carrouges and Ecouche but was repulsed at Montreuil-au-Houlme. Richard Bassett was one of the "new" men that Henry I brought over to England and honoured with positions of great importance. Richard married Maud Ridel, daughter of Geoffrey Ridel, whose wife, Geva, obtained Drayton (Bassett) from her father, the Earl of Chester. This grant, made to her in frank marriage, was confirmed in a charter dated c1120, to be found among the Randal Holme's MSS in the British Library (Harleian MS 2060). Hugh Lupus, Earl of Chester received the manor of Drayton (Bassett) from the king in the 1100s.

From Richard Basset can be traced seven successive Ralph Bassetts of Drayton Bassett. From the Bassetts of Drayton descended the Bassetts of Cheadle and of Blore and Hints. It is the Bassetts of Blore that the following chapters consider

SIR JOHN BASSETT KNT, MP, SHERIFF, JP - Cheadle, Blore and Grindon. *Born 1345 Died 1410/11*
Or three piles in point gules on a canton argent a griffin segreant of the second

The first member of the Bassett family to hold Blore Manor was Sir John Bassett of Cheadle. He was born, in 1345, son of John Bassett of Cheadle, descendant of the Bassetts of Sapcote. His political career began in 1367 before he was 22 years old. John received his knighthood and began to establish himself within the county of Staffordshire. He adopted a variation on the Bassett of Cheadle coat of arms. Attached to a charter, dated 1379, is a seal in which the canton is charged with a griffin, instead of ermine. It is this coat of arms that the Bassetts of Blore proudly displayed for the next two and a half centuries.

In 1374/5, Sir John was appointed Sheriff of Staffordshire; one of the most important and powerful figures in the county. As Sheriff, he was responsible for the militia, administration of the King's Court and justice, as well as looking after the royal revenue.

Sir John is reputed to have had two wives. His first wife is generally not named but Challinor in his pedigree, of the Bassetts, dated 1613, states that her name was Catherine. Most authorities suggest that his first un-named wife was the mother of two sons: Edmund and Rafe. If Sir John married Joan Brailsford around 1375, this means that the two sons would have been born before that date. Rafe married in 1404, so he must have been over thirty, much older than usual for arranged marriages. It is equally curious that his elder brother, Edmund, is reputed to have married after Rafe. It was the normal custom that the older brother and heir to the estates was married first. It has not been possible to solve these discrepancies.

Following Sir John's marriage, his wife's father tried to retain part of the inheritance which was due to her. Sir John sued Sir Henry for a pyx, containing certain documents. He retrieved the documentary evidence and sued his father-in-law for the land belonging to his wife, Joan.

In 1380, Sir Henry Brailsford conveyed the manor of Brailsford to three trustees: Thomas de Pykkesthorp, parson of Brailsford, John de Fyndern and Thomas de Wombewell. The grant provided that Sir Henry should continue to hold the manor for life. After his death, the manor was to descend to Sir John Bassett, and his wife Joan.

As part of his wife Joan's inheritance, Sir John held the advowsons of Brailsford Rectory. He was named as Patron of Brailsford in the year 1393. As Lord of Brailsford he was also patron of Blore Church in 1395, when he presented William Yorke as rector. In 1406, the new rector of Brailsford Church made his oath of office before him.

Joan brought to him the manor of Blore and lands in Grindon, Slindon and Bescot, handed down to Joan, through Brailsford, from the family of De Hastang. Proof of his wife's descent from de Hastang are contained in deeds relating to Grindon dated 1314, 1332 and 1351, Slindon dated 1343 and 1353 and Bescot in 1314.

Sir John, by his wife Joan, had a son called Thomas, who inherited the Brailsford portion belonging to his mother. Thomas's daughter, also named Joan, subsequently married Ralph Shirley, and the Brailsford estate passed to the Shirley family.

Edward III's rash spending in the wars against France had drained the national coffers. The corruption of the Royal Council brought the government to near bankruptcy. Sir John was a member of the so-called "Good Parliament", inspired by the Black Prince, and under the leadership of Sir Peter de la Mere. It was this parliament which demanded the impeachment of the Chamberlain, Lord Latimer, and a London financier, Richard Lyons. Parliament also appointed a new council and demanded that Richard II should be named as heir to the throne.

In 1381/2, during the reign of Richard III, Sir John was elected to the Parliament which enacted the poll tax. This sparked off the Peasants Revolt among farm workers in south east England. From 1382 to 1392, he was one of only four Justices of the Peace for Staffordshire. The justices were very powerful and were required to hear cases, as well as bring them. They were required to keep the peace; arrest and punish those who were illegally armed; enquire into all felonies and trespasses, punish beggars and vagrants; be responsible for the treatment of the poor, deal with brewers, hawkers, and control the licensing of badgers, kidgers and grovers.

The Hundred Years' War (1337-1453) continued intermittently between England and France. In 1380 a treaty was signed between England and Brittany, in which they jointly agreed to take arms against the French. The names of John Bassett, Thomas Bassett and neighbour Philip Okeover appear in the French Roll, in the retinue of William de Wyndesore. The English forces sailed to Calais. After marching to Brittany, it was discovered that the Duke of Britanny had made a treaty with France, and refuted his agreement with the English. In January 1381, without the support of the Bretons, the English returned to England.

In 1386, Sir John was appointed as one of the Commission of Array to select 200 archers from Staffordshire. The Commission was required to send the archers to London, to defend against a threatened invasion from France. The wages of 6d per day for each archer were to be paid by those who stayed behind. King Charles of France did not fulfil this threat to invade, and the men returned to their homes. Sir John settled the Blore and Cheadle estates on his sons Edmund and Rafe in a charter dated 1404, witnessed by Robert Fraunceys, Thomas Beek and John Bagot. Sir John Bassett died in 1411 at the age of 65, and was succeeded by his son Edmund as Lord of Blore Manor.

EDMUND BASSETT *Born ? Died 1429/30*

Edmund, the elder son of Sir John Bassett's first wife, is stated by some authorities to have been born before 1375, but he did not marry his wife Matilda until 1405/6. At thirty years old, he was unusually old for a first marriage. It was vital that the eldest son, as heir to the Bassett Estates, was married as soon as possible. Edmund's brother Rafe is reputed to have been married at an earlier date than Edmund. This is equally unusual, so doubt must be cast upon the generally accepted information relating to the birth and marriage of Edmund.

In 1405 his father, Sir John Bassett, settled most of his estates on his two sons Edmund and Rafe; Edmund got Blore and Rafe inherited Cheadle. A deed signed by Edmund in 1408 bears the same seal as his father, with a boar's head couped and armed gules gorged with a chain of silver. When Sir John Bassett died in 1410/11, Edmund continued to hold Blore.

He and his brother Rafe accepted liveries from Lord Ferrers. They were involved in Ferrers' resistance against the Erdeswickes of Sandon. Hugh Erdeswicke was just like a fictional robber baron. His bands of armed men terrorised the counties of Staffordshire, Shropshire, Cheshire and Derbyshire - robbing, pillaging and killing. Sir Edmund Ferrers was able to resist and avoid the one thousand strong army. In retaliation for the atrocities carried out by the Erdeswickes, Ferrers ambushed and killed Sampson, the brother of Hugh Erdeswicke. This attack was particularly horrible, because after Sampson was badly wounded, his toes were cut off and stuffed into his mouth - he was left to die. Hugh Erdeswicke survived and ultimately became a favourite of Henry V.

It was in the interests of the Crown to restrict the powers of the nobility and in particular, to limit their private armies. On the basis that it was illegal for anyone below the rank of **banneret** to retain his own followers, Sir Edmund Ferrers was charged in the Court of King's Bench. He was accused of illegally presenting liveries to his followers. However, it was readily proved that the King himself had confirmed Ferrers as Baron Chartley by Letters Patent. Letters Patent had the same effect as a Royal Charter. They were issued on any matter that the King wished to make public, and were witnessed by the King alone.

The King's Court was thwarted and so had to tackle the problem in a different way. It was illegal for anyone below the rank of esquire to be retained so those who had received the liveries were charged with the offence. Edmund and his brother Rafe, among others, were each fined the sum of forty shillings.

The Hundred Years' War dragged on against the French. In 1419/20 Edmund was summoned to serve the King in defence of the realm against the French. It is doubtful whether he performed this military service, because Henry V married Catherine de Valois, averting war, and bringing temporary peace between the two nations.

In 1425 Edmund Bassett was patron of Blore Church, when he presented John Brokesby as rector following the resignation of William Hancock. After his brother's death, Edmund, by an indenture dated 1426/7, transferred all his lands in Dilhorne, Fosbrook, Fulford and Kingsley to his brother's son, Ralph Bassett. He outlived both his father and his brother. Having no children when he died in 1429/30, the Bassett estates reverted to his brother's son, Ralph Bassett

RAFE BASSETT *Born ? Died: February 1420/1*

Rafe Bassett of Nuplace, Cheadle and Blore, the second son of Sir John Bassett, married Maude, daughter of Sir Thomas Beke in 1404, and had three sons, Ralph, Richard and William. According to Glovers Visitation, his wife (Matilda) Maude died in 1407, but if this is the case he had two wives both named Maude (Matilde). Wm Salt MSS 459 states that his wife Matilde died in 1422/3, when his son Ralph was 16 years old. He is also reputed to have had a daughter who married Sir John Tiringham of Tiringham, Bucks, although no trace has been found in the Tiringham Pedigree.

The Final Concords of 1404 confirm the transfer of lands in Dilhorne, Kingsley, Cheadle, Fulford,

Fowall and Fosbrook, to Rafe on his marriage to the daughter of Sir Thomas Beke. After the death of his father in 1410/11, Rafe was involved in a legal suit to establish his rights to the Manor of Cheadle. It was found that Cheadle was split into separate manors: Cheadle and Parkhall, and although Cheadle was his by right, the manor of Parkhall had descended to Simon Bassett of Sapcote, Leicestershire. The suit also established the descent of Rafe from the Bassets of Sapcote:

In 1412, one year before King Henry IV died, Rafe was accused of 'enormous transgressions' against the King, and fined twenty pounds. His brother Edmund had to vouch for his future good behaviour. With his brother Edmund, who then held Blore, Ralph of Cheadle was charged with accepting liveries from Edmund Ferrers of Chartley and fined 40 shillings. Rafe died on the Feast of Purification in the Eighth Year of the reign of King Henry V, 1420/1 and when his brother Edmund subsequently died without issue in 1429/30, Blore reverted to Ralph, the son of Rafe.

RALPH BASSETT, Sheriff *Born 1406/7   Died 1455*

Ralph Bassett, the son of Rafe, was born in 1406/7. He married Margaret, the daughter of Reginald and Thomasia Dethik, and widow of Richard Montgomery. They had a son, William, and two daughters, Thomasine and Cicely.

A deed recorded in the archives of the College of Arms confirms that the son, William, was William (I). He was born around 1430, and married Joan, one of the daughters of Richard Byron. Thomas Okeover and Ralph Bassett made a covenant in 1439 for the marriage of Philip Okeover and Ralph's daughter, Thomasine. They settled upon their children lands in Blore, Coldwall, and Woodhouses. In accordance with an indenture of marriage, dated 1455/6, the other daughter, Cicely, married Hugh, son of Henry Erdeswicke.

Ralph had a brother William (0), who married Alice Moton, and is often wrongly referred to as the son of this Ralph.

Thomasia Dethik, née Meynell, Ralph's mother-in-law, married as her second husband Hugh Erdeswicke, the robber baron. Thomasia had safeguarded her Meynell inheritance. In 1439, when she was too old to produce further children, she settled the manor of Meynell Langley, together with lands in Newall and Snelston, upon Ralph and her daughter Margaret. Meynell Langley and Snelston remained with the Bassetts until sold by the Duke of Newcastle in the seventeenth century.

Ralph was elected Sheriff of Staffordshire in 1438 and came face-to-face with the problems caused by the rivalries between the Houses of York and Lancaster. This was only a foretaste of what was to come. Over the next twenty years, his personal problems were equal to anything he ever met as sheriff.

In 1442, Ralph sued Nicholas Fitzherbert of Norbury for trespass. He was obviously dissatisfied with the response to his action, because he took the law into his own hands to remedy the matter. As a result he was required to make an undertaking not to harm Fitzherbert and his men, on the pain of being made to pay £100 in the King's Court. In 1443, Ralph Bassett charged Fitzherbert and thirteen others with cutting down one hundred oaks at Snelston and carrying off two hundred loads of underwood. He took the law into his own hands again and as a result he was called on to make a further undertaking, to the value of £500.

Ralph held Repingdon (Repton) in Derbyshire, which had been given to him as a gift by Giles Swynerton. He was taken to court by Richard Lane and John Bromley who claimed the land themselves. Ralph was successful in defending the case, and the lands in Repingdon remained with the Bassetts.

In order to recover rent from bad payers, Ralph was involved in a number of legal actions. New Place, Cheadle, was part of the Bassett estate. Because the rent was unpaid, Ralph sued Henry Atherley for putting cattle on his corn and grass at New Place. He similarly accused John Beresford, William Pursglove and John Bagenhall of depasturing cattle on his land in Grindon and Musden - the Bassetts were leaseholders of land in Musden Grange. He accused John North of Rocester and John Parker of Denstone of breaking into a close in Rocester. By these rather devious tactics he ensured that he established his rights to the lands and got the rent overdue plus his costs.

Another contentious issue was the right to present the parson to the church of his manors. As the Patron of the Church at Kingsley, he successfully sued Thomas Stafford of Alveton (Alton), for a charter and muniments concerning the patronage which Stafford had unjustly detained. In another case, he lost the legal battle made against him by the Master of the House of the College of St Michael of Cambridge. This case was over the presentation of William Beke, probably one of Ralph's mother's relatives, to the church of Cheadle.

In 1444 Thomas Okeover legally surrendered all his land to Ralph Bassett and John Brown, on condition that they paid their debts to Thomas and £40 towards the marriage portion of Isabel, daughter of Thomas. This was a roundabout way of making sure that an estate was handed down without hindrance from the courts. When Ralph died before his neighbour, the Okeover papers show that Thomas Okeover disclaimed this enfeoffment of use.

He was involved in a long-standing dispute with his neighbour Sir Sampson Meverell, over the tithes of Throwley. The tithes belonged to the church of Ilam, and the Vicar of Ilam had granted them to Ralph. Sir Sampson Meverell claimed that, as Lord of Throwley, the tithes should have been granted to him. In 1441, Sir Sampson and others were sued by Ralph for going to Throwley, armed with swords, bows and arrows, and treading down and consuming sixty cartloads of hay. The Vicar of Ilam, John Southworth, was waylaid by forty armed persons and threatened with death - unless he gave up the society and service of Ralph Bassett. The Vicar laid a curse upon Sir Sampson and because of this was excommunicated. When a special commission was set up by the Church to investigate the matter, Sir Sampson was called but did not appear and as a result was himself excommunicated. In 1447/8, Sir Sampson and his wife, William Rufford, John Bersford, John the Abbot of Dieulacres, Nicholas Montgomery, Thomas Meverell, John Holys, John Stathome, William Londesdale and others were sued for breaking into houses at Blore and taking twelve oxen and twelve cows. They were accused of insulting and beating Ralph's servants, John Hude, John Baxonden, and John Cole. Ralph claimed that the servants were beaten so badly that they were incapable of work for six months. He claimed £40 in damages. Although this type of allegation was often exaggerated to create maximum effect, in and out of court, there is no doubt that Sir Sampson often used force to achieve his own ends. Sir Sampson was sent to jail but obtained a pardon from Henry VI and was discharged. He then countersued Ralph for conspiracy, on the basis of the accusations of Vicar John Southworth.

Sampson appealed to the Archbishop of Canterbury complaining of the "wronges and extorsions". He said that he could get no remedy at law, because of Bassett's "grete myght and support". In making these complaints Sampson was probably trying to justify his absence from the special commission, but there was undoubtedly a large element of truth in his allegations. Ralph's rough handling of the Fitzherberts and readiness to join his neighbour Philip Okeover in active defence of his property, confirms his might. As a retainer of Stafford, Duke of Buckingham, and a close friend of John Curson JP and his allies, the Bagots and Bradbournes, Ralph was sure of great support. The only real success that Sampson Meverell had against Ralph was in his activities outside the law, rather than in the courts.

Ralph Bassett, and his friend and neighbour Philip Okeover, had become involved in a feud with the Cockaynes of Ashbourne and Vernons of Haddon. This feud was based upon the politics and rivalries of the Houses of York and Lancaster. It was further fuelled by local differences over the Bassett and Okeover estates. The feud between the Cockaynes and the Bassetts probably dated back to a rival claim to the Grey of Codnor moiety of the Cheadle estate.

In 1449, Ralph made a petition to Parliament complaining that on the last Thursday in October the Cockaynes and the Vernons, with a large mob of people, laid siege to Blore Manor. He alleged that their intent was to kill him, his brother Richard, tenants and servants, and to burn his house. The mob burned cartloads of hay and peas and stole two bows and a thousand arrows. John Curson, Richard Bagot and Henry Bradbourne, with their own band of armed men, came to their rescue and drove away the mob. John Curson was related to Philip Okeover by marriage, and was one of the more influential local justices of the peace. One week later, while neighbour Philip Okeover was in London, attending Parliament, the same mob attacked Okeover. They broke down the fences of the park and slaughtered 115 of the 120 herd of deer. They attacked Okeover Hall and broke down the doors. They used the doors, tables and trestles to build fires to roast the slaughtered deer. The value of the damages was assessed at 400 marks, and the Sheriff of Staffordshire was ordered to arrest the malefactors.

In order to defend themselves and their property, Philip Okeover and Ralph's brother Richard gathered together a band of fifty armed men. At Christmas 1450, one of this band, David Trigg, wounded Thomas Mane with an arrow in his left thigh, from which injury he died. Charges were laid against David Trigg but he received a King's Pardon, and the charges against the others were dropped.

In 1451, after protracted legal action, John Cockayne was fined 100 shillings for trespasses committed against Ralph; William Cockayne and eighteen others were fined from 30 to 40 shillings each. Ralph was granted costs of £80 and £20 against the Cockaynes, but having proved his point decided not to prosecute the other defendants.

During the period 1440 to 1460, the Yorkist Earl of Warwick and the Lancastrian Duke of Buckingham (a Stafford by birth) were each trying to extend their power in Staffordshire. Each magnate tried to attract the more influential gentry into their own camp. Ralph became a Buckingham retainer thus giving allegiance to the Lancastrians. In 1451 Ralph was one of a group of Staffordshire gentry who accompanied Buckingham to Kenilworth to attend on Henry VI. Unfortunately, the allegiance to Buckingham meant that Ralph found himself in the same grouping as Cockayne and Vernon. All attempts by Buckingham to mediate between the rivals were unsuccessful. This ongoing clash was a major factor in the change of allegiance to the Yorkists, by Ralph's son William (I) Bassett.

In 1451, Ralph was still having problems with Sir Sampson Meverell and his wife, and John Beresford. He accused them of breaking into his close at Blore and carrying off twelve oxen and twelve cows and beating his servants.

The Bassetts were always keen huntsmen and not above following the hunt over other people's land. In 1454 John, Earl of Shrewsbury, sued Ralph Bassett, William Bassett and Richard Bassett and others for taking game in his park at Alton.

Ralph died around 1455 and his wife eleven years later, in 1466. Ralph did not see the end of the feuding before his death. His brother, Richard of Tutbury, who stood by him throughout all the troubles, was murdered. This was probably by Nicholas Montgomery of Sudbury, one of the ringleaders of the opposing bands, in 1457. It is perhaps surprising that Margaret, who was the widow of Richard Montgomery, before her marriage to Ralph Bassett, then married Sir Nicholas Montgomery, after Ralph's death.

William (II) Bassett was commissioned to arrest John Vernon in 1461 and John Cockayne in 1463. Two generations later (Sir) William (IV) Bassett married Anne Cockayne which brought together two of the feuding families. According to the Rev William Beresford, in his book on the history of the manor of Beresford, there were a number of marriages between the members of the Bassett family and the Beresfords. John de Beresford (living 1411, 1431 and 1438) married Elizabeth, daughter of William Bassett of Blore. John's great-grandson, another John Beresford, who was living 1470, 1510 and 1513, and who died in January 1523, married Margaret, daughter of William Bassett of Blore in 1470. These marriages are recorded in the family tree of the Berisford family published in "The Ribbon People: Berisfords - The Story of a Family Business". first published 1958.

The son of Ralph Bassett was called William and, confusingly, the five Lords of Blore Manor were called William Bassett. The author has attributed a number (0) to his brother (he is included because there is so much disagreement about his position in the Bassett family) and the numbers (I) through (V) to each successive William Bassett.

WILLIAM (0) BASSETT The non-existent line *Born ? Died 1456?*
This chapter really concerns the authors' years of frustration trying to solve a mystery. In comparison with the rest of the Bassetts of Blore, there is an almost complete lack of information concerning William (0) Bassett. It is almost as though he did not exist.

According to the pedigree given in Glover's Visitation of Staffordshire in 1583, there were six William Bassetts, in succession, but no name is given for the wife of the first. The date 34 Henry VI (1455/56) is given, which is assumed to be the date of death. This date appears to have been copied in a number of subsequent pedigrees: Sleigh's "History of Leek", Derbyshire Collection No. 3522 and "Beauties of England and Wales".

In two pedigrees, only five William Bassetts are named: Blore MSS Cambridge University Library,

Topographer Magazine 1790 - the missing Bassett is William (0] Bassett. There was a pedigree by William Challinor, in 1613 (1615?), which has disappeared from the Derby Library Collections. That pedigree showed William Bassett of Blore married Alice, daughter of Sir Robert Moton, of Peckleton, in Leicestershire. Maxwell Craven offers support of this, with references from Jeayes "Derbyshire Charters": references: 1512 and 2137. These two references could equally refer to William (0) or William (I) Bassett. The marriage to Alice Moton (Moston) is also given in the Pedigrees in the Hadfield Collection, DAJ 1887 "Manors of Kirk Langley", Morris pedigrees in Shrewsbury Library and Stebbing Shaw's "History of Staffordshire".

On the death of Ralph Bassett, last baron of Sapcote, in 1379, according to the Inquisito Capta, the Cheadle estate passed to his two daughters, Elizabeth, wife of Richard, Lord Grey of Codnor, and Alice, age 30 years, wife of Sir Robert Moton of Peckleton. According to Collections for a History of Staffordshire, 1926, pages 154 to 164, there was a partition of Cheadle Park in 1451, between Sir Robert Moton and Elizabeth his wife, and Ralph Bassett. This is as noted by Harwood's Erdeswick p.505. According to SHC, 1938, page 7/8, this Sir Robert Moton died 34 Henry VI (1455/6). As stated above, there are a number of references which give the marriage of William (0) Bassett to Alice Moton.

In the College of Arms, Ref Vincent 133, page 81, there is a deed which reads:

> "Ego Willi[el]mus Bassett de Blore armiger filius et haeres Radulphi Bassett et Margaretae uxoris suae dedi Thomae Entwyssell esq omnes terras et tene[men]ta mea in Langeley Dat apud Langeley 18 E 4 Sigillum Willi de Bassett"

This translates as:

> "I William Bassett of Blore armiger son and heir of Ralph Bassett and Margaret his wife have given unto Thomas Entwyssell esq all my lands and tenements in Langley
> Dated at Langley 18 E 4 [1478] Seal William Bassett

This clearly states that William Bassett is the son of Ralph and Margaret and the date 1478 confirms that this refers to William (I). The Inquisition Post Mortem of William (I) Bassett, dated 13 H VII (1497), states:

> "Thomas Entwysell, esquire, Ralph Cantrell clerk, vicar of Chesterfield, late rector of Bloure and Charles Dethyk, clerk, were seised of the undermentions manor in fee, and being so seised gave it by charter to the said William Bassett and Joan, then his wife, and the heirs male of his body begotten, with remainder in default in right heirs".

Thus, Thomas Entwyssell is given as enfeoffed of the Bassett estates, which confirms the original deed.

The relationship of William (I) Bassett, as son of Ralph Bassett, is referred to, obliquely, in a case held at the Kings Bench, ref KB29/88 rot. 33. This relates to the murder of Ric Bassett, the UNCLE of William (I), by Nicholas Montgomery, of Sudbury, in the mid 1450s. As Richard Bassett was the brother of Ralph Bassett, he was, therefore, the uncle of William (I) Bassett. This gives possible confirmation of the relationship of William (I) to Ralph.

Ralph was born around 1406/7, and William (I) was born in 1430, which means there are twenty four years between these two births. If William (0) had been born in between the two of them, it would mean that Ralph and William (0) would both have been married, *and produced children,* by the time they were each around twelve years old. As Ralph was born c1406, he would need to have married around 1417/8, in time for William (0) to be born. Then, in turn, marry and produce Wm (I) by 1430. The Bassett family, like other gentry of the period, always tried to arrange an early marriage, to avoid the complications of wardship of heirs. The possibility of very early marriage, in both instances, has been propounded by other researchers. However, we think that to have produced children at such a young age, in two succeeding child heirs, is highly improbable.

Even though Ralph Bassett is the father, and William (I) Bassett is the son, there is still no positive evidence, which establishes how William (0) fits into the picture. The only way the author has been able to account for William (0) is in the "uncle" references mentioned above - an unsubstantiated brother of Ralph. However, the findings illustrated above mean that there is an error in the information, provided by the Visitation of 1583. It, also means that all pedigrees showing the descent through William (0) and his wife Alice Moton, must be revised.

WILLIAM (I) BASSETT MP, Sheriff, Commissioner, JP. *Born c1430. Died 15 November 1497*
William (I) Bassett was born around 1430. He married Joan, one of the daughters of Richard Byron, son of Sir John Byron. In 1452 he made a recognizance to Richard Byron's brothers, Nicholas and Ralph, that he would not make any claim against any Byron land, other than that belonging to Richard Byron.

At the bottom of the east window, of the north aisle in St Bartholomew's Church, Blore, used to be stained glass. This depicted William (I) in his surcoat of arms, and his wife, Joan, wearing a mantle with the arms of Byron. They both kneel before St William, with a scroll, in Latin, translated as "O holy William pray for us". Pieces from this original window still exist in a jigsaw of glass in the chancel.

As a boy William saw his family feuding over local differences in support of their Yorkist loyalties against the Vernons and Cockaynes. The family feuds simmered and boiled. At Cubley, in 1457, William became involved in a quarrel over the murder of his uncle, Richard. As a result of the quarrel, he killed a man, and was indicted for murder. It must be assumed that he was found not guilty, because a year later he was counter-suing Nicholas Montgomery, Thomas Meverell, Thomas Sapurton, Nicholas Agarde and one hundred others for insulting and wounding him in the same incident at Cubley.

Humphrey, Duke of Buckingham, and John, Duke of Shrewsbury, intervened in the Bassett/Meverell dispute and bound over both of the men to shelve their differences and drop all lawsuits, under penalties of £200. Bassett and Meverell were not overawed by the power of the magnates. Although there may have been a temporary truce, the feud continued on and off until the end of the century.

Like all his forbears, William enjoyed his hunting and in 1454 was named, with Ralph and Richard Bassett, for poaching on the Earl of Shrewsbury's estate at Alton. He was probably out hunting in 1457 when he shot a man with an arrow, from which the man died. It appears to have been an accident, because although he was brought to court in 1459, he received a full pardon.

In the 1460s, the process of law was gradually replacing the anarchy of the Wars of the Rose, and the Yorkists were in the ascendancy. As an important member of Staffordshire/Derbyshire gentry, he was often called upon for his influence and ability. In 1461 he was appointed as one of the commissioners for the arrest of John Vernon and again in 1463, to arrest John Cockayne and bring him before the king. This was one of the final acts, leading to the cessation of hostilities between William, his ally Philip Okeover, and the Cockaynes. On 6th November 1465 William was offered, and accepted, an indentured contract with William, Lord Hastings, a powerful magnate and favourite of the King. William (I) was one of the first Staffordshire men to be approached by Hastings, who was seeking to extend his sphere of interest in the Midlands. William was an obvious candidate for indenture. The King required that the names of up to four candidates were submitted each year for the post of Sherrif. King Edward IV had pricked (made his small mark or tick against the selected candidate) William (I) Bassett as Sheriff of Staffordshire earlier in 1465, and this must have been known to Hastings.

As Sheriff, among his responsibilities he was required to bring accused men to trial before the justices of the peace. He appointed sub-sheriffs to carry out this task, under a bond. In 1466, he sued John Wright of Warslow, for £20, for not bringing a labourer, Richard Mole, before the justices.

William was Lord of Blore Manor and had extensive holdings in Staffordshire: Grindon, Fosbrooke, Cheadle, Newplace, Bescot, Kingsley, Dilhorne. He also held lands in Derbyshire: the Manor of Meynell Langley, and land in Mayfield, Tissington, Fenny Bentley, Leigh, Hollington, Hognaston, Cold Eaton, and Thorpe.

From 1465 to 1467, William was suing various people for illegally breaking and entering his property in Blore and Dilhorne and Cheadle. These were probably no more than local cattle rustling and minor affairs, in comparison with the open warfare and mob violence of a few years previously. William (I) still continued to have problems with some of his neighbours over disputed property. In 1474, the close at Musden was broken into by John, Abbot of Croxden Abbey and one of his monks, Stephen York of Wighton. They were accused of stealing twenty cartloads of hay, and three hundred sheaves of oats, valued at 20 marks. This was probably as a result of a dispute over a lease of Musden Grange.

He was the patron of Blore Church and in 1465 presented Ralph Canterell as rector of the church, following the resignation of the previous rector, William Sont. His appointment as sheriff, on three occasions, in 1465/6, 1472/3 and 1480/1, was undoubtedly in part as a result of his Yorkist allegiance. In

1472/3, after the return of Edward IV, it may have been influenced by William's relationship with Lord Hastings. Even after the execution of Hastings, William was still re-elected as sheriff, which demonstrates the high esteem in which he was held by successive rulers and their advisers. The office of sheriff was a very prestigious one but it was also onerous and time-consuming. His duties meant that he was travelling, and away much of the time. William had to appoint a number of men to collect the rents and monies due to the Crown. Following his term of office, in 1472/3, William (I) was suing a number of his agents to account for the money they had received during his absence on other sheriff's duties.

It was the custom to appoint local gentry as commissioners, to carry out the wishes of the Crown. Membership of such commissions was normally politically biased. Dependent upon whether the ruling power was Yorkist or Lancastrian, so the appointment favoured the supporters of the particular party. In 1470 he was one of the Commissioners of Array, whose task was to raise troops in Staffordshire. He did this on behalf of the Yorkists against the rebellion of Warwick the Kingmaker and the Duke of Clarence. In 1473, after the restoration of Edward IV, William (I) was a member of the commission to investigate the ancient estates of the Crown in Staffordshire. When Edward IV died, in 1483, and Richard III assumed the throne, he was elected Member of Parliament. Subsequently, he was one of the Commissioners appointed to assess the Subsidy on Aliens, which had been levied by that Parliament. Again in 1485, after Richard III had been killed at the Battle of Bosworth Field, Henry VII issued a Commission of Peace. William was among those appointed as a Commissioner for Staffordshire.

Membership of a commission brought greater contact between individuals and their families. This offered the opportunity to expand their interests and associations farther afield. Three fellow commissioners on some of the commissions, were Sir John Aston of Heywood, Hugh Egerton of Wrine Hill and Sir Nicholas Montgomery. William's son John married Elizabeth Aston, son Ralph married Elenor Egerton and son Nicholas married Elinor Montgomery. The marriage between a Bassett and a Montgomery helped to heal the rift between the two families, caused by the killings in the 1450s. His daughter Mary married William Beaumont of Cole Orton. There may also have been a daughter, Catherine, who married Edward Pilkington, whose name appears in the Powtrell pedigree.

Justices of the Peace were mainly appointed by the Crown from among the local ruling class. These were the knights and gentry, whose local knowledge best suited them to administer law in their own county. During the first half of the fifteenth century, the power of the justices was often misused, to protect and further their own interests. To reduce the collusion and corruption, and to dissipate the powers of certain individuals, the Crown made a significant increase in the number of justices. This increase contributed to the reduction in the number of local disputes and disorders. The appointment of justices was not always a purely political choice, although in the case of William (I) Bassett it was obviously a contributory factor. From 1471, until his death, William (I) was a Justice of the Peace. His term was briefly interrupted in 1483, at the time of the Buckingham rising, when the Lancastrians took away his office.

In 1488, he was a member of the Commission of Array, to raise and muster archers for Henry VII's campaign, in Brittany. He was, probably, a member of parliament again in 1489/90. He died, in 1497. A brass inlay, on a marble-like slab of Purbeck stone, was laid in the North Aisle of Blore Church, to his memory, and to the memory of his wife, Joan. This memorial bears the Latin inscription:

ORATE PRO ANIMABUS WILLIEMI BASSETT ARMIGER DOMINI DE BLORE ET LANGLEY ET JOANNE UXORIS EJUS UNIUS FILIARUM ET HEREDUM RICARDI BURYN ARMIGER FILLI ET HEREDIS JOHANNIS BURYN MILITIS QUI QUIDEN WILLIEMUS OBIIT XII DIE MENSIS NOV ANNO DNI MILLIMO CDXCVII ET EADEM JOANNO OBIIT DIE MENSIS ANNO DOMINI QUORUM PROBITRIETOR DEUS AMEN

which translated means:

PRAY FOR THE SOUL OF WILLIAM BASSETT ESQUIRE LORD OF BLORE AND LANGLEY AND JOAN HIS WIFE ONE OF THE DAUGHTERS AND HEIRS OF RICHARD BYRON ESQUIRE SON AND HEIR JOHN BYRON KNIGHT WHICH SAID WILLIAM DIED NOVEMBER 1497 AND JOAN DIED THE DAY OF MONTH ANNO DOMINI UPON WHOSE SOULS GOD HAVE MERCY AMEN

Joan his wife was still living in 1499 and the absence of a date may indicate that she was not buried at Blore. The head of the figure on the brass was removed, some time before 1848. William (I) Bassett had four sons Ralph, John, William and Nicholas and a daughter, Mary. His son Ralph was still living in 1474/5, but died before 1488 when his brother John was named as son and heir. John died sometime after 1490, also during William's lifetime. Blore Manor descended to the third son, William (II) Bassett, aged 24, at the death of his father on 15th November 1497.

William (I) Bassett was an outstanding example of a powerful landowner, who was held in great respect within his own county, and by each successive king. He was the calibre of man who could be relied upon to maintain law and order within his own county, no matter what the changing face of central politics, and government.

MARGARET KEBELL née BASSETT
Daughter of Ralph Bassett, brother of WILLIAM (II) BASSETT *Born c1477 Died c1550*

Marriage by Force
Margaret Kebell was the daughter of Ralph Bassett, brother of William (II) Bassett. Around the age of 21, Margaret married the ageing Thomas Kebell, sergeant-at-law and leading advocate. Her husband died on the 26th June 1500, at the age of 61. He was buried, at Humberstone, Leicestershire, and his effigy in robes lies on a tomb in the church.

As a result, at the age of 25, Margaret found herself a widow, with one third of the Kebell estates, and an income of £260. She was the heiress to the property belonging to her grandmother, Joan Bassett, née Byron. In addition she was also next in line to the Bassett estates, should anything happen to the seven-year-old heir William (III) Bassett. Not only a wealthy widow, with many suitors, she was obviously a very attractive prize.

At the end of January 1502 a small group of friends and relatives had travelled to Blore Hall to celebrate the betrothal of Margaret Kebell to Ralph Egerton, of Wrinehill. Ralph Egerton was the half-brother of Margaret's mother, Ellen Bassett, née Egerton, and heir to the Egerton estates.

Across the River Dove, in Derbyshire, the Vernon family reigned supreme, with never any qualms about establishing, or maintaining, their interests by force. One member of the family, Roger Vernon of Wirksworth, was a young tearaway. Four years earlier he had been accused of murder, but escaped punishment, most probably because of the intervention of his father, the all-powerful Sir Henry Vernon. Roger undoubtedly felt that a prize like Margaret was worth snatching, especially with the backing of his powerful family and friends.

In the early hours of 1st February 1502, under the cover of darkness, Roger Vernon, supported by Thomas Foljambe of Walton, Chesterfield, John Alsop of Alsop-en-le-Dale and a gang of over 100 men, forded the river and rode up to Blore Hall. At six o'clock in the morning, before most of the household and guests were up and about, they forced their way into the hall. Brandishing weapons, they grabbed Margaret, filled a basket with some of her belongings, and forced her on to a horse. Outnumbered and unprepared, all that the family and guests could do was stand by and watch helplessly as she was snatched away. The abductors rode down to the River Dove, across the ford, and on into Derbyshire to Darley Dale.

Roger made it quite clear that he would stand no nonsense from Margaret. The following day, accompanied by a smaller number of his supporters, they rode to Derby, where a willing priest performed the marriage ceremony. It had been a well-planned operation.

However, once over the shock, Margaret began to voice her objections very strongly. She made it quite clear that she would not succumb, or cooperate, in any way. To avoid any rescue attempt, Roger took his unwilling bride to his uncle's place in Netherseal, and then on to the home of Sir Richard Delaber of Clehonger, near the Welsh border.

At the first opportunity, she escaped from her abductor, when a band of Bassett supporters, who had been following their tracks, appeared. She set off for London with the band of rescuers but Roger went after them. Catching up with the party, he insisted upon joining them, protesting that Margaret was his wife and was just being difficult. In fact, Roger's father, Sir Henry Vernon, was in London, and Roger went to him to plead for his intervention.

Margaret was staying at a lodging house, in Fleet street, called The Saracen's Head. On the advice of his father, Roger sent a peace offering, in the form of a large pike, but, when Margaret realised the purpose of the gift, she sent it back - to his father. Sir Henry Vernon took part of the fish and returned the rest to her. Again, Margaret sent it back but, by this time, the fish was going bad. However, Margaret did agree to listen to Sir Henry, just to see what he had to say. All to no avail.

Margaret gained a personal audience with the King. Although he heavily fined Sir Henry Vernon for his part in the affair, the King did not nullify the marriage. For over six years Margaret, her mother and her late husband's legal friends pursued the matter through the courts - without success. They tried every court in the land, and every possible legal avenue. They hounded all the participants, and a large number were forced to make settlements. However, Margaret was unable to secure an annulment of the marriage.

It was not until 1509 that Margaret was freed from her marriage to Roger Vernon, and she was able to marry her first love. As Ralph Egerton and Margaret were distantly related, it was necessary to obtain special dispensation from the Pope.

Whether it was a good match or not is questionable, because Sir Ralph Egerton admitted to more illegitimate children than any other man of his time. In his will, Sir Ralph acknowledges one bastard son, Raufe, one bastard daughter, Mary, and other bastard daughters unspecified. At least three illegitimate daughters have been identified: two daughters, Elizabeth and Alice, by the daughter of Bracy of Bulkeley; one unnamed daughter, described as wife of Ball of Upton, by the daughter of Henry Fisher.

Ralph Egerton distinguished himself in battle, when he accompanied Henry VIII to France in 1513. He fought at the Battle of the Spurs, Siege of Terouenne and taking of Tournay, and was knighted by the King on the 25th September. In January 1514, in recognition of his services, he was appointed Standard Bearer of England. He was given the manor and lands of Ridley and a salary of £100 per year for life.

Margaret's experiences at law had made her a very formidable adversary. After she had succeeded in obtaining her freedom, she immediately entered the courts again to claim her rights to the Kebell estates. She succeeded in claiming the jointure of £40 from Sir Walter Hastings, who was forced to release a large portion of the Kebell estates.

On her marriage to Ralph Egerton she first moved to the Egerton home in Wrinehill, and later, to Ridley, Cheshire. She produced a son and heir, Richard. One of her grandsons was Thomas Egerton, the famous Lord Chancellor Ellesmere. In the oratory at Bunbury, which was founded by Sir Ralph Egerton, there used to be an altar-tomb. On the tomb, was a monumental brass representing the figure of the knight, in plate armour, and that of his wife. The arms of Egerton, Bassett and Byron were placed on the tomb, along with the following inscription:

> OF YOUR CHARITYE PRAY FOR THE SOULES OF SIR RAPHE EGERTON KT AND DAME MARGRET HIS WIFE, WCH SIR RAFE WAS LATE STANDARD BEARER TO OUR SOVRAINE LORD HENRY VIII AND ALSO TREASURER OF THE HOUSEHOLD OF THE LA[DY] PRINCES[S] HIS DAUGHTER, AND THE SAID SIR RAPHE DYED THE 9 DAY OF MARCH M.CCCCC XX.VIII AND THE SAID DAME MARGARET DYED THE ..... DAY OF IN THE YEARE OF OUR LORD GOD M.CCCCC..... ON WHOSE SOULES JESUS HAVE MERCY. AMEN

WILLIAM (II) BASSETT, JP   *Born 1473/4 Died 1506*

William (II) Bassett was born in 1473. In 1491/2, he married Elizabeth, daughter of Thomas Meverell of Throwley, descendant of Sir Sampson Meverell, with whom the Bassetts had been quarrelling thirty years before.

Unlike his father, William (II) kept out of the limelight of public office except for five years, from 1501 to 1506, when he was a Justice of the Peace for Staffordshire. He continued to extend and consolidate the Bassett estates, and vigorously defend any unlawful trespass. In 1500, he sued Henry Stubbs of Grindon for trespassing on his land. When Henry Stubbs did not appear in court, he was outlawed. However, the matter was settled, and Henry received a pardon for his trespass.

William bought lands in Kirk Langley from George Smalley and Thomas Twyford, and consolidated his estate around Meynell Langley, in Derbyshire.

As a relic of the feudal system of retaining a knight for military service, the lords and magnates continued to retain followers. These followers were military supporters, legal advisers and others who would be valuable in the pursuance of their political, and business activities. William's father, William (I), had been retained by Lord Hastings, the most powerful magnate in the Derbyshire/Staffordshire area.

Although strictly illegal since the 14th century for men below the status of baronet, William (II) made an agreement, in 1499, to pay retainer fees to four of his neighbours. Giles Button and Richard Hood, of Swinscoe, Thomas Joly and John Starkey, together with William (II), himself, were summoned to court for entering into this illegal agreement. They appear to have evaded the legal action by numerous postponements of the case.

Around 1500 Eleanor Bassett, née Egerton, the widow of his brother Ralph, came to live at Blore. Her daughter, Margaret, who had married Thomas Kebell, a lawyer, joined her mother after Thomas died, in 1500. As described, in the previous chapter, in 1502 Roger Vernon abducted Margaret and forced her into marriage. She took the matter to the courts and the legal wrangling went on for years.

It was of paramount importance to the Bassetts to ensure the continuation of the family name, to maintain its landholding, and its position in society. According to custom and law, the eldest son normally inherited the estate, and his father did everything he could to ensure that the inheritance was not impeded. If the son was under the age of 14 at the death of his father, the Master of the Wards could take the son into custody. The Crown could claim the rents and income from the estates during the period of wardship. William (II) made an arrangement that his son should marry the daughter of Thomas Cockayne, of Ashbourne. In order to cover the eventuality of his death, before his son came of age, William agreed that special conditions should apply. If the Crown exercised its right of wardship, Cockayne could claim up to 300 marks against the Bassett estate to pay the Master of Wards to release the boy, to marry Cockayne's daughter.

That William (II) should agree to the marriage arrangement, was especially unusual because the two families had been on opposing sides for half a century. The Cockaynes were aligned with both the Earl of Shrewsbury and the Vernons of Derbyshire. Bassett was of the opposite political faction: the magnates Hastings and Lord Grey were in opposition to the Earl of Shrewsbury. Bassett was a retainer of Hastings, and was distantly related to Grey of Codnor - one of Grey's forebears had married a Bassett daughter. The Vernons, with whom the Cockaynes were so closely allied, even at the time of the marriage, were in direct conflict with the Bassetts over the abduction of the widowed Margaret Kebell.

The Cockaynes were in financial trouble. John Cockayne, the grandfather, had arranged the marriage of Thomas Cockayne, Senior, with Barbara Fitzherbert, to buy himself out of debt. As a result of that deal, the Cockayne land had been held by the Fitzherberts until five years after John Cockayne's death. This left Thomas Cockayne, Senior, also in a difficult financial position and a deal with the Bassetts must have been a very bitter pill to swallow. Margaret Kebell's husband, Thomas Kebell, serjeant-at-law, probably brokered the deal between the Cockaynes and the Bassetts. Kebell had had previous dealings with the Cockaynes, before his marriage to Margaret Bassett.

William died on 3rd April 1506, at the age of 33, leaving four sons: William, Thomas, Francis and Nicholas, plus three unmarried daughters, Elizabeth, Anne and Dorothy. The Bassett estates descended to his son and heir, William (III) Bassett, who was then aged twelve. It has not been clear whether due process of the law was instituted, but William (III) Bassett did marry Ann, daughter of Thomas Cockayne. According to the pedigrees for the Hunt Family, the youngest daughter Dorothy married Christopher Hunt of Aston. Some pedigrees for the Alsop family suggest that Anne Bassett married Thomas Alsop of Kniveton, but it has not been positively confirmed that it was Anne the daughter of William (II).

Following his death an inquisition was held to establish the extent of his landholdings and whether there were any lands which the Crown was entitled to hold during the minority of his heir.

William (II) Bassett was acknowledged to be Lord of the Manors of Grindon, Cheadle and Parkhall and Blore. Blore was valued at 20 marks. He also held lands locally in Swinscoe and Woodhouses, as well as in more distant places in Derbyshire and Warwickshire. The relationship that had been established between the Cockaynes and the Bassetts continued after his death, when William's widow, Elizabeth, married Henry Cockayne.

THOMAS BASSETT and THE BASSETTS OF HINTS

From the 12th to the 14th centuries, the Meynells held the Manor of Hints. On the death of Sir Hugh Meynell, of Meynell Langley, the estates were divided amongst his four daughters, Elizabeth, Margaret,

Thomasia and Joan. Thomasia acquired Hints as her portion and she married Reginald Dethick. Their daughter Margaret Dethick married Raufe Bassett of Blore in the 1400s and Hints became part of the Bassett estate.

William (II) Bassett died in 1506 and settled lands in Kirk Langley upon his sons. His will states that, if his eldest son and heir, (Sir) William (III) Bassett, should wish to have any of the land specified, then he could do so, by giving land of equal value to his brothers. Sir William chose to have Kirk Langley for himself and used Langley as his principal residence for a number of years. It is assumed that Thomas Bassett received Hints as his inheritance, and it was here that the Bassetts of Hints held court for around one hundred years.

In 1537/8, an agreement was made between Thomas Bassett and his wife Margaret, and Christopher Hunt Armiger, in respect of 10 messuages, 100 acres of land, 24 acres meadow, 260 acres pasture, 120 acres wood, 300 acres furze, and heath, in Hints. Christopher Hunt acknowledged the tenements to be the right of Thomas and Margaret. They granted to Christopher, and his heirs, an annual rent of four pounds from the tenements. Sometime during the 16th century, the Sacheverells acquired land in Hints.

In 1544, Thomas Bassett was recorded as living at Barton Backpuche, subsequently known as Barton Blount, near Broughton in Derbyshire. He was in dispute with Ralph Sacheverell of Melbourne, over lands in Hints. As a result of independent arbitration, Thomas Bassett was awarded "the site and precinct of the Manor Place of Hints" plus 266 acres of land and the right to graze four hundred sheep and forty beasts, on the common land at Hints. For his part, he was required to pay £4 per year in rent to Ralph Sacheverell.

In Shaw's "The History and Antiquities of Staffordshire" there is a picture of Hints Hall and Chapel. According to the inscription on a monument in the chancel of Hints Church in the 18th Century, Thomas Bassett had two wives, Margaret and Jane. Thomas Bassett of Hints was married to the daughter of Cockayne of Ashbourne.

On 6th September 1554, after Ralph Sacheverell died, his son Ralph, of Normanton upon Soar, Nottingham, sold to Thomas Bassett his interest in the land in Hints for £515.19.2d. On the 14th February 1558, Thomas married Johanne Perry and from this marriage they had a son Edward. On 5th July 1564, the marriage was arranged between Edward Bassett and Jane Lynne, niece of Mary and Humphrey Wellys of Hoar Cross. Mary Wellys was the daughter of Wm Chetwynd of Ingestre; her sister had married a member of the Lynne family by whom she had a daughter, Jane. Humphrey Wellys was a very rich and important man: Member of Parliament, Justice of the Peace and Sheriff. He died a year later in 1565, but in his will there is no mention of Edward and Jane. Thomas Bassett was one of the appraisers of the inventory of Humphrey Wellys, valued at £622.11s.0d.

Thomas Bassett agreed that on his death the land in Hints should descend to Edward his son. Humphrey Wellys, for his part, agreed to provide a dowry of £200 for his wife's niece, Jane. The boy Edward was to be properly dressed and equipped for the marriage by his father, in accordance with his standing. Jane's uncle agreed to see that she was dressed in accordance with her position. He also agreed to supply the food, drink and accommodation for the guests at the wedding.

Jane, a daughter by the second wife of Thomas Bassett of Hints, married Robert Fitzherbert of Tissington. She died on the 27th October 1574, and was buried in St Marie's Church, Oxford. They had five sons, William, Thomas, Rafe, Hoffry, Samson and three daughters, Anne Elizabeth and Dorothy. Dorothy married Edward Whorwood of Compton, and had two sons, Thoma, and William.

There is no record in the Hints parish register of the marriage of Edward and Jane. In 1565 and 1566 two children, both called Thomas, are recorded as being baptised at Hints. The first child died at birth and the second only lived for a year. On 10th December 1567 the baptism of a son, Walter, is recorded. They had seven other children, Thomas, John, Dorothy, Ann, Mary, Magdalen and Jone.

In 1586, when the eldest son Walter was 19, his father Edward arranged the marriage with Sconsolate, one of the daughters of Sir Fulke Greville. Edward conveyed lands in Hints to Walter and Sconsolate, and granted to Sconsolate £10 per year for life, should Walter die before she did. There is some doubt about their children, but there appears to have been ten of them: Edward, Fulk, William, Thomas, John, George, Margaret, Elizabeth, Dorothy and Jane.

There is an undated reference in the "Memorials of the Dead" Ireland F.E. Vol VIII, page 192, which reads: "BASSETT Edward of Hince, Staffordshire Father of Joyce second wife of Groot Madden."

On 6th May 1594, Edward gave Walter the manor of Hints and all his lands in Staffordshire. One of the tenants on the Hints Estate was Richard Flyer. In 1599, Walter and Sconsolate sold parts of their estate in Hints, one part to William Underhill, of Utlicote, and second part to Raffe Fitzherbert, of Hints.

In 1601, Walter sold "all that capital messuage or house called Hynts Lodge" to Ralph Floyer. Ralph acquired the rest of the estate fourteen years later, in 1623. On the death of Ralph Floyer in 1793, his nephew, Cawley, took the name of Floyer and the manor and estate. It remained with the Floyer family, until the late 1800s.

In 1606/7, Walter and his father Edward sold to John Endisor, haberdasher of London, and Christopher Endisor, a further part of the estate. Thus the entire interest of the Bassetts in the manor of Hints had passed to other hands. This was the end of yet another chapter in the story of the Bassetts. Walter Bassett was buried, at Hints, on 9th September 1632.

SIR WILLIAM (III) BASSETT   King of the Moorland. Knight, MP, Sheriff, JP.
Born 1493   Died 1553

Sir William (III) Bassett, Knight, Member of Parliament, Sheriff, Justice of the Peace, was born at Blore on the Moorlands of North East Staffordshire, in 1493. Leland during his travels, visited Blore and referred to Sir William as "The King of the Moorland." On the death of his father William (II) Bassett in 1506, the twelve year old William (III) was taken into the Cockayne household. He married Anne Cockayne, his first wife. Their son, and heir, William (IV) was born a year later, followed by another son, Thomas, and a daughter, Margaret.

Brought up in the Roman Catholic faith, William (III) and his wife Anne spent large sums of money on major improvements to St Bartholomew's Church, at Blore. They built the entrance porch and increased the height of the nave and the chancel. The bone aching pews, the pulpit and the beautiful screen of hundreds of pieces of carved oak, were installed. For the use of chaplains and monks during the singing of daily offices, the oak choir stalls were added. Stained glass was placed in a number of windows, one of which depicted William and his wife kneeling before a crucifix. Below this picture was an inscription in Latin which translated, read "Pray for the Good Estate of William Bassett Esq. and his wife Anne who erected these windows and built this chancel AD 1519." There still remain in the south window of the chancel remnants of the stained glass from the old windows in the church. In a window in the north wall of the church there are nine coats of arms, including three showing the three cocks of the Cockayne family. Anne died shortly afterwards.

William married his second wife, Isabel, daughter of Sir Rd Coton, and widow of John Bradbourne, of Ashbourne. The marriage was arranged in 1523/4 but was very short. Isabel died suddenly around 1524/5.

In 1527/8, he married his third wife Ellen, daughter of Thomas Lytelton, widow of John Cotes of Cotes. Ellen was the sister of Edward Lytelton MP, of Pillaton, Staffs, who subsequently became strongly anti-Catholic. William's marriage to Ellen could indicate a typically pragmatic approach to his political and economic future. A year later, on 3rd November 1529, William received his knighthood from King Henry VIII at York Place, now called Whitehall, in London. He was present at the coronation of Queen Anne Boleyn.

In 1532, the Archdeaconry of Stafford compiled a Prayer List, or list of communicants, for the whole of the County. This covered the majority, but not all, of the population. Sir William, his wife Dame Ellen, his two previous wives, Ann and Elizabeth (Isabel), and all their children are mentioned. The population of the Parish, including Swinscoe, was more than 130 people. The tiny village of Blore was then a thriving place, but has now virtually disappeared. All that now remains are the church, Blore Hall, two houses, and evidence of previous habitations in nearby fields.

In 1532, the Spanish Ambassador to the Court of Henry VIII reported that the King was *determined to reunite to the Crown the goods which churchmen held of it."* Sir William was selected for a Commission to investigate the lands and goods of the nearby priory of Calwich. The Commission reported that the priory had fallen into disrepair and was no longer used for divine service and pious work.

This religious property was among the first to be claimed, in the name of Henry VIII, by his henchman Thomas Cromwell. The success of this early claim may have provided the incentive for Cromwell to appoint Richard Layton and Thomas Legh to visit every monastery and report on the activities and conduct of the occupants. Their reports condemned the small monasteries and this gave Cromwell the justification for closing all those of less than £200, in value.

William (III) was elected as a Member of Parliament for the first time, in 1536. Parliament lasted for only five weeks but was responsible for *"having finally extinquished Papal Authority in England."* Sir William was at Langley, when he received instructions, from Thomas Cromwell *"that such Images as you know so abused with pilgrimages or offerings you shall for avoiding that most detestable offence of Idolatry forthwith and take down."*

Sir William carried out his task, and replied to Cromwell, as follows:

"Right honourable my inespecial good lord, according to my bounden duty and the tenor of your lordship's letter lately to me directed, I have sent unto your good lordship by this bearer, my brother Francis Bassett, the images of St Ann of Buxton and St Modwen of Burton upon Trent which images I did take from the places where they did stand, and brought them to my own house within 48 hours after contemplation of your said lordship's letter, in as sober manner as my little and rude wits would serve me. And for that there should no more idolatry and superstition be there used I did not only deface the tabernacles and places, where they stand but also did take away the crutches, shirts and sheets with wax offered, being things that did allure and intice the ignorant people to the said offerings, also giving the keepers of both places admonition and charge that no more offerings should be made in those places till the King's pleasure and your lordships be further known in that behalf. My lord, I have locked up and sealed the baths and wells at Buxton and none shall enter to wash them till your lordship's pleasure be further known. Whereof I beseech your lordship that I may be ascertained again at your pleasure and I shall not fail to execute your lordship's commandment to the uttermost of my little witt and power. And the trust that they did put in those images and the vanity of the things, this bearer, my brother can tell your lordship better at large than I can write for he was with me at the doing of all and in all places, as knoweth good Jesus, whom ever good lordship in his blessed keeping. Written at Langley with the rude and simple hand of your assured and faithful orator and as one ever at your commandment, next unto the King to the uttermost of my little power."

WILLIAM BASSETT Knight

The distance from Langley to Buxton, then to Burton and back to Langley, is about one hundred miles. Even allowing for exaggeration, to travel such a distance within 48 hours, over the roads and terrain of the 16th Century, was quite a feat of horsemanship.

St Modwen's Holy Well was in a chapel on Andrew's Island, between two branches of the River Trent at Burton. According to Dr Plot, St Modwen's Well was famous for the cure of King's Evil, and other extraordinary cures. The water had long been used by the monks, for brewing the famous Burton Ale, and pilgrims came to partake of the water, and possibly the ale too. The offerings received from the pilgrims visiting the shrine in 1535 amounted to £2.0s.0d.

Even though the shrine in Buxton was closed and the chapel subsequently pulled down, visitors soon started returning to take the famous waters of Buxton Spa again. Sixteen years later, the Buxton Bath Charity was formed, possibly by Bess of Hardwick, with a scale of charges according to social status.

On 1st September, Thomas Thacker, steward to Thomas Cromwell, wrote to his Master. He reported that Francis Bassett had delivered to Austin Friars in London, the image of St Ann, and the image of St Modwen *"with her red cow and her staff which women labouring of child in those parts were desirous to have with them to lean upon and to walk with."*.

Sir William also went to Ingestre, destroyed the images, removed the statue of St Erasmus and closed the healing shrines. Later, when Thomas Cromwell was arrested, in 1540, an inventory was taken of his belongings, which showed an extensive collection of paintings, and sculptures. It has not been possible to identify the images of St Ann and St Modwen mentioned in the letter, nor the statue of St Erasmus.

In an attempt to satisfy the greed of King Henry VIII, the brilliant but unscrupulous Thomas

Cromwell carried out an assessment of the vast riches of the church. His overt reason was that church property had been undervalued for tax purposes for the previous 250 years. With the possibility of lessening their own tax burden, many taxpayers readily accepted that the church had evaded its fair share. Cromwell called for a complete revaluation, and set up local commissions to carry out this task.

Sir William Bassett was appointed as a member of the Commission, for assessing the Valor Ecclesiasticus. Within the jurisdiction of his commission were the religious houses of Tutbury, Rocester and Croxden. His brother, Francis Bassett was closely involved with these monasteries as a Servant of Cranmer, Archbishop of Canterbury. As auditor, Francis had received the fee of £2.0s.0d from Tutbury Priory. He was also able to learn a lot about the value of its lands. The Valor for these establishments was increased:

Tutbury	to £358.2s.0d
Rocester from £100. 2s.10d	to £129.6s.3d
Croxden from £102.15s. 7d	to £157.1s.2d.

Cranmer wrote to Thomas Cromwell, recommending that these monasteries should be dissolved. In December 1538 Cranmer also asked that the lands be given to his servant, Francis Bassett. Among Cromwell's personal papers is a reminder to speak to the King for Francis Bassett, and a note that Musden Grange had a yearly value of 20 marks.

Francis went to see Thomas Cromwell to ask him to intercede with the Abbot of Garendon regarding the lease of land at Royston Grange. It must have been with some trepidation that the Abbot replied to Cromwell giving reasons why Sir William's lease could not be extended.

On the 14th September 1538 Sir William and his son Thomas, Francis Pole, William Leigh and John Bulkeley, were witnesses to the Deed of Surrender of Tutbury Priory. Subsequently, in March 1539, Sir William obtained the lease of land from Tutbury Priory and a house there, which he left in his will to his wife. Tutbury Priory had a working fountain and its own water, supplied by channels and lead pipes. In Tutbury, he also acquired land, belonging to the Yotton Chantry in Lichfield.

Two days later, Sir William was present at the signing of the Deed of Surrender of Rocester Abbey. This time his elder son, William (IV), and Thomas and John Fitzherbert, were the witnesses. In the 14th Century Rocester had acquired extensive land in the village of Swinscoe, from the Okeovers. The monks had established a chapel "surrounded by ditches" there. Sir William increased his holdings by the acquisition of some of this Rocester Abbey land.

The Deed of Surrender of Croxden was signed on 17th September 1538. Following the Dissolution, the land was leased to Francis Bassett for twenty one years, at an annual rent of £16.16s.5d. Seven years later he sold the lease to Godfrey Foljambe for £577.2s.8d, a very handsome profit. Francis bought four of the five items offered for sale at Croxden, at very low prices:

Lyttle Gatehouse on the northsyde of the comyn way	13s.4d
Loft under the organs	10s.0d
Lyttle smythes forge	4s.8d
Roffe of the dorter (dormitory)	33s.4d

It may be that he bought the roof on behalf of Sir William, for the house at Blore. There are 14th Century re-used timber beams at Blore Hall, which pre-date the 15th/16th Century part of the building. There is no record of any sale, but Sir William's son and heir, William (IV), acquired the monumental brass from Croxden Abbey. He took it to Norbury, where it was re-used for the monument of his father-in-law, Sir Anthony Fitzherbert.

From 1540 onwards Francis Bassett was again involved in claiming for disputed land. He was claiming from the Abbot of Combermere for land in Hartington, and threatening to sue in the Court of Augmentation. The title for the land was in dispute and there were other claimants, all clamouring to get their hands on more property.

Burton Abbey surrendered on 14th November 1539. It was re-established as the Burton College for Canons in 1541, but only lasted for four years. At the sale, following the closure of Burton College in 1545, Sir William bought two small organs, possibly for his residences at Blore and Langley. He also bought a pair of great candlesticks and a number of vestments and cloth.

In 1539, King Henry VIII became worried about the alliance between Francis I of France and Charles of Burgundy. He called for the country to be put into a state of readiness, in case of attack. All ablebodied men in the Hundred of Totmonslow were recorded in the Muster Roll of 1539, under the direction of Sir William Bassett and Sir Phelyp Draycott. In the other hundreds the muster records the names of the parishes from which the men came, but in the case of Totmonslow no split occurs.

None of the names of local yeomen from Blore or Swinscoe appear in the list. Nicholas Bamford, Giles Button, Richard or William Eyton would have been eligible. The Muster Roll for Totmonslow may be faulty, or part missing.

Sir William, his first two wives and his family were very closely related to the Fitzherberts. The Fitzherberts were renowned for the strength and steadfastness of their Catholic faith, throughout the oppressions of the 16th Century. His wife Anne was the daughter of Sir Thomas Cockayne and Barbara Fitzherbert. His son, William (IV), married Elizabeth Fitzherbert, whose brother Sir Thomas Fitzherbert was named as the most important papist in the Country. These relationships must have been acutely embarrassing to Sir William. He never openly showed any Roman Catholic leanings. His involvement in the activities of the Establishment was an opportunity to enhance his position and wealth, rather than acceptance of the new faith. With his brother Francis so closely connected with Cranmer, and the associations with Thomas Cromwell, what other line could he take? However, in his will, he calls for a priest to sing the Catholic Vespers for the Dead and the Catholic Dirge. Even though he had taken full advantage of the chances to plunder the Old Church, Sir William had secretly retained his Catholic belief.

The associations with the Fitzherberts were not just based upon religion. They were close neighbours, and had in common an interest in making the most of their extensive landholdings. In 1523, Sir Anthony Fitzherbert published "The Boke of Husbandry" that became the standard work on agriculture in the 16th Century. It discussed different types of land usage, the advantages of enclosure, the value of manure and the practice of drainage. The value of the Bassett Estates and their income continuously increased throughout the 16th Century. This confirms not only their ability as entrepreneurial landowners and land-grabbing dissolutionists, but also their application of the good husbandry advocated by the Fitzherberts.

Blore was not Sir William's only home - he held Meynell Langley in Derbyshire. On the 20th June 1545 there was a great storm which "went to Syr Willam Bassett's place.... and pullyd a great part of it downe". He rebuilt the house, covering three sides of a square with a stateroom panelled in wood and decorated with the arms of the Bassetts. There is a stained glass window showing a version of the Bassett Motto "Espoir D'Avoir" in the building, which used to be the Meynell Arms Hotel. The Hall, at Meynell Langley, stood for over two centuries, until it was partially dismantled in 1757, leaving only the stateroom, lobby and stairs to the chapel. The old chapel remained until 1834, when it too was torn down, together with the rest of the original building.

Sir William (III) Bassett was a Member of Parliament in 1547, when the Government became bankrupt due to the dishonesty and mismanagement of John Dudley, Earl of Warwick. Sir William died 31st October 1553, and his will, dated 12th January 1553/4, was proved at Lichfield.

During a very difficult period of dramatic change, Sir William extended his influence and landholding. Personally, he took full advantage of the "benefits" to be gained from the dissolution of religious houses. As Sheriff and Justice of the Peace, he was involved in Law and Order in Staffordshire and Derbyshire. As a Member of Parliament, and Knight of the Realm, he was involved with some of the most far-reaching events of the Era.

WILLIAM (IV) BASSETT   Lord of Blore, Grindon, Cheadle, Parkhall and Slindon.
         Born 1507/8 Married:21st September 1519. Buried at Blore:17th Feb 1563
William (IV) Bassett was born in 1507/8, when his father was only fourteen years old, and his mother Anne Cockayne, was only a couple of years older.

In 1519/20, an agreement was made between Sir William (III) Bassett and Sir Anthony Fitzherbert, of Hamstall Ridware, Justice of the Common Bench. It was agreed that William (IV) Bassett should marry Elizabeth, daughter of Sir Anthony. However, it was agreed that should young William die before marriage, or before carnal copulation took place after marriage, then his brother should be married to

Elizabeth. William was only about thirteen years old when he was married to Elizabeth Fitzherbert.

At the age of twenty one William was nominated as one of the trustees of Isabella Bradbourne Widow, his father's second wife. As a trustee, he was among the patrons of Boyleston Church at the appointment of the Rector, Richard Reve, on 9th December 1528. The other patrons nominated were: Ralph Longford, Humphrey Comberford, Ralph Purfrey, Richard Coton and William Dethyk gent and Edward Redferne Clerk.

William's marriage to the daughter of an avowed Catholic and related events confirm that he was an adherent to the Roman Catholic faith. Her brother, Sir Thomas Fitzherbert, was a devout Catholic who because of his refusal to denounce his faith was imprisoned a number of times. Thomas was finally sent to the Tower of London, where he died peacefully in 1591, at the age of 73 - still professing his Catholic faith. His wife's sisters, Dorothy and Catherine Fitzherbert, married Ralph Longford and John Sacheverell. The extreme Catholic views of the Fitzherberts affected all of those around them. According to the Derbyshire Archaeological Journal, William and these two gentlemen were repeatedly and heavily fined. He and John Sacheverell endured long terms of imprisonment. Their wives, Elizabeth, and Catherine, were given into the custody of puritanical conformists and forced to pay for their own maintenance.

In 1538 he and his father, Sir William, were witnesses to the Deed of Surrender of Croxden Abbey. William (IV) acquired old monumental brass from the Abbey, and took it to Norbury, where it was reused for the monument of his father-in-law, Sir Anthony Fitzherbert. This was in spite of Sir Anthony's dying wish that his children should not acquire monastic land or property. This was not just a matter of conscience. As an eminent judge, versed in English Law, he was well aware that the Crown had the right to take into Wardship a surviving underage heir, if any of the land was held of the Crown. His intention was to preserve the Fitzherbert estates from the kind of fate that sixty years later befell William's granddaughter, Elizabeth Bassett, and the Bassett Estates.

At his father's death in 1553, William was stated to be forty years old. According to records discovered in the British Library, he was born in 1507/8, and so did not inherit the Estates until he was about 46 years old. William's Catholic tendencies were a source of great embarrassment to his father, and to his uncle, Francis Bassett, auditor and servant to Cranmer, Archbishop of Canterbury. In his father's will, William (IV)'s inheritance is fully specified, but his name is mentioned indirectly only once. His brother Thomas is named a number of times. The reason for the lack of mention is that the disposition of the estate would have been subject to the terms of his marriage settlement. His steward, Nicholas Bamforth (Bamford), farmed the land at Blore. When Nicholas died in 1558 he left twenty shillings to his mistress, Elizabeth Bassett, twenty shillings to her son, William (V), and one cow to Joan Bassett, wife of Thomas. Could this Joan have been the newly married Joan Perry, wife of Thomas Bassett, of Hints? Thomas Bassett married Joan at St Bartholomew's Church, Hints on 14th February 1558, one month before Nicholas Bamford made his will on the 21st March 1558. The generosity seems a bit excessive for a "stranger", and therefore it must mean that Joan was already well known to Nicholas. No mention is made of William (IV) Bassett, which may confirm the unsubstantiated suggestion, in the Derbyshire Archaeological Journal, that William (IV) served sentences in jail for his Catholic tendencies. William was still alive, because his will was made in 1561.

William (IV) Bassett died, and was buried at Blore on the 17th February 1563. No memorial exists. There is a broken memorial stone on the floor in the Bassett Chapel, which appears to be part of the bottom of a robe. According to Rector Rev T.J.S. Roberts, this memorial was inscribed to one of the Bassetts. William's remains would be interred in the vault, below the chantry. In his will, dated 8th September 1561, he instructed that twelve poor men should be chosen, and provided with a black gown for his funeral. In return for loyalty and good service he made special provision for his waiting servants and yeomen, by providing each of them with a black coat and a whole year's wages. His will also guaranteed their places for at least forty days after his death. His yeomen stewards - Richard Cotton at Langley, Thomas Cotton at Grindon, George Warner at Cheadle and Humfrey Brown at Parkhall - were each given the tenancy of their farms for their lifetime. Richard Bamford was confirmed as "Keff" of Langley Park also for his lifetime. Richard Bamford was probably the nephew of Nicholas Bamford, who died in 1558.

The Bassett Lands were very extensive in Staffordshire. Within the Manors of Blore, Grindon, Cheadle, Parkhall and Slindon, he held over one thousand eight hundred acres plus thirty four houses, property with rentals exceeding £31, two watermills, and the advowsons of three churches: Blore, Grindon and Kingsley. William (IV) bequeathed to his wife Elizabeth, the Manor of Meynell Langley, for her lifetime, and the Manor of Blore until his son and heir reached the age of 21. To his sister Margaret, and her husband William Copwood, he left the house and lands at Fole, where they were then living. To Margaret's two sons, William and Bassett Copwood, he bequeathed £13.6s.8d each, to be paid on their reaching the age of 21.

His wife died in 1574 and was buried with her husband. Her will has survived in the Lichfield Record Office and in the inventory taken following her death, her estate was valued at £225.6s.8d.

WILLIAM (V) BASSETT, MP, SHERIFF, JP   *Born 1552 Died 9th November 1601*
Buried 10th December 1601 at Blore

William (V) Bassett was born on the 18th August 1552. From the age of 12 years, when his father died, he was brought up in the household of his uncle, Sir Thomas Fitzherbert. He received his education from the Catholic Priests and Schoolteachers who served the Fitzherbert family. In 1566, at the age of 14, he was at St John's College Oxford and was admitted to the Middle Temple in 1571. On his tombstone, he is referred to as "courtier" and that, together with his association with the Earl of Dudley, could indicate that he held some minor position at court when he was a young man. In 1579 he, along with Mr Poole, Mr Sacheverell and Mr Gell, was instructed by the Privy Council (Lords Chancellor, Treasurer and Admiral and Vice-Chamberlain) to adjudicate in a land dispute. Again, in 1591, he was called upon, by the Privy Council, to act in a dispute at Duckmanton. He certainly made frequent visits to London, riding on horseback along Watling street - the present A5 - and visiting Skinners, the lodging and eating house in the City.

Following his grandfather's footsteps he continued to extend the Bassett landholding. He acquired Kirk Langley from German Pole, thus bringing together the two manors of Meynell Langley and Kirk Langley. They have remained together to the present day, in the hands of the Meynell Family. He bought Barlaston from the House of Stafford. In 1583, William gave to his Aunt Margaret, Bubnell Hall in Derbyshire, which had belonged to another branch of the Bassett Family three centuries previously.

In 1583, William accompanied Robert Dudley, Earl of Leicester, to the Netherlands to maintain an army against the Spaniards. Dudley quarrelled with his captains. At the first opportunity Bassett deviously persuaded a friend to write him a letter, urging his return to England to attend to urgent matters concerning the Bassett Estates. On his return, an accusation was made against him. It was alleged that he had threatened to burn down a neighbouring landowner's home and prepared a fort, at Grindon.

In 1586/7, Philip Okeover, as Sheriff of Staffordshire, was instructed to nominate in the elections "those who were elected before". Philip ignored these instructions and nominated his friend and neighbour, William (V) Bassett. William was elected as a Member of Parliament. This Parliament appears to have been very hurriedly brought together so that the alleged Babington Plot to assassinate Queen Elizabeth could be considered. As a result of their deliberations, Mary Queen of Scots was beheaded in 1587.

On his appointment as Sheriff, William was required to nominate Bailiffs, for each of the hundreds of Staffordshire. Their duties were to execute the instructions of the court, and distrain any goods. On the 27th December, William appointed Hugh Rowlston, yeoman, of Codsall, as Bailiff for the hundred of Seisdon and he, with two others - Humfrey Hopkis and Sampson Eginton - signed a Bond for £200 as surety for his term of office in the Bailiwick.

William had a cousin, Thomas Fitzherbert, who betrayed the hiding place of his own father, a Catholic, John Fitzherbert, in 1586. This Thomas Fitzherbert offered Richard Topcliffe the enormous sum of £5000, to "persecute to death" his father John, his uncle Sir Thomas Fitzherbert and his cousin, William (VI) Bassett. Richard Topcliffe was one of the most evil men of these harsh times. He was a notorious torturer and blackmailer, who had a private torture chamber and rack for extracting confessions from Catholic "Traitors". He was on the payroll of Lord Burghley in 1581 and slowly grew in strength and influence over the next ten years.

Topcliffe laid many charges against William Bassett. William was accused of receiving a letter from another Thomas Fitzherbert "his dearest darling and a Spanish Traitor", who had escaped to exile in Spain. This letter was supposed to have asked for money and promised repayment when the Spanish Armada invaded England. If this allegation was true, then William (V) Bassett's contribution of £25 towards the defence of the realm against the Armada must be questionable. In 1587 Robert Sutton, a Seminary Priest, was executed in "a most villainous butcherly manner" for saying mass in the town of Stafford. William was Sheriff of Staffordshire, at the time. It was alleged that he did not stop the execution because Sutton would have revealed that Bassett's cook had made candles for him. As Sheriff, William accompanied Topcliffe to Norbury, in search of traitorous material, allegedly hidden there by Thomas Fitzherbert. Topcliffe found a spider in his milk and accused William of trying to poison him. William said it was not a spider, but a bee. Topcliffe replied that he had found the legs, but if Bassett could find the wings, then he would believe it to be a bee.

It was also alleged that he had been involved in witchcraft twelve or thirteen years before, when he had entertained Thomas Allen, of Oxford, at Langley. Thomas Allen (1542-1632) was a mathematician, philosopher and astronomer, at Oxford University, who also studied Astrology, as many did during this Age. Thomas had previously been accused of using magic to effect a match between his Patron Robert Dudley, Earl of Leicester, and Queen Elizabeth. William (V) was in the service of the Earl. The meeting with Thomas Allen was used as another of the evidential half-truths at which Topcliffe was so adept. The alleged witchcraft ceremony involved placing a hammer on an anvil to await "the very prick of noon". If the sun shone on the anvil, precisely at noon, then the hammer would strike three times, and Bassett would be able to ask of the Oracle any question he chose. The priest Robert Gray, under interrogation by Topcliffe, in 1593, confessed to visiting Margaret Thomson, a recusant, who lived at a house on Bassett's Estate. William (V) was accused of giving Robert Gray two saddles and a sum of money on one occasion when they had met on the road to London.

Many of the allegations infer that William (V) was a Catholic like his father. However, Robert Healde, the rector of Blore in 1607, swore that there had never been any recusant, or half-recusant, at Blore, during his thirty years of office. William (V), as Lord of the Manor, undoubtedly conformed, but most evidence points to his Catholic faith.

In 1594 Topcliffe sued Thomas Fitzherbert for the £5,000. Fitzherbert, in defence, stated that his father and uncle had died of natural causes, and that Bassett was still flourishing. It is difficult to comprehend how any Court could accept such a suit as this and probably relates to the powerful patronage which supported Topcliffe's activities. The court did, however, decide to hold the proceedings in camera. It is assumed that Topcliffe was successful, because he did acquire Padley, one of the Fitzherbert Estates.

William (V) Bassett married Judith, daughter of Thomas Osten of Oxley Hall, Bushbury, by special licence at St Mary's Church, Stoke Newington, near London, on 11th May 1598. She was the widow of William Boothby, wealthy Haberdasher, by whom she had seven children. A year later, in 1599, when William was 49, and Judith was 33, their only child was born, a daughter, Elizabeth.

William continued to extend his landholding. In 1599 he bought from Edmund Cockeyne the greater part of the Manor of Calton, for the sum of £400. This comprised 20 messuages, 10 cottages, 20 gardens, 20 orchards, 600 acres of land, 400 acres of meadow, 300 acres of pasture, 60 acres of wood, 500 acres of furze and heath, 30s of rent. Thirty years later William Senior produced a series of maps for the Duke of Newcastle. The maps and surveys detail the names, fields and acreage of Calton, Blore and other manors which the Duke acquired by his marriage to Elizabeth Bassett.

The Circuit Judges of Assize visited Stafford in August 1601. Even though the custom had been specifically banned in 1574, they were provided with accommodation, food and drink by the Sheriff and local gentry. William's contribution was; a buck, two capons, twelve rabbits and six pigeons, valued at five shillings. The buck and the rest of the items could have come from Blore Park. After William's clash with Topcliffe and the allegations of Catholic sympathies he needed every friend he could get!

William (V) Bassett, the last male heir, in line of descent, of the Bassetts of Blore, died, on the 9th November 1601, and was buried at Blore, on the 10th December. The magnificent tomb was erected in Blore Church by his wife Judith, and bears the inscription in verse, written by Sir William Cavendish, Elizabeth Bassett's second husband:

Here lyes a courtier souldier handsome good
Witty wise valiant and of pure blood
From William's conquest and his noble sword
In the same lyne many a noble lord
That time hath lost in paying thus Death's debt
In this unparallel'd William Bassett
But by high virtue with thy ancient name
Shall ever swell the cheeks of glorious fame

His wife Judith continued to hold Langley and part of Cheadle. After his death she married, for a third time - to Sir Richard Corbet. In 1640, at the age of 74, she died a very wealthy woman. She left her estates to her sons of her first marriage to William Boothby, and £3000 to her favourite daughter, Elizabeth, née Bassett, Countess of Newcastle.

JUDITH ASTYN (OSTEN/AUSTEN)*Baptised at Bushbury 16th May 1566*
Married (1) William Boothby at St Mary Colechurch 16 May 1586
Married (2) WILLIAM(V) BASSETT at Stoke Newington 11 May 1598
Married (3) Sir Richard Corbett c1603
Buried at Blore 28 Aug 1640

Judith, the daughter of Thomas Astyn (Austen), of "the Graunge nigh Wolverhampton" and his first wife, Mary, née Cresswell, was born at Bushbury, near Wolverhampton, in the year 1566.

On the 16th May 1586, at St Mary Colechurch, Judith married her first husband, the Staffordshire born businessman, and landowner, William Boothby. He lived and worked in the City of London and was a member of the Company of Haberdashers. They lived in one of the "many fayre houses" in St Laurence's Lane, not far from Blossoms Inne, popularly known as Bosoms Inn! Blossoms Inn was the terminus of the Norwich to London Carrier, in the 15th Century. Curiously, on its site was a receiving office of the London and North Eastern Railway in the 1950s. The Lane, on the western edge of the old Jewish Quarter, had always been an important residential area. William de Ferrers, Earl of Derby, had a house there prior to his death in 1294. The Lane was named after the large parish church, of St Laurence's, at the Guildhall end.

William and Judith had seven children, all of whom, including son Robert born four months after his father's death, were baptised at St Laurence's Church, Old Jewry. The church, the lane, and most of the surrounding area were later destroyed in the Fire of London, 1666. Sir Christopher rebuilt the church in 1676. It was destroyed again during the blitz, in December 1940 and rose from the ashes, in 1954-1957.

William Boothby held lands in Staffordshire, Derbyshire, Leicestershire and Oxfordshire. He held land in Hackney, Kingsland and Stoke Newington, the upper class residential area three or four miles outside the City. Kingsland probably acquired its name from King Henry VIII. He is thought to have had a hunting lodge there from which he enjoyed his favourite pastime - the chase. St Mary's Church, Stoke Newington, like St Laurence's, was held under the patronage of the Dean and Chapter of St Paul's. Queen Elizabeth I is reputed to have been a visitor to St Mary's church.

Judith's first husband, William Boothby, died and was buried at St Laurence's church, Old Jewry, on the 14th July 1597. Judith received one third of his estate, another third was divided among his six children, and the remaining third, amounting to almost £600, plus a number of legacies, were distributed to relatives.

Staffordshire families have always established close bonds. It would be natural for William (V) Bassett, on his travels to London, to come into contact with the Boothbys. Forty years previously his grandfather, Sir William (III) Bassett, sold land in Tutbury to William Boothby's father, Thomas. One of William Boothby's four sisters, Ellinor, married a member of the Hurt Family. There were Hurts at Castern, three miles from Blore. One member of the Hurt family, Dorothy Hurt, in 1641, is recorded as "of Blore". Of course, the wealthy bachelor William Bassett would make an ideal suitor for such an eligible widow as Judith Boothby.

They were married by special licence at St Mary's, Stoke Newington, on the 11th May 1598. A year later, in 1599, their daughter and sole heir Elizabeth was born, but no record has been found of her place of birth.

The year 1601 was a tragic one for Judith. On the 9th April 1601 her father Thomas Austen of Oxley, near Bushbury, died. An alabaster gravestone, near the north door, of the chancel, of Bushbury church, shows the image of a man between two women and at their feet, six children: Judith, Martha, Anne, John, Mary Nith and Sarah. There was an inscription which read as follows:

HERE LYETH THE BODY OF THOMAS AUSTYN GENT WHO DEPARTETH THIS LIFE THE
9TH DAY OF APRIL IN THE YEAR OF OUR LORD GOD 1601 AND HE WAS THE AGE OF 63
YEARS AND HAD TWO WIVES

Over the man's head was written, Thomas Austyn of Oxley, gent. Over the woman, on his right hand, is written Mary, the daughter of Ric Cresswell, first wife of Thomas Austyn. Over the woman, on his left hand, is written Elinor, the daughter of Edward Sebright, second wife to Thomas Austyn.

Seven months later, her husband, William (V) Bassett, died on the 9th November 1601, at the age of 49, and was buried at Blore on the 10th December 1601. Judith later erected a magnificent tomb in Blore church, in memory of her husband, William Bassett. The tomb bears an inscription in verse, composed some years later by her daughter's second husband, Sir William Cavendish:

Baby Elizabeth was only 2 years 2 months and 13 days old when her father died. Judith found herself in a very difficult and harrowing situation when William died. The Master of the Wards, Sir Robert Cecil, was intent upon proving that William (V) had held land of the Crown. As Judith's baby, Elizabeth, was sole heir to the extensive Bassett estates, evidence was needed to bring the estates, within the jurisdiction of the Court of Wards. The Bassett estates were very valuable - worth over £4000 per year in rentals. Furthermore, according to feudal custom, the Master of Wards would have the right to impose a marriage upon the widow. Although this legal right had been allowed to lapse during the 16th century, the threat still existed.

Sir Robert Cecil summoned to London the Bassett Solicitor and Counsel, John Baxter. Cecil specifically instructed Baxter to search for evidence that William (V) had held lands from the Crown. John Baxter appears to have been rather tardy in providing the information. This incurred Cecil's displeasure and when Baxter asked to receive some benefit from the Bassett estates, his plea was ignored.

Baby Elizabeth was made a ward of the Crown. Judith pleaded with Sir Robert Cecil for the wardship of her own child, but was refused. There were a number of contenders; Sir Michael Hickes, a close friend of Cecil's, was told that *"it would stir too much envy to give it to you"*. The wardship was given to Henry, Lord Cobham, the brother-in-law of the Master of the Wards. A couple of days later, in a private arrangement, Cobham sold the wardship, and the right to arrange the marriage, to Sir Walter Raleigh. Some months later, Lord Cobham agreed that Judith could have "custody of the body" of her daughter. In return, Judith was required to pay £40.0s.0d, until Elizabeth was ten years old. After that, a further 100 marks (£66.3s.4d) was to be paid until she reached the age of sixteen years.

Further disturbing pressures were placed upon Judith from other sources. Sir John Davies, one-time Attorney General of Ireland, had a home in the City, not far from St Laurence's Lane, where Judith had lived for many years. Sir John Davies wrote to the Master of Wards: *"There is nothing left but to repair my fortunes by some marriage. If it be agreeable to your Honour I do not know any whom I better fancy than Mrs Bassett over whom your power is so great..."*

It had become common knowledge that baby, Elizabeth and the Bassett Lands were to be taken into wardship. Sir John Davies continues: *"a few favourable lines to intimate your readiness in gratifying her with the wardship of her daughters lands if for your sake she entertained my suit."*

Judith somehow managed to avoid the suit of Sir John Davies. She married Sir Richard Corbett, Knight of the Honourable Order of the Bath, who was a member of the Middle Temple, in the City of London.

After Sir Walter Raleigh was thrown into the Tower of London, the Court of Wards decided that the obligations of the late Lord Cobham for the wardship of Elizabeth, should be cancelled. In 1605, Judith with her husband Sir Richard as "Next Friends" of the Ward, were still trying to establish at law the "true grantee of her wardship and marriage". The marriage to Sir Richard Corbett gave Judith the chance to act as match-maker for one of her daughters by her first husband. Elizabeth Boothby was married to Sir Andrew Corbett; they had at least sixteen children. Unfortunately, Judith's marriage to Sir Richard, was also only very short. He died and was buried on the 29th September 1606 at Moreton Corbet, in Shropshire.

Judith's sister, Martha, was married to Sir John Fitzherbert, which maintained the close relationship with the Fitzherberts. She leased a large part of her land to Sir John Fitzherbert: Claydon, Clattercoat, Cropredy in Oxfordshire, Ashbourne, Coldeaton, Mappleton in Derbyshire, and Cheadle Parkhall, Alderlie, Kingsley and Broadoak in Staffordshire, and Marston in Leicestershire.

Three times a widow, and with her Austen inheritance, Judith was a very wealthy woman. She moved around her estates quite extensively. In 1623, she is referred to as "the lady Judith Corbet of Clattercut". Judith died at Meynell Langley in Derbyshire in 1640 at the age of 74. In her will she left all her land to the sons of her first marriage. She left £3000 to her favourite daughter, Elizabeth, Countess of Newcastle.

Judith specifically requested that she should *"be buried in the Church of Blore in the vault which I made there"*. Her wish was granted, and she was buried in the vault, below the Bassett Tomb, on the 28th August 1640. An effigy of Judith lies beside that of her second husband, William (V) Bassett, on the Bassett tomb in Blore church. Her daughter and granddaughter kneel at the head of the tomb. The effigy itself has been sliced along the arms, at each side, suggesting that it was cut down in size, to fit the tomb. This was probably a mistake in measurement by the stonemason, as a similar slicing occurs on one of the kneeling figures.

It is from Judith, through her daughter Elizabeth, née Bassett, wife of the Duke of Newcastle, that the descent to HRH Charles Prince of Wales can be traced.

ELIZABETH BASSETT *Born 1599 Died 17th April 1643*

In the Art Gallery at Ranger's House, Blackheath, London, there is a portrait of the lovely and petite Elizabeth Bassett, widow of Henry Howard, third son of Thomas, Earl of Suffolk and heiress to the Bassett Estates. The exquisite gown in black belies her state of mourning, and emphasises her slim figure and beautiful features. The massive chair, close to which she stands, shows off the dainty petiteness of her stature. This painting is reputed to be one of a group of portraits specially done by the portrait painter William Larkin, to show off the charms of young ladies eligible for marriage.

Elizabeth was born in 1599, the only daughter and sole heir of William (V) Bassett of Blore, Staffordshire, and Meynell and Kirk Langley, Derbyshire and his wife Judith, daughter of Thomas Austen, and widow of William Boothby.

In 1602, following the death of William Bassett, his ex-Solicitor and Counsel, John Baxter, was taken to London to be interviewed by Sir Robert Cecil, Master of Wards to the Queen. Baxter was interrogated, and specifically instructed to seek evidence that William Bassett had held land from the Crown. Where the heir was under age, and any land belonging to the deceased had been held from the Crown, the heir became a ward of the Crown and the

William Cavendish

Elizabeth Bassett
*Photograph reproduced by permission of
Mrs Anne French, Iveagh Bequest, Kenwood*

Margaret Cavendish

Thomas Rivett
*Reproduced by kind permission
of Mr D C Rivett-Cormac*

profits derived from the estates became the right of the Crown. The Master of Wards had the right to transfer the wardship to the most suitable applicant, which was usually the highest bidder, but sometimes the biggest briber.

Elizabeth became a ward of the Queen. Her mother must have been heartbroken when, in spite of her pleading to become guardian of her own daughter, this was refused by Sir Robert Cecil. Cecil sold the wardship to his brother-in-law, Lord Cobham, on 18th May 1602. Two days later, Lord Cobham privately transferred the wardship, and marriage, for an unspecified sum of money, to Sir Walter Raleigh, who in turn entered into a private agreement with Cecil. It was agreed that in the event of Cecil's death the benefits of the wardship and the Bassett Estates would go to the heirs of Sir Robert Cecil. By this underhand method Cecil would ensure some form of benefit from this valuable wardship, even though he could not be seen to take it himself directly.

On the 16th November 1602, Henry Lord Cobham made an agreement that "the body of" Elizabeth should be released into the custody of her mother Judith. In return, Judith was to pay £40 per annum until Elizabeth was ten years, and then 100 Marks (£66.3s.4d), until she reached the age of sixteen. Sir Walter Raleigh retained the benefits of wardship and the right to arrange the marriage of Elizabeth. With the apparent consent of Cecil and Cobham, the four year old Elizabeth was betrothed to Raleigh's ten year old son, Walter. In 1603 Lord Cobham was committed to the Tower of London, for plotting against King James I. Cobham implicated Sir Walter Raleigh who was also thrown into the Tower.

By 1604 Raleigh was stripped of all his rights and properties. According to official records, the wardship belonged to Lord Cobham, but Sir Walter was seen to be the guardian. Cecil was obviously unwilling to implicate himself, or to show any close involvement with Raleigh or Cobham. After the execution of Lord Cobham an order was issued by the Court of Wards that the obligations of the late Lord Cobham, for the wardship, should be cancelled.

In 1605, her mother Judith, and her mother's third husband, Sir Richard Corbett, were still trying to regain the wardship, and marriage, of her daughter Elizabeth. They sued Sir Roger Dallison, Sir Walter Raleigh and Dame Elizabeth, his wife, young Walter Raleigh, John Shelbery and Robert Smith. John Shelbury was brought to court for examination, but Dame Elizabeth did not appear, and the Court refused to grant an attachment. The Raleigh family were still a force to contend with. A number of authorities confirm that the betrothal to young Walter was broken, although just when this took place in not known.

However, around 1613 the marriage was arranged between Henry Howard, third son of the Earl of Suffolk, and the young Elizabeth Bassett. Her first child was a son, James, who lived for only a short time, and was buried at Blore, on the 14th December 1614. This was followed by a second child who was stillborn. In 1616, Elizabeth was pregnant again but her husband, Henry Howard, died before this third and only surviving child, a daughter Catherine (Elizabeth?) was born. Catherine (Elizabeth?) lived to marry Sir John Harpur of Swarkestone, reputably the richest man in Derbyshire. An effigy of the daughter is one of the two kneeling figures on the Bassett Tomb at Blore, with the Arms of the Harpur family carved on the rails above the tomb.

The fiery young Walt had plenty of reason to dislike the Howards. Lord Henry Howard, Earl of Suffolk had been responsible for the arraignment and Conviction of his father, Sir Walter Raleigh, at Winchester in November 1603. Howards had also been witnesses for the prosecution at the trial. Young Walt's broken betrothal and Elizabeth's subsequent marriage to a member of that family must have rankled. He quarrelled with one of the Howard family retainers, Robert finett or Tyrwhit, who he killed in a duel and as a result had to flee the country.

Henry's sister, Frances, was involved in a notorious divorce case, and subsequently was accused and found guilty of poisoning Sir Thomas Overbury, a friend of her second husband. Henry Howard died "suddainly at the table," and was buried at Blore, on 10th October 1616. Elizabeth's brief marriage to Henry Howard had given her further opportunity to move in high circles. After Henry's death, his brother Thomas, created Earl of Berkshire in 1626, arranged for the commissioning of his sister-in-law's portrait.

She was courted by Kit Villiers, the brother of the Earl of Buckingham, a rather drunken and coarse young man. It was the courtly manners and gracious ways of the wealthy Sir William Cavendish, son of the Earl of Ogle, that won her over. His letters and poems are preserved in the Portland Collection, which is held in the Nottingham University Library. He tells of his love and pleads with Elizabeth to end her mourning.

In October 1618, Elizabeth married Sir William and took to him the Bassett Estates. According to Margaret, second Duchess of Newcastle, the estates were valued as follows:

The Manor of Blore with Caulton	£ 537. 13. 4.
The Manor of Grindon, Cauldon with Waterfall	£ 822. 3. 0.
The Manor of Cheadle with Kingsley	£ 259. 18. 0.
The Manor of Barlaston etc	£ 694. 3. 0.
	£2349. 17 4.
plus	
The Manor of Litchurch and Mackworth	£ 713.15. 1.
Church and Meynell Langley Manor	£ 850. 1. 0.
Mapleton and Thorpe	£ 207. 5. 0.
	£1771. 1. 1.

This £4120.18.5. represented almost 20% of the total rental of £22,393.10.2, which the Duke of Newcastle was reputed to be worth. It has not been possible to confirm the additional £6/7000 cash that Elizabeth is also reputed to have taken to her new husband.

Sir William was himself not very tall, so that he and the diminutive Elizabeth made a well-matched couple. Many years later Sir William's second wife wrote that God *"made him happy in his first marriage,"* and that Elizabeth was a *"very kind, loving and virtuous lady,"* approved of by his mother.

Elizabeth joined her husband on the family estate at Welbeck. She soon found herself having to act as hostess to Royalty. King James and his royal party called at Welbeck on the 10th August 1619, on his way north to York. Around the same time, her first son, William, was born, but died a year later in 1621. Her husband received letters of condolence dated 20th and 21st April 1621, from The Earl of Arundel and the Earl of Pembroke. A second son was born at their London home, and he was named Charles, in honour of his Godfather, the Prince of Wales, later to become Charles II. Elizabeth returned to Welbeck, but sadly her son died, and she fell seriously ill. With the permission of the King, her husband absented himself from Parliament in March 1621 and stayed at home to be with her for the rest of the year. In 1622 Elizabeth gave birth to the first surviving child of the marriage - daughter Jane, who subsequently married Charles Cheyne.

Sir William commissioned a Dutch portrait painter, Daniel Myton, to paint her portrait. She was 25 years old when it was completed, just in time for it to be shown to King James, who made his second visit to Welbeck in August 1624. The full length portrait of Elizabeth, in a black dress, still exists in the Portland Collection, at Welbeck. The childbearing and serious illness had obviously taken their toll. This portrait does not have the youthful beauty of the previous one.

Another son, also named Charles, was born, in 1626, and he was the first son to survive and subsequently to marry the daughter of Mr Richard Rogers. A daughter, Elizabeth, was born in 1627. In 1639 at the age of 12, too young to be bedded, daughter Elizabeth was married to John Egerton, who later became Earl of Bridgwater. After bearing five sons and one daughter, Elizabeth died in childbirth.

In 1628, Sir William Cavendish attained the rank of Earl of Newcastle and his wife Elizabeth became Countess of Newcastle. In 1630, Elizabeth had another son, Henry, who survived to become Earl of Ogle and married Francis, daughter of William Pierrepoint. After his father's death in 1676, Henry inherited the title of Duke of Newcastle, but outlived his only surviving son. On his death, in 1691, the estates passed to his third daughter, Margaret, who married John Holles, Earl of Clare, for whom the title of Duke of Newcastle was re-created in 1694. It is through this line that the descent of our present Prince Charles of Wales can be traced back to Elizabeth Bassett of Blore and coincidentally through another line, Sarah Ferguson, ex-wife of Prince Andrew.

In 1631, Richard Andrews, an apothecary, or herbalist, in London, wrote: *"I pray heartily for a good hour for my Lady, which I hope this time is come."* This would appear to refer to a pregnancy of one of the seven babies who "died young". No living child is recorded, for that year.

In 1633, Elizabeth was pregnant again and received from Richard Andrew a letter which reads:
May 10, London

"I understand your Ladyship is with child and that therefore you desire to be furnished with such help in physics as shall be fit, and such you have had heretofore. I have therefore sent down to you first a powder to hasten the birth and make it more easy. It is made of cassia, saffron and borax. When you are in travail I would have you take of the powder as much as will lie upon a groat in a spoonful of burnt white wine or beroar water, or spirit of saffron. If you should be long in labour and grow faint, there is an excellent cinnamon water to take a small spoonful of to refresh your spirits. But there is a water in a little glass, called Adrian Gilbert's water, which is commended above all others in childbirth. There are other comfortable waters and spirits sent down in a little "seller" of which you may make use now or at any time. There is also a glass of "Confectio Alchermes" to take a little of when you are fainting, and in the evening you may take the quantity of dry bean, either alone or mingled with cordial water, and four or five grains of beroar stone. I have also sent you an eagle stone which in time of labour being tied about the thigh will make labour easier. I pray that when your time comes you may prove a joyfull mother and make my Lord a glad father when he returns out of Scotland, that so he may the sooner forget his late losses."

The "physics" prescribed were used medicinally to promote various needs of childbirth. Cassia is most probably cinnamon cassia, which was used as a mild laxative, and caused a reaction in the muscles of the lower body, thus assisting childbirth. Saffron was used to relieve flatulence, promote sweating and promote menstruation. Borax is a mild antiseptic. Bezoar (beroar) stone derives from a secretion in the stomach of a goat, but there is no indication of its alleged properties. Confectio Alchermes was a syrupy liquid, probably extracted from Wild or Spanish Bugloss. It was coloured red with cochineal,and recommended for "women with childe to strengthen the childe and preserve life". So far, Adrian Gilbert's water has not been identified.

Her third daughter, Frances, subsequently married Oliver, Earl of Bollingbrook. Frances and her sister Jane, remained behind after Newcastle fled to the continent following the defeat at Marston Moor, in 1644.

King Charles I paid two visits to Welbeck and Bolsover in 1633 and 1634. Sir William and Elizabeth presented for the King's entertainment two special masques, written by the playwright Ben Jonson. The first masque, "The King's Entertainment at Welbeck", and the associated entertainment, food and drink, cost £5,000. However, on 16th June 1634 entertainment was provided, the like of which had never been seen in England before, and probably never since. The cost of the Masque "Love's Welcome at Bolsover", and entertainment, was £15,000 - a lot of money now, but an unimaginable sum in those days.

Her husband lost a fortune - estimated by his second wife at almost One Million Pounds - in the service of the King during the Civil War, when he was Commander-in-Chief of the Royalist Forces in the North. During his many absences from home,he still wrote loving letters to his "Dearest Heart", and continued to write his poetry of love, for her.

Judith, Elizabeth's mother, had married for the third time, to the very wealthy Sir Richard Corbett. In 1640, she died leaving £3,000 to her daughter. It was Elizabeth's mother who arranged for the erection of the magnificent monument in St Bartholomew's Church, Blore. The central figure is Elizabeth's father, William (V) Bassett, and, on his right, is Henry Howard. The figure of Elizabeth is kneeling, in mourning, at the head of her first husband, Henry Howard. The second kneeling figure is Elizabeth's daughter, kneeling at the head of Judith, mother of Elizabeth, and wife of William Bassett. The inscription on the tomb was composed by the Earl of Newcastle, her second husband, who was a prolific writer of verse and prose.

Elizabeth had ten children from this marriage, and three from her previous marriage. A total of seven died in childbirth, or very young. Her health declined over the years, and so it was that while her husband was away at war in Yorkshire, she died at the age of 44. The Marquess of Newcastle rushed home but was too late to be with his wife before she died. She was buried in the family tomb at Bolsover on 19th April 1643.

Elizabeth Bassett lived during a very eventful period of English History, and was closely involved with many of the principal events and characters of that era. Most of all, she was a loving and caring wife who shared the splendours of Welbeck and Bolsover with her devoted husband, surrounded by a loving family.

HENRY HOWARD   *Born 1592 Died September 1616   Buried October 1616 at Blore*

Henry Howard was a member of one of the most powerful families in the Land; Herewards (Howards) had been an important family long before the Norman Conquest. His father's uncle, Henry Howard, Earl of Northampton, was Lord Privy Seal. Another uncle, Charles Howard, Earl of Nottingham, was the Lord High Admiral who commanded the fleet that beat the Spanish Armada. His father, Thomas Howard, acquired the position of Lord Chamberlain, under James I. Thomas was created first Earl of Suffolk and became successor to the most powerful men of Elizabethan times, the Cecils - Lords Treasurers and Masters of the Queens' Wards.

It may have been that his father, Thomas, Earl of Suffolk, used his influence to acquire the wardship of Elizabeth Bassett of Blore. Elizabeth's mother could have no objections to her daughter marrying into such an important family. Not that her objections would have any sway with the Master of the Wards as Judith knew to her cost, from dealings with Robert Cecil.

Around 1613/1614, Henry Howard married Elizabeth Bassett and took up residence at Blore Hall, only twenty miles from his sister Frances's home at Chartley.

Henry and Elizabeth had three children, one stillborn, one son who died in 1614, and a daughter, who was born after Henry's death, in 1616. Subsequently, this daughter Catherine, (some authorities refer to her as Elizabeth), married the richest man in Derbyshire - Sir John Harpur, of Swarkestone.

In addition to holding the position of Lord Treasurer, his father, Thomas, was Justice of the Peace for Staffordshire. Henry joined his father on the bench, and was Justice of the Peace, from 1613 to 1616.

Through the influence of his father, in December 1613, Henry acquired the lands at Manshall Park (Monsal Dale), in Derbyshire, in spite of the fact that these lands had been granted to someone else. In 1614, he inherited considerable property from his father's uncle, Henry Howard, First Earl of Northampton, who had never married.

He was one of seven brothers, Lord Theophilus of Walden and Sir Thomas Howard were older, he was number three. He also had three sisters, Elizabeth, Frances and another.

Through his sister Frances, Henry was involved, although remotely, in one of the most scandalous affairs in British History, that later became known as the Overbury Affair. On 5th January 1606, his sister Frances, at the age of thirteen, was married to the fourteen year old Robert Devereux, Earl of Essex. Immediately after the ceremony the young earl was separated from his bride and sent off to the continent for a period of three years. On his return in late 1609, he found that his wife had fallen in love with Robert Carr - a favourite of King James I. Frances refused to have anything to do with her legal husband, and demanded that her marriage should be made null and void. The grounds for annulment were based upon Robert's alleged inability to consummate the marriage. Henry Howard took his sister's part, and questioned the virility of the Earl of Essex. This resulted in Essex challenging Henry Howard to a duel. They set off separately for the Continent where duelling was legal. Henry's uncle, the Earl of Northampton, was very concerned and instructed the Governor of Calais to watch out for either of the pair. They were intercepted before the duel could take place. King James interfered in the affair, and arranged for a specially selected Commission of Bishops to examine the case. Although there was dissent among the Bishops, five Bishops agreed to vote yes and five refused. The King circumvented this situation, by appointing a further two Bishops who voted yes. So the King's wish prevailed and in 1613 young Frances had her marriage annulled, on the grounds of the impotency of her husband. Subsequently, on the 26th December 1613, she married her sweetheart - Robert Carr, Viscount Rochester, who a few weeks before the wedding, had been created Earl of Somerset.

However, the affair did not stop there. Frances had developed an extreme hatred for Sir Thomas Overbury, a friend of her new husband, who had protested vehemently against the divorce and remarriage. To reduce the tension, and get him out of the way, King James offered Overbury a diplomatic position overseas. Overbury refused the offer, but in such a manner that the King himself took offence, and had Overbury thrown into the Tower. Frances, with vengeance in her heart, bribed various people to arrange that Overbury should be murdered, by poisoning. It was two years before the murder came to light and Frances and her husband were brought to trial, along with those who actually performed the deed. Their trial took place on the 25th May 1616, and great prices were charged for seats in Westminster Hall. John

Chamberlain, a prolific writer whose letters have been preserved amongst the state papers, records that he paid ten shillings for a seat. Frances and her husband Robert were found guilty, but escaped execution by receiving a pardon from the King. They were first imprisoned in the Tower but later allowed to stay together, and placed in "honourable" confinement for the rest of their lives. Frances died in 1632 and her husband in 1645. The poisoners employed to carry out their dirty deed were executed.

It is not known whether Henry Howard was himself involved in the later stages of this affair. He did persist in trying to see Frances whilst she was under arrest, but without success. However, there is no doubt that all members of the Howard Family were affected. The Howard Dynasty was effectively destroyed and a new star, Villiers, later Earl of Buckingham, rose in their place in the position of power next to the King.

Although there was no indication of cause of death it was reported that Henry *"dyed suddainly at the table"*, at the age of only 24 years, in September 1616. In a letter dated 9th October 1616, his uncle, Lord William Howard of Naworth Castle, writes that Henry Howard, who *"he esteemed most of all,"* is dead. Henry was buried on the 11th October 1616, and his effigy lies on the Bassett Tomb, in the side chapel of St Bartholomew's Church, Blore.

SIR WILLIAM CAVENDISH   Duke of Newcastle   *Born 1593 Died 25 December 1676*

William Cavendish was born at Handsworth Hall, near Sheffield. An entry in the register of Handsworth Church reads: "1593, Dec 16th, William son of Sir Charles Cavendish, baptised". Handsworth Hall was owned by Gilbert, Earl of Shrewsbury, a close friend of his father, Sir Charles Cavendish and his mother, Catherine, daughter and heir, of the Baron Ogle. It was from the Earl of Shrewsbury that his father had bought the old ruins of Bolsover Castle. His father commissioned Huntingson Smithson to rebuild Bolsover which William Cavendish enjoyed for much of his lifetime.

William was privately educated and, later, attended St John's College, Cambridge, but did not take a degree. William was knighted, at the age of 18, and progressed through the peerage to become Duke of Newcastle. He led a life in the grand style, and was renown for his elegance, his courtly manners and his generosity. As a rich patron of the arts, writers, poets and philosophers such as Ben Jonson, Hobbes and Rene Descartes gathered at his table. He was a discerning judge of men, and at time of war gathered around him men of ability, action and leadership. George Goring, James King created Lord Eythin, Sir Marmaduke Longdale were Royalist Officers, of note, under his command during the Civil War.

In 1617, William's father died, and William was left with the task of completing the work on Bolsover, which his father started around 1612. Known as the "Horsemanship Duke", his lifelong interest was in training horses in the menage. He began the building of the famous Bolsover Riding School around 1620, and it was completed in 1630. He also built another riding school at Welbeck in the years following 1623.

When Sir William was 26 years in 1618, he married the petite and lovely Elizabeth Bassett. She brought to him her inheritance of the Bassett Estates, valued at over £4000. For twenty four years, they lived happily together at Welbeck and Bolsover, acting as hosts to Royalty and entertaining in lavish style. In the Pillar Room, at Bolsover Castle, still exist the arms of Lord Newcastle with the motto "Cavendo Tutus", a play upon the name Cavendish, meaning "Safety by caution". The arms of his wife, Elizabeth, "Esperance d'avoyr" meaning "Live in hope", also remain. It was Elizabeth's mother, Judith, who erected the monument in St Bartholomew's Church, Blore, in the memory of The Last of the Bassetts. On this tomb, the epitaph to William (V) Bassett, was composed by Sir William Cavendish, who fancied himself as a writer and poet.

His wife, Elizabeth, had three children by her first husband, one was stillborn, one died as a baby and the daughter lived to marry Sir John Harpur of Swarkestone. By her marriage to Sir William Cavendish, Elizabeth bore ten children, although only five of these lived to reach maturity.

In 1623, his mother was declared Baroness Ogle, in her own right, and there were great celebrations at Bolsover. In 1627, when she died, Sir William inherited still greater wealth, as well as title to the Ogle Estates.

In 1628, he was created Earl of Newcastle and from 1628 to 1638 was Lord Lieutenant of the County of Derby. In this role, he was responsible for all the militia in the County, which became his own private army, clothed, fed and paid by him.

Sir William was pleased to accept King Charles I, and his Queen, to Welbeck, on their progress to the North, in 1633. He presented a masque, by Ben Jonson, for their entertainment. In the following year, he provided even more lavish entertainment to the King and Queen, at Bolsover, with an extravagant banquet, and another masque, by Jonson, called "Love's Welcome to Bolsover".

The Earl of Newcastle was not popular at court. In a letter to his wife, dated 8th April 1636, he writes: *"There is nothing I either say or do or hear but it is a crime, and I find a great deal of venom against me, but both the King and the Queen have used me very graciously."*

When King Charles I created his son as Prince of Wales, he appointed the Earl of Newcastle as his Governor. Newcastle, by word of mouth, by written instruction and by example, had a great influence upon the boy who was to be the future King. It was Newcastle who instructed his protege to pay respect to all great ladies. Charles II, subsequently, interpreted this advice too freely in his numerous love affairs. Although he was Governor, to the Prince of Wales, for only three years, from 1638 to 1641, it is reputed to have cost him £40,000. His influence with Charles II continued by close association over the years, and, also, through Queen Henrietta Maria. The Queen was a great admirer of the elegant and gentlemanly ways of the Marquess.

When the Scots invaded England, Newcastle formed his own troop, under the banner of the Prince of Wales. He went north, to join forces with Lord Holland, at Kelso. Unfortunately, there was no love lost between Newcastle and Holland. Holland dismissed Newcastle to the rear, rather than the van, where Newcastle felt his Prince's Troop should be. A personal feud developed, and, with honour at stake, the two of them started to make plans to settle their differences in a duel. Queen Henrietta Maria, as she was to do on several occasions, intervened and cajoled Newcastle into swallowing his pride and forgetting the duel.

In 1641, Charles heard Newcastle's name mentioned in connection with the Army Plot, and, although false, relieved him of his post of Governor. Although Newcastle expressed disappointment at the loss of his post, he was not too put out because he had found some of his duties and associates irksome. He had to share table with Dr Duppe, the tutor to the Prince, who was of low birth and low social standing.

King Charles I was in conflict with Parliament. The situation deteriorated to such an extent that, in 1642, Parliament proposed that the King should surrender his sovereignty - Civil War was inevitable.

Newcastle rallied to the King's cause, and demonstrated his support, by forming his own troop. The War spread to all parts of the Kingdom. The Marquess marched to the relief of York which was besieged by Lord Fairfax, and his son, Sir Thomas Fairfax. He drove off the Parliamentarians.

In April 1643, Newcastle received the news that Elizabeth, his wife, was dying. Newcastle hurried back to Bolsover but arrived too late - she had died. He stayed to arrange her funeral, and burial, in the vaults at Bolsover.

His marriage, to Elizabeth Bassett, had been a happy and fruitful one. She had produced ten children, but, in doing so, her health had obviously been affected.

He replaced Lord Cumberland as Commander in Chief of the Northern Forces. With a very large army at this command, he captured Newcastle-on-Tyne and took over the northern coalfields. From his headquarters in York, he controlled the North. In July 1643, his army severely defeated the Parliamentary forces at Adwalton Moor near Bradford. The leader of the opposing forces, Lord Fairfax, escaped from the battlefield and fled south towards Lincolnshire, but his wife and daughter were captured. Ever noble and courteous, Newcastle personally arranged for Lady Fairfax, and her daughter, to be taken to safety in his own coach.

After the battle of Adwalton Moor, Newcastle and his forces were in command of the whole of Yorkshire, with the sole exception of Hull. His army moved south and drove the Parliamentary forces out of Lincolnshire. He was persuaded to halt his advances southwards, so that the formidable stronghold of Hull could be reduced to submission. However, the halting of his advance to the south allowed the Parliamentary forces to reassert themselves, attacking and subdueing Kings Lynn which had declared for the King.

Newcastle tried to use his wealth to seduce the commander of Nottingham Castle, Colonel Hutchinson, into surrender. His attempted bribes were refused with lofty contempt.

During the long hard winter of 1643/4 there had been little need to defend the northern border. However, by the end of March, the weather improved and the Scots started to advance. It was necessary for Newcastle to move his three thousand Whitecoats and cavalry to meet them. As they marched north, Lord Fairfax and his son, and their army, attacked and chivvied Newcastle's flanks.

The Scots, with a very large army, captured Durham. The Marquess learned that Selby had fallen to the enemy advancing from the South. So with Parliamentary forces closing in from three sides, the only possibility left for him was to seek refuge within the formidable walls of York, until reinforcements could arrive. Three large armies totalling more than 25,000 men lay outside the gates of York. In spite of bombardment of the walls, and frequent attack, Newcastle repelled the enemy. He called on Prince Rupert, nephew of the King, great military hero, and leader of the Royalist Forces, to send reinforcements. Rupert was delayed in his march. In June 1644, he led an army of 15,000 men to the relief of York, and by an unexpected manoeuvre, brought his army to the walls of York, without intervention. He then sent orders to Newcastle, instructing him to march against the enemy immediately.

Newcastle, and his troops, were weary and expecting rest, and perhaps even praise, after their long and hard fought defence of York. Newcastle took offence, and his objections had some justification. He was slow in reacting to the call. The two opposing armies formed, facing each other, on Marston Moor, 25,000 Parliamentarians and Scots against 18,000 Royalists. Newcastle's Whitecoats arrived late, and were placed in the rear, rather than at the front, where their experience and strength would be most useful. As he had always done in previous battles, Prince Rupert wished to attack Cromwell's Army immediately, but was advised by Newcastle, and Lord Eythin, not to do so. In the late evening, the Royalist forces started to relax, and break ranks. At 7.30, one hour before sunset, Cromwell and his cavalry charged. With the benefit of surprise, and the speed and ferocity of his attack, Cromwell was able to rout the feared Royalist Cavalry. His infantry quickly overwhelmed the Lancastrians, and cut their way through to Newcastle's Yorkshire Whitecoats, who fought on, even though hopelessly outnumbered.

The Marquess of Newcastle, with his two sons beside him, stayed with his valiant troops. When defeat became inevitable, he fled from the battlefield, to York declaring, "I will go to Holland. I will not endure the laughter of the court". Newcastle believed his actions had been those of a loyal, and honest, gentleman, and felt that Rupert was totally responsible for all that had happened. Two days later, accompanied by his brother, Sir Charles Cavendish the mathematician, his sons, and a number of other Royalists, he sailed from Scarborough to the continent. He arrived, in Hamburg, with £90 in his pocket, to live in exile for fifteen years. His daughters stayed behind at Welbeck. Two of them, Lady Jane and Lady Frances, were allowed to continue to hold Blore Manor, and Blore Park, "during the pleasure of Parliament". This special dispensation did not last long, because, in 1652, Blore was stated to be in forfeit, to the Commonwealth Commissioners, for treason. It was sold by a Commissioner, called Robert Mellor, to someone of the same name, Richard Mellor of Blore, and John Goring of Kingsley.

Whilst Newcastle was in exile, he called upon the Queen in Paris. He met the lovely, but eccentric, Margaret Lucas and fell in love again. His love letters and love poems to Margaret swept her off her feet. By the end of 1645, they were married, and went to live in his home in Paris.

He moved to Antwerp and then Rotterdam, and back again to Antwerp in August 1647, in the hope of joining forces with Prince Charles. He, and his wife, set up home in the unoccupied house of the painter Rubens. It was in Antwerp that Newcastle set up a riding school and established himself as a leading authority on horsemanship. Some years later, in 1658, he published a very fine book on horsemanship "La Methode Nouvelle et Invention Extraordinaire de dresser Les Chevaux".

His King, Charles I, was executed in January 1649. Newcastle was denounced as a traitor, with the penalty of death on his head. All his lands and property were confiscated.

In November 1651, his wife, Margaret, and his brother, Sir Charles, returned to England, for a period of almost eighteen months. On the 10th December, Margaret made her claim for one fifth of her husband's estate, on the grounds that she had no other means of livelihood. The Committee refused the claim, as she had married Newcastle since he became a delinquent, so that at the time of marriage he had no estate. In the previous year, his two daughters Jane and Francis had successfully claimed one fifth of the estate. Welbeck, and Bolsover, had been badly damaged, and, subsequently, needed a lot of repair and attention.

Sir Charles remained in England and died in May 1659, a great loss to his brother.

When King Charles II returned to the throne in 1660, Newcastle hurried back to England to join him. He left his wife behind in Antwerp, as a guarantee against his many debts. Luckily for Margaret, he was able to raise sufficient cash to get her out of pawn, but for many years after he was in severe financial trouble. His vast wealth had been severely depleted in supporting the cause of King Charles I.

By Royal Assent, on the 13th September 1660, all his estates were returned to him. It was necessary to sell off some of them, in order to repair and maintain those he loved best. He set about restoring his principal estates to their former glory. He re-established a riding school at Bolsover, and with it his authority in horsemanship. In 1661, he was installed as Knight of the Garter, but due to illness at the time, his son Henry went to Windsor to act as his proxy. It was in this year that he was appointed Chief Justice North of the Trent. Newcastle sent a letter to the King, and in return received the following reply:

"King Charles II to Marquis of Newcastle
1664 June 7 Whitehall
I have received yours by your son and am resolved to grant your request Send me therefore word that title you desire to have or whether you will choose to keepe your old and leave the rest to me. I do not tell you I will despatch it tomorrow; you must leave the time to me to accommodate it to some other ends of myne; but the differing it shall not be long nor with any circumstance that shall trouble you. I am glad you enjoy your health for I love you well.   Signed Signet"

On the 16th March 1665, the Marquess of Newcastle was created Duke of Newcastle and drove, with his wife, to London to thank the King personally.

His wife, Margaret, in an effort to support her husband's claims for financial support from the King, wrote his biography " Life of the Duke of Newcastle". This book was full of praise, and adulation, but not entirely in keeping with the true facts. It was published in 1667. The book was particularly notable, because it was written, and published, by a woman - one of the first lady authors. Whether by coincidence, or not, Newcastle obtained repayment of £3,500, the balance of a loan owed to him by the previous King Charles I.

In 1670, in an effort to raise funds, Newcastle sold Meynell Langley, part of the Bassett Estates, to Richard and Isaac Meynell, the sixth and seventh sons of Godfrey Meynell. He was paid £12,524.11s.6d for the Manor plus part of Kirk Langley, excluding the advowson.

Later in 1671, the King gave his consent for a tomb to be erected in Westminster Abbey. In 1671 Newcastle bought, from the Duke of Buckingham, the place where King Charles I had unfurled his banner, on 22nd August 1642 - Nottingham Castle. In 1674, at the age of 83, he began the building of the Renaissance palace which is now the site of the Nottingham museum. The rebuilding was completed by his son, at a total cost of £14,002.17s.9d.

At the age of 50, Margaret died very suddenly in London and was buried, with much pomp, in Westminster Abbey, on the 7th January 1674. Sadly, her husband was too old to travel to attend the funeral.

Three years later, on Christmas Day 1676, the Duke of Newcastle died and his body was carried in state to London, and laid to rest beside his wife, with all the ceremony befitting a rich and noble Lord.

Newcastle had a profound influence upon the events of the Civil War, and upon its ultimate conclusion. He was a proud and honourable man, who worked to a very strict code of principle, and was a loyal and faithful servant to two Kings.

CAVENDISH - HOLLES - HARLEY

After the death of William Cavendish Duke of Newcastle in 1676, all his lands, including Blore, were inherited by his son Henry Cavendish, 2nd Duke of Newcastle, who married Frances Pierrepoint in 1653. He lived at Bolsover and commissioned a painting of the castle which is in the collection at Welbeck Abbey. Henry died in 1691 without male heir, and his third daughter, Margaret Cavendish, became heir to the Newcastle Estates.

In 1690, Lady Margaret Cavendish married John Holles, Fourth Earl of Clare, who revived the title Duke of Newcastle. When the earl died, there was again no male heir, so that the estate passed to their daughter, Henrietta Cavendish Holles, who married Edward Harley, 2nd Earl of Oxford, in 1713. The Countess of Oxford founded a school at Bolsover, and moved many of the paintings and the furniture from Bolsover to Welbeck.

In 1755, the estates once more passed through the female line to Margaret Cavendish Harley. She married the Second Duke of Portland with whose descendants the estates have remained, to the present day.

THE RIVETTS OF DERBY AND BLORE

Per pale argent and sable on a chevron between three lozenges as many martles countercharged; Crest: a cubit arm erect vested bendy argent and sable cuffed of the last holding in the hand proper a broken sword of the 1st hilt and pommel; Motto: "Holde faste"

The story of the Rivetts, and their holding in Blore, is partly based upon the book by the late Mr D.C. Rivett-Carnac OBE, "The Rivett Family of Repton and Derby (1538-1909)". The Author is grateful to Mr Rivett-Carnac for his encouragement and also for his permission to share the information.

Thomas (III) Rivett was born in 1678/9. He married Elizabeth Eaton of Derby, on the 9th December 1708, at St Peter's Church, Derby. Around 1708, he gave up the family trade of Maltster and concentrated on local affairs and extending the family landholdings. In 1715/16, he was elected Mayor of Derby. Around 1718, he acquired Blore Manor, and with it, the right to present his own nominee to the Rectory of Blore Church. Thomas (III) died, in 1724, leaving his wife, and seven young children.

Thomas (IV) Rivett, the fourth child and eldest son of Thomas (III), was born in Derby in 1713. His education had been well provided for by a Tuition Bond, signed jointly by his mother and his mother's aunt, Elizabeth Eaton.

In 1728, still under age, he was required to exercise the right to nominate a new Rector for Blore Church. Together with his mother, as his guardian, he nominated Rev William Blackwall, in a presentation deed dated 16th September 1728. Rev Blackwall was probably related to Elizabeth Rivett, whose grandmother, the wife of Richard Eaton, was born Blackwall. Unfortunately, Rev Blackwall died in 1732. It was necessary for Thomas and his mother to make a further presentation to the Church. This time he nominated Rev Charles Sibley of Bath, under a deed dated 4th April 1732. Thomas Rivett subsequently married Anna Maria Sibley, the daughter of Rev Sibley. Rev Sibley died at Blore on the 24th May 1740.

Thomas (IV) attended the Inner Temple, in 1731/2, and was called to the Bar in 1739. He made a third presentation to the Rectory of Blore in 1740. Rev Aden Ley had been curate of Blore some years previously, and was Vicar of Ilam at the time of this presentation to Blore Church. The Rev Ley retained his vicarship of Ilam until his death on 21st April 1752, and was buried at Ilam.

Thomas Rivett became a Justice of the Peace on 13th July 1744, and was appointed Deputy Lieutenant of Derbyshire in 1745. The position of Deputy Lieutenant has always been much sought after, for the recognition and the social prestige it bestows upon the holder. However, one important purpose of the office was to muster all able men within the shire and form the militia to provide home defence. In the year 1745, Bonnie Prince Charlie marched down from Scotland. Any social prestige of the position of Deputy Lieutenant was blighted by the necessity to find solutions to a potentially very serious national problem, within the bounds of Derbyshire.

With the approach of the Scottish Army, the Lord Lieutenant of the county, the Duke of Devonshire, instructed that two regiments should be formed under his command. Among the local gentry there was some support for the Jacobite cause, and for Bonnie Prince Charlie, the lawful contender for the throne - a number of men refused Commissions. Whether he liked it or not, and whatever his own beliefs, there was no way that the Deputy Lieutenant could refuse a Commission in one of the companies. Thomas Rivet Esq is listed as a Captain of one of the two Derby Companies of The Derbyshire Blues. Mr Fra Rivet, most probably his brother, was given a commission as Lieutenant.

The Scottish Army was reputed to be seven thousand strong. The militia that were mustered, were only six hundred in number; which probably demonstrates the serious lack of support. With such weakness in numbers, discretion was obviously the better part of valour as the Scots approached Derby.

The Duke of Devonshire ordered a withdrawal, and he, and his Derbyshire Blues, retreated to Nottingham, and then to Mansfield.

When Bonnie Prince Charlie, and his army, entered Derby, the Duke of Perth lodged, during his brief stay, with Thomas's mother, Mrs Rivett, at her home at 14 Tenant street .

On 25th October 1746, his mother died, and was buried at All Saints Church, Derby. Her will named Thomas as sole executor, and legatee, which together with the legacies from his father, gave him total control over all Rivett Properties.

Sir Robert Walpole, Prime Minister, referred to Thomas Rivett as the Duke of Devonshire's "chief friend and manager". However, in 1748, Thomas allowed himself to be nominated as Candidate in opposition to the Duke's own candidate - Mr John Stanhope. Thomas was elected as Member of Parliament for Derby by a significant margin of 71 votes: 382 Votes for Rivett, 311 for Stanhope. One of his staunchest supporters was Miss Anna Marie Sibley, daughter of the late rector of Blore, who was still living in the Rectory at Blore. She is reputed to have worn a Blue and White Cockade during his election campaign. This blue and white rosette that Anna Maria wore on her hat, may have had special significance. Blue was (and is) the colour of the Tories, and white the colour of the party of the White Rose - the Jacobites. Derby was a major stronghold of Jacobite supporters, and the fact that his wife-to-be wore their colours, may, indicate his own following. The fact that Thomas subsequently stood against the Whig Candidate, would also support this view. His mother provided lodgings for the Duke of Perth. If Thomas was of Jacobite persuasion, would he have influenced the withdrawal from Derby, by The Blues, not just because they were outnumbered? According to the "Gentleman's Magazine", Thomas Rivett married "the celebrated" Anna Marie Sibley in April 1749.

The fourth presentation to the Rectory of Blore during his lifetime, was in 1752: Rev George Gretton, Anna Maria's Grandfather.

Thomas Rivett remained a Member of Parliament for five years, until 1754. He was persuaded not to stand again, by the promise of a place in some of the inferior commissions and in the meantime £300 per year, from a special fund, known as secret service money. This fund was used for "pensions", and other such payments, which were regarded as expedient by the government and crown. In this case, a "pension" was to ensure that Thomas would not compete again in the by-elections. He continued to receive his £300 annual payment until he died in 1763.

The 3rd Duke of Devonshire died in 1755. By 1757, under the 4th Duke, any rift had obviously been mended, helped perhaps by the "pension". Whatever the past differences with the 4th Duke's father, Thomas had obviously regained a high esteem. He was made Deputy Lieutenant of Derbyshire once again, followed by High Sheriff of Derbyshire in 1757/8. In 1761/1762, he was elected Mayor of Derby, and, in 1762, he was appointed Deputy Lieutenant for the third time.

Thomas Rivett held extensive lands in Calton. As Lord of the Manor, he held Court Baron on 13 October 1752, 5th May 1759 and 20th May 1761, dealing with the rights of Lord and Tenant within the Manor.

In 1763, a Master in Chancery approved the appointment of twelve new trustees for the Catherine Port Chantry, including Thomas Rivett.

Thomas (IV) Rivett died at Bath on 6th April 1763, and his will was proved at Lichfield on 10th May 1763. On the 26th February 1764, the Manor of Calton was sold by Anna Maria Rivett and Francis Rivett, to John Sparrow (later Port), of Ilam, being devisees in trust for the will of Thomas Rivett. His interest in Blore Manor was sold to Samuel Shore of Norton Hall, South Yorkshire.

THE SHORES

Argent two chevronels sable between three holly leaves slipped vert
Crest: a stork reguardant argent ducally crowned beaked and membered gules holding in dexter claw a pebble
proper gorged with a collar gemel sable in the beak a holly leaf slipped in vert. Motto: "Non dormit qui custodit"

The family of Shore, who held Blore, from 1758 to 1868, were descended from a long line of bankers, merchants and landowners in Yorkshire and Derbyshire.

The most famous member, of the Shore family, was Florence Nightingale, the Lady with the Lamp, who nursed the soldiers during the Crimean War. Her father, William Edward Shore, assumed the maiden name of his grandmother, Nightingale, by Royal Sign in 1815. He inherited the estates of his maternal great uncle, Peter Nightingale, and thus, Florence inherited the name Nightingale.

William Edward's grandfather, Samuel Shore of Meersbrook, married Urith Offley, of Norton Hall, on 15th March 1759, six weeks after his 21st birthday. They moved into Norton Hall, then in Derbyshire, but now within the Metropolitan District of Sheffield. A year later, at the age of only 22, Samuel Shore was appointed as High Sheriff of the County of Derby.

Samuel Shore's father, also named Samuel, acquired Blore in 1758. By a family settlement in 1768, he released to his son extensive estates in Bedfordshire, Essex, Sussex, Suffolk, and Norfolk, plus the Manor of Blore and Blore Park in Staffordshire.

George Gretton was the Rector of Blore, but rarely visited the Parish, and a curate ministered the Parish for him. When Samuel Shore, junior, became Lord of the Manor, the Rector was quick to make an arrangement to exchange the tithes of Blore for seventeen acres of Blore Dale Pasture and a small croft called Grimley Gap. Being an absentee Rector, it was obviously beneficial to acquire land rather than receive the doubtful benefit, to him, of grazing fifty two sheep, and a horse, and a twinter, and collecting the tithes of corn and hay in kind.

Although Samuel Shore was a dissenter, he still maintained his responsibilities as Lord of the Manor and Patron of Blore Church. In 1786, he presented the Rev William Bayliffe as Rector of Blore.

Mr Shore was one of the leading citizens of Sheffield. In 1819, he chaired a vast public meeting, of many thousands of local people, assembled to join the countrywide complaint about the "Manchester Massacre". Manchester Magistrates had ordered troops to attack, and disperse a meeting, which resulted in a number of deaths.

His wife shared his status. She was one of the "Madams" of Sheffield. As part of their "uniform", these high-ranking ladies often wore their gowns with cane hoops near the bottom, forty or more inches in diameter, and to enter a door they had to pull their gown bottoms aslant to obtain entrance.

Samuel Shore never lived in Blore, but had a series of well-to-do tenants at Blore Hall. In the British Library, is an extract of the lease of Blore to Mr John Sutton dated 1764. In 1792, John Sutton left an estate valued about £2,000, and recommended his wife, and son, to *"my worthy landlord Samuel Shore Esquire"*, as Joint Tenants to his farm at Blore.

Samuel Shore died 1st November 1836 and in his will, left his property to be divided among his children. Offley Shore received the Blore Estate, as part of his inheritance.

After Samuel's death, the surviving members of the family lacked the deep interest and involvement in the running of the family business - Parkes, Shores & Blackelock Bank, based in Snig Hill, Sheffield. This lack of involvement contributed to the serious difficulties which overtook the Bank. In 1843, the Bank closed its doors, causing widespread ruin and disaster for the Customers, and for the Shore Family. The Bank had operated under the old UNlimited rules, which meant that the private estates of the Family had to be sold off to satisfy their Creditors. It took eighteen years to settle the banks affairs, and even then, only 13s.0d in the £ was paid out.

In 1861, Harrington Offley Shore married Isabel Emma Coke, but 3 years later on the 11th November 1863, Isabel died at the age of 25. Harrington erected the memorial East Window of Blore Church in memory of his wife.

In 1865, he remarried, to Eleanor "Annie" Thomson and shortly afterwards the Shore holding in Blore was sold to the Okeover Family. At this time the saleable value was estimated at £35,000 against which a mortgage of £11,415 was held.

THE BASSETTS AND THE OKEOVERS

The Bassetts were important members of the traditional ruling group of Staffordshire/Derbyshire Gentry. They established and maintained their position in this group by judicious social economic and political relationships. Of premier importance was their relationship with the Okeovers of Okeover.

The Okeovers are one of the oldest recorded families in England. Their descent is traceable with absolute certainty to the Eleventh Century and with high probability before that to Noble Saxon Ancestors.

A history of the Okeover family was written by Major General G. Wrottesley, Antiquarian, and Staffordshire Historian, and published in Collections for a History of Staffordshire (SHC) Volume New Series VII.

During the period that the Bassetts were Lords of Blore there is plenty of evidence of the unusual harmony and understanding between the two families. This was established by geography, friendship, marriage, economics, politics, military service and mutual defence. Okeover is geographically located in Staffordshire, in an isolated area of the Peak Foothills, and shares common boundaries with Blore. Okeover and Blore are isolated to the East and South by the Rivers Dove and Manifold, and to the West and North by the bleak upper moorlands of Swinscoe. Swinscoe is within the Parish of Blore-with-Swinscoe but has been held in part by the Okeovers for eight hundred years.

In friendship, the two families were able to make exchanges of land, and each consolidate their own landholdings, without argument or disagreement. No evidence of land or boundary disputes have been found in spite of common boundaries and geographical proximity. They were always available to each other as witnesses to important documents, particularly those which needed close and trusted allies and friends. With common interests, they were among the principal subscribers to the foundation of Ashbourne Grammar School.

Philip Okeover married Thomasine Bassett, daughter of Ralph Bassett, in 1439, and being underage, grew up as a member of the Bassett household. He subsequently is referred to as "Philip Okeover late of Blore". One hundred years later, in 1536, Ralph Okeover married Mawde Bassett, daughter of Sir William (IV) Bassett of Blore.

Philip Okeover, as Sheriff of Staffordshire, nominated his friend and neighbour William (VI) Bassett as Member of Parliament in 1586/7.

In response to calls to arms against the Welsh, and the Scots, and the French, the Okeovers and the Bassetts served together in the Wars. During the turbulent 15th Century, they maintained a common front, and jointly formed their own band of armed men to defend their estates. William (II) Bassett and Philip Okeover were together members of the 1461 Commission of Array, to call Staffordshire men to arms against the Lancastrians.

Although the Okeovers were Lords of the Manor of Swinscoe for many centuries, it was not until the middle of the 19th Century that the opportunity arose for them to acquire Blore. Due to severe financial problems in the Shore family, Blore was taken into Chancery. Over the period from 1850 to 1865, the Okeovers negotiated the purchase of Blore, including The Waterings comprising 743 Acres, valued at £35,000 and an annual rental of £940.

LOCAL TALES AND FOLKLORE

There are many interesting tales relating to the Parish and its people, and some of these
are recounted once again:

RISEN FROM THE DEAD

With the kind permission of Mrs C Heath, of Onecote, the following is a copy of a tattered handwritten document in her possession. The following is a Summary of the contents of the Manuscript, which, unfortunately, is undated:

"A TRUE STORY"

"I am a man in years and a story comes to my mind which my grandfather told me when I was a boy." In the Moorlands there is a Church in the Parish of Bloor on the border of Staffordshire. Near the Church is a large farm.

During the early part of last century there lived a family by the name of Bassetts within the Parish above mentioned. The family are all dead many years ago and are interred in a vault beneath the Altar. Years afterwards a family named Smith lived on the farm, near the church. There were six servants, three men and three women. Mary Brown, one of the three servants from the farm, cleaned the Church, and Arthur Johnson, a man servant, also from the farm, went into the Church and told Mary Brown that he would go into the Bassett's Vault. He found the key in the vestry, entered the vault and in a short time came out carrying a human skull, which he said was Bassetts. Mary Brown hurried out of the church and hastened to the farm where she told the occupants what she had seen. Arthur Johnson returned the skull to its resting place, placed the key where he had found it in the vestry, locked the Church door and took the key to the farm house. The next day, Mrs Smith complained of being unwell and early in the evening the Master advised her to go to bed and in a while they would bring her something to do her good. Later that evening Mr Smith and the servants were in the kitchen sitting round the fire. The men servants were dressing feathers, one woman was knitting, one sewing and one darning stockings. As they worked they told ghost stories and the Master said he would give half a guinea to any one of them who would fetch Bassett's skull out of the vault at twelve o'clock. The younger servant, Sarah Hassett, said she would fetch it, but would not take it back that night, so they all sat up until twelve o'clock. She then lighted a candle, put it into a lantern, and made her way through the small planting that led to the church. She entered the Church, took the key of the vault from the vestry, brought out the skull, re-locked the door of the vault and placed the key in the vestry where she found it. The story appears to be continued in her own words "In retracing my steps through the planting after locking the Church door I saw the figure of a woman whom I thought was my Mistress, walking before me to the front door of the farm house. She then disappeared. Of course I felt greatly afraid, but I entered the house and laid the skull on the table. I said 'Its there' the Master said 'Well, you are a brave girl' and gave me the half guinea and we all went to bed. The next morning, I, Sarah Hassett, and my fellow servant, Mary Brown, conveyed the skull to the vault."

During the next day a doctor was sent for to visit Mrs Smith as she was very ill - she kept getting worse and in a few days the Doctor testified that she was dead. In due course the funeral took place and she was interred in a vault near the Chancel inside the Church. It appeared that the Sexton at a late hour at night entered the Church with the intention of robbing the dead as he thought. He had made preparation, lantern and candle lighted in it. He took a knife and screwdriver with him, entered the vault and took off the coffin lid. Mrs Smith had some valuable rings on her finger which he attempted to take off, but was unable to do so without the use of a knife. In cutting off the rings he cut the finger of the "dead" woman and it began to bleed. She then began to open and shut her eyes. The moment the Sexton saw her movements he was afraid and in his fear ran out of the Church. He left the light in the vault and not stopping to lock the Church door made off for home. About two o'clock in the morning there was a loud rap at the door of the farm. One of the servants named Emma Morris got up to the window and asked who was there. The answer was 'Mrs Smith'. Emma Morris went and knocked at the Master's bedroom door and told him that Mrs Smith was at the front door. He answered "Get off to bed with you, you know your Mistress was interred in the vault yesterday". Emma Morris said "Vault or no vault, the Mistress is at the front door with a light in her hand." The Master got up and looked through the window, and at once

Dovedale Hill

Dovedale Hill from Ox Leisure (Ilam Meadows)

recognised her as his wife. In haste downstairs, opened the door and let her in. She has a lantern and candle lighted in her right hand. The left hand was bleeding. Mr Smith said to his wife "that is William Baddeley's lantern. Where have you had it from?" She replied "I found the light on the floor of the vault, the Church door was unlocked and I made my way home." Mr Smith sent Arthur Johnson for William Baddeley the sexton, as he recognised the lantern, but he would not come. He sent again the aforesaid servant to tell the sexton he need not be afraid for what he had done, for it was his intention to reward him for his bravery. Mr and Mrs Smith afterwards lived happily together for a number of years, and after this incident had a family of three children."

Although some research has been carried out, to try and partially verify this "true story", nothing of any significance has come to light. Blore Hall Farm did used to have a "planting" between it, and the church. None of the servants names given in the "true story" have been found in the Blore Parish Registers of Births, Marriages or Deaths: Mary Brown, Arthur Johnson, Sarah Hassett, Emma Morris; although, as servants they would not necessarily have been recorded within the Parish Records. There is no trace of a Sexton named William Baddeley, although there was a field called Baddeley Meadow on Ellis Hill Farm; fields are often named after people who have farmed them. Smiths have lived at Blore Hall, from time to time, but it has not been possible to relate them to the Smiths, of our story.

Bill Oldham, of Doveridge, a descendant of a family of Smith who lived at Blore Hall, repeated what may be a corroborative story, that his father often told: *"A Mrs Smith had died, and was being carried in her coffin, when one of the bearers stumbled. One of the other bearers yelled, "Don't wake the old bugger up AGAIN!!!"* This story mentions the key to the vault, which is kept in the vestry. The vault itself has no door; the entrance is down steep and awkward steps beneath heavy flagstones, just inside the entrance to the Bassett Chapel. There are double doors in the screen at the entrance to the Bassett Chapel, which implies that it was the door in the screen that was locked. However the present slabs, placed over the entrance, are much too heavy for one person to move. It is hard to believe that the coffin was placed in the vault, without the vault being closed or sealed, but this could have been the case, immediately after the funeral.

It must be recorded, that a very similar story about a young wife buried in a tomb in Chapel Wood, opposite the entrance to Charnes Hall at Croxton, is related in "Staffordshire and the Black Country" by Michael Raven. Similar stories are common folklore.

THE BASSETT SKULL Another story, relating to the Bassett Skull, in the vault in Blore Church. According to the Rev J.H. Young, the vault below the Bassett Tomb was plundered for the lead coffins, or more likely, their valuable contents. He tells of a report that the skull of the Last of the Bassetts was left behind. Subsequently, the skull was taken from the vault by a cleaning woman at the Church, and given to a doctor who lived in Uttoxeter. When the doctor died, the skull was publicly sold along with the rest of his effects, and was reputed to be in the hands of a well-known Ashbourne tradesman in 1903. In spite of advertising for information concerning the skull, nothing has been found.

MYSTERIOUS VISITOR The Deanery Magazine, March 1894, tells the following story:
"A gang of mules and asses in the charge of 'Old stout' were passing Blore Lime Kiln after having delivered Coal to Ilam Hall. 'Old stout' found a gentleman lying exhausted and unable to carry on. The ganger put him on the back of a quiet mule and took him to the Inn at Calton Moor kept by a family named Gilman. The stranger asked to stay for a few days as he felt very unwell. Next morning he was no better and after first consulting a cow-leech, who could do nothing, it was suggested that a doctor should be called, but the stranger refused. However after a few days the situation became serious and Dr Hall was called. The doctor carried out his examination only to find that the stranger was a lady.

At that time the Rev Frederick Day was private tutor to the sons of John Russell at Ilam. The Rev Day was called and he talked to the Lady who admitted to being of noble birth but pledged him to secrecy. Her death occurred a day or two later and a special messenger was sent to a Country Seat in Cheshire. Her funeral at Blore Church was attended by a heavily veiled elderly lady who arrived in a hired coach from Leek.

Who or what the deceased lady was is not known but an entry in the Parish Register reads as follows: "Ellen H—- of C—-- Aged 21 buried 10th March 1844 Frederick Day, Officiating Minister. This young woman had wandered about in the disguise of a man's clothing for 'several years, through England, Wales and Ireland and died at Calton Moor House.' (Since this entry was originally made in the Register, the name and place have been completed: Ellen HATFIELD (alias HADFIELD) of Chapel-en-le-Frith).

After a few days the grave had sunk and it was assumed that the body had been stolen. The Rector, Rev Hugh Wood, instructed the Sexton, George Bott, to reopen the grave. Mr Bott always swore that he found the coffin burst, and saw the hand of the corpse, but two others, Robert Yates and Thomas Stubbs, of Swinscoe, both firmly believed that the lady's friends had taken the body away.

ROUNDHEADS AND CAVALIERS
Local folklore says that Cromwell and some of his troops were stationed at Throwley, and that the Cavaliers were at Tissington. But the association of Throwley is with Thomas Cromwell, the henchman of King Henry VIII, not with Oliver Cromwell. Thomas Cromwell acquired Throwley and it duly descended to the Earl of Cathcart, who still held it in the 1860s. The roundheads are reputed to be associated with the removal of the hands of the effigies on the Bassett Tomb. It was more likely just plain vandalism, which unfortunately still continues to the present day.

Tissington was one of the strongholds of the fervent Catholic, and Royalist, supporters - the Fitzherberts. It is possible that the Cavaliers were at Tissington but no specific record has been found.

ELI, THE FRIENDLY GHOST
A ghost is reputed to wander up and down Yerley Hill, between Mappleton and Blore Hall. A number of people report having seen a tall thin figure dressed in black, like the man on the Sandeman Port bottle, but wearing a tall hat. One resident of Mappleton says that she saw the ghost quite often when she was a young girl. At Mappleton Post Office, a chair caught on fire and the occupants tried frantically to get the burning chair out of the house, but without success. A slim tall man in black suddenly appeared, took the chair, and threw it into the garden. He then disappeared as quickly as he had arrived. The owners tried to find the man, but were told by a little girl that he had gone, but his name was Eli, her friend. A farmer on Yerley Hill says that he has seen the ghost on a couple of occasions, near or walking past his farm. A retired couple who used to live at Lees House, report that they both saw Eli a number of times, although George and Mo Mansfield, ex-tenants who moved to The Waterings, say they never saw the ghost. There are stories of a similar figure being seen at Blore Hall.

SPIRITS AND GHOSTS OF BLORE HALL
A Clairvoyant who visited Blore Hall reported that there are three other ghosts in different parts of Blore Hall. There was a young stable lad aged around 18 who was beaten to death by his Master. This is the ghost who switches the TV on and off. A very pretty young girl who wears a mob cap has been seen. In one of the holiday cottages that used to be called Grindleford, someone had a nasty end.

GHOST OF SCOTTISH SOLDIER
The cottage, called Fairbrook, next to the Dog & Partridge in Swinscoe, was used by visiting cabaret artists. One of those was Diana Dors, a radio, TV and film star, who during one of her visits reported that she had seen a ghost in the cottage. The ghost was thought to be one of the Scottish soldiers, from Bonnie Prince Charlie's Army, who were reputedly killed on their retreat from Derby.

BIBLIOGRAPHY

British Library CLEO EIV 285
College of Arms Vincent 133   Historic Manuscripts Commission
Collections for a History of Staffordshire
Victoria County History of Staffordshire
North Staffordshire Field Club Journal
Derbyshire Archaeological and Natural History Journal
Letters and Papers Henry VIII   HMSO
List of Sheriffs   HMSO
Calendar of Patent Rolls   HMSO
Okeover Charters,   Matlock Record Office 231M
Rutland MSS
Blore Parish Registers,   Public Record Office, Stafford
Salt Manuscript, 459 ii,   William Salt Library, Stafford
Harlaeian Manuscript 818, 45b
Wills and Administrations   Lichfield Joint Record Office
"The Complete Peerage"
"Dictionary of National Biography"
"The Deanery Magazine/Our Parish Magazine"   Deanery of Alstonefield"
"Derbyshire Life" January 1983
"Ashbourne Telegraph"
Genealogical Research Directory 1986 - 1992
Family History Knowledge 1991 - 1992/3
N.W. Alcock "Old Title Deeds" 1986
T. Allen "Blore-with-Swinscoe   Parish Magazine Historical Notes"
T. Allen "Roll of Blore Church Clergy" (also Hutchinson " Archdeaconry of Stoke-on-Trent")
Archeologia Vol 42 1869 "Inventory of Earl of Northampton"
Armitage, Harold "Chantrey Land" 1910
Ashmole "Staffordshire Arms & Inscriptions 1662" - Wm Salt Ref 252 dated 10 August 1661 p 81, 82, 83 (own doc no.42)
T.C. Banks "Dormant Baronage"
T Bateman "Ten Years Digging in Celtic & Saxon Grave Hills in County of Derby, Stafford and York" 1861
C.F. Broughton The History and Topography of Ashbourne, The Valley of the Dove and the Adjacent Villages" 1839
Burke "Landed Gentry"
S.A.H. Burne "Essays in Staffordshire History"
Dom Bede Canon "Forgotten Shrines"
Stanley D. Chapman "The Early Factory Masters" 1967
C.R. Cheney "Handbook of Dates"
Joy Childs "Tudor Derbyshire" 1985
J. Cox "Churches of Derbyshire"
J. Cox "Three Centuries of Derbyshire Annals"
Maxwell Craven "A Derbyshire Armory"
P Cunnington "How old is your house"
R.K. Dent & J. Hill "Historic Staffordshire" (1896/1975)
Douglas D.C. "History" Vol XXVII pp 127 - 147 1943
Dugdale Derby MS 3461 "Bassett Pedigree - Visitation 1583"
Dugdale "Monasticon"
Duignan "A Survey of Staffordshire Place Names" 1902
Duncan, Jonathan, "The Dukes of Normandy from the times of Rollo to the Expulsion of King John" 1839
Eardley Simpson "Derby and the Forty Five" 1933
Edward Edwards "Life of Raleigh" 1868
Rev R.W. Eyton "Domesday Studies"
P.A. Faulkner " Bolsover Castle Official Handbook"
H.P.R. Finberg & V.H.T. Skipp "Local History" 1967
Michael J. Fisher "Dieulacres Abbey"
Susan Foster "Tudors & England - Collections and Collectors" "History Today" Dec 1985 p 22
DV Fowkes&GR.Potter "William Senior's Survey of Estates of the First and Second Earls of Devonshire 1600-28"
H.J.H. Garratt "Derbyshire Feet of Fines 1323-1546" 1985
Irene Gladwin "The Sheriff" 1974
Glover & Riden "William Woolley's Derbyshire"
Eileen A Gooder "Latin for Local History" 1961
Douglas Grant "Margaret the First" 1957
John Richard Green " Short History of the English People"
Greenslade & Stuart "A History of Staffordshire" 1965
S.M. Harrison "Henry VIII and The Dissolution of the Monasteries" 1985
Rev Thos Harwood "A Survey of Staffordshire by Sampson Erdeswicke" 1844
F.A. Hibbert "The Dissolution of Monasteries" 1910
C.P. Hill "Who's Who in History" Vol III 1603 - 1714
W.G. Hoskins "The Age of Plunder" 1976
W.G. Hoskins "Local History in England" 1972

W.G. Hoskins "The Midland Peasant" 1957
W.G. Hoskins "Fieldwork in Local History" 1982
W.G. Hoskins "The Making of the English Landscape" 1955
J. Hurstfield "The Queens Wards"
Lucy Hutchinson "Memoirs of the Life of Colonel Hutchinson"
E.W. Ives, R.J. Knecht & J.J. Scarisbrick "Wealth and Power in Tudor England" - "Against the taking away of Women"
S.A. Jeavons "Staffordshire Glass, Fonts & Woodwork"
I.H. Jeayes "Derbyshire Charters"
T.S. Jennings "History of Staffordshire Bells"
F.J. Johnson "Settlement Patterns of North East Staffs" 1964
Rev C. Kerry "Volume of Pedigree" 1901
Kunitz & Haycraft "British Authors before 1800"
Agnes Latham "Sir Walter Raleigh's Farewell Letter to his wife in 1603" Essays and Studies XXV 1940
Leader "Sheffield in 18th Century"
Lecomte, Edward "The Notorious Lady Essex" 1969
Leigh "History of Ashbourne"
Leland's "Itinerary of England and Wales"
Lindley, David "The Trials of Frances Howard"
Margaret, Duchess of Newcastle "The Life of William Cavendish"
Matter, Joseph Allen "My Lord and Lady Essex"
K.B. McFarlane "The Nobility of Later Mediaeval England" 1963
Rosemary Milward "Glossary of Household, Farming and Trade Terms from Probate Inventories" 1986
J.B. Mitchell " Historical Geography" 1954
George Morris "Shropshire Genealogies"
J.F. Moxon "Old North Staffordshire I & II" 1972
Murrays "Handbook of Derby, Notts, Leicester & Stafford" 1892
Arthur Mee "King's England - Staffordshire"
J.E. Neale " The Elizabethan House of Commons"
Duchess of Newcastle "The Life of the Duke of Newcastle" 1667
Nicholls "History and Antiquities of Leicestershire"
J. Nightingale "Beauties of England and Wales - Stafford" 1813
D.M. Palliser " The Staffordshire Landscape" 1976
William Pitt "Topographical History of Staffordshire" 1817
R. Plant "History of Cheadle" 1881
Robert Plot "Natural History of Staffordshire"1686
Lindsey Porter "The Staffordshire Moorlands" pictures from past
R.B. Pugh "How to write a Parish History" 1954
P.H. Reaney "Dictionary of British Surnames" 1976
Redfern "History & Antiquities of Uttoxeter"
J. Richardson "The Local Historian's Encyclopedia" 1974
D.C. Rivett-Carnac "The Rivett Family of Repton and Derby" 1980
ROLLS SERIES "Chronicon Monasterii de Abingdon"
Marie Rowlands "West Midlands
Trevor Rowley "The High Middle Ages 1200-1550"
I.D. Rowney Univ of Keele Thesis "Staffordshire Political Community 1440 - 1500" 1981
Christine Smith "The Drayton Dynasty" 1980
Stebbing Shaw "History and Antiquities of Staffordshire"
W.A. Shaw "The Knights of England"
Eardley Simpson "Derby and the Forty-Five" 1933
John Sleigh "History of Leek"
Christine Smith "Drayton Dynasty"
Robert Speake "Audley - An out of way quiet place"
William Stebbing "Sir Walter Raleigh" 1899
John Stow "The Survey of London
D. Stuart "A Social History of Yoxall in 16th/17th centuries"
D. Stuart "Croxden Staffordshire" 1984
W.E. Tate "The Parish Chest"1983
P.D. Thomson D.D. "Parish and Parish Church" 1935
Kate Tiller "English Local History" 1992
Tilley "Old Halls"
Geoffrey Trease "Portrait of a Cavalier" 1979
David Tredale "Local History Research and Writing" 1974
Eva Tuff "Graves and Memorials - The Church of St Bartholomew Blore 1994"
C.V. Wedgwood "The Kings Peace 1637 - 1641" 1983
C.V. Wedgwood "The Kings War 1641 - 1647" 1983
White, Beatrice "A Cast of Ravens"
Anne Whiteman "Compton Census"
John Winton "Sir Walter Raleigh" Michael Joseph 1975
Margaret Wood "The English Mediaeval House" 1965
Susan M. Wright "The Derbyshire Gentry in 15th Century" 1983

INDEX

Bott, Hannah 113, 125
Bott, John 125
Bott, Joseph 125
Bott, Louisa 101
Bott, Mary Ann 113, 125
Bott, Mary Elizabeth 125
Bott, Mr 128
Bott, Mrs 123
Bott, Samuel 101, 125
Bott, Sarah 113
Bourne, Hugh 35
Bourne, James 35
Bowring Hanbury, Mrs 127
Bradbourne, Henry 158
Bradbourne, John 167
Bradbury, Bert 147
Bradbury, Daniel 147
Bradbury, Doreen 49
Bradbury, Enid 147
Bradbury, Enid Rosemary 147
Bradbury, Ivy Elizabeth 147
Bradbury, James 28, 147
Bradbury, James David 37, 147
Bradbury, James William 147
Bradbury, John Antony 147
Bradbury, Margaret Rose 37, 147
Bradbury, Nancy 147
Bradbury, Owen 147
Bradbury, Richard 28
Bradbury, Ruthe 28
Bradbury, Tony 147
Braddock, William 106
Brailsford 155
Brailsford, Joan 154
Brailsford, Sir Henry 59, 153, 155
Brassington, Charles 105
Brassington, Clarice Sarah 105
Brassington, J W C 115
Brent, George 104
Brickkiln Close 61
Briddon, Frank 117
Briddon, Jessie 128
Briddon, Joan 105, 128
Briddon, Mary 128
Broadbotham, Alice 145
Brokesby, John 27
Bromley, John 157
Brown, Emma 139
Brown, Humfrey 171
Brown, John 157
Brown, Richard of Shelton, 142
Brunt, Mr 109
Bubnell Hall 172
Buckingham, Duke of 158
Buckingham, Humphrey, Duke of 161
Buckler, J 20, 143
Bucknall Rev J W 31
Bukham Wm. 65
Bulkeley, John 169
Bull, Miss 49
Burgess, G H O 30
Burton Abbey Cartulary 72
Burton, Edith 140
Burton, James Arthur 140
Burton, William 124
Button, Giles 61, 164
Button, Richard or William Eyton 169
Buxton Spa 168

Buxton, Elizabeth 72
Buxton, George 115
Buxton, Martha 75
Byron 25
Byron, Richard son of Sir John Byron 157, 160
Calton Moor House, 68
Calwich 167
Calwich Abbey 40
Campagnac, Jeremy 105
Campagnac, Susan 105
Campbell, John 140
Canterell, Ralph 27, 160, 161
Carr, Alexandra 144
Carrier, Rev W 37
Carrington Smith, William 139
Carrington, S 61
Carver, Dorothy 125
Cavendish 24
Cavendish Harley, Margaret 184
Cavendish, Henry 184
Cavendish, Sir Charles 181, 183
Cavendish, Sir William,
    Duke of Newcastle 25, 65, 138, 177, 178, 181, 184
Cecil, Sir Robert 175
Chadwick, Elizabeth 104, 111
Chadwick, James 111
Chadwick, John 114, 121
Chadwyk, Thomas 27
Chandos, Duke of 60
Charles I, King 183
Charles, Anna Maria 26
Charlesworth, Edwin 99
Chatham, Rev C L 30
Cheadle 155, 156, 158, 161, 165, 171
Cheavin, Edward 143
Chetwynd, Wm 166
Cheyne, Charles 178
Clewes, Alice 41
Clewes, Arthur 108
Clewes, Ernest 108
Clewes, John 41
Clewes, Louisa 41
Clewes, Phyllis 108
Clowes Thomas 122
Clowes, Adrian, Elizabeth 118
Clowes, Beryl 117, 122
Clowes, Charles 38, 117, 122
Clowes, Charles William 117, 122
Clowes, Cynthia 117
Clowes, Doris Clowes 122
Clowes, Elaine 37, 112
Clowes, Frances Elizabeth 122
Clowes, Joan Irene 37, 112
Clowes, John 117
Clowes, Margaret 38
Clowes, Marian 122
Clowes, Marilyn 47, 110
Clowes, S 36
Clowes, Sam 40
Clowes, Sarah 122
Clowes, Sylvia 117
Clowes, T 123
Clowes, Thomas Frederick 37, 112
Clowes, Tom 39, 110, 112, 117, 122
Clowes, William 35
Cobham, Lord Henry 176

Cockayne, Anne 159, 167
Cockayne, Henry 165
Cockayne, John 158-159, 161, 165
Cockayne, Sir Thomas 165, 169
Cockayne, William 158
Cockaynes 23, 158
Cockeyne, Edmund 173
Coke, Isabel Emma 187
Cold Eaton 161
Coldwall Bridge 71
Cole, John 158
Collear, Mary 28
Colombo, Angelo 105
Colombo, Lupino 105
Colombo, Naomi 105
Comberford, Humphrey 170
Common End 68
Constable, Gordon 119
Cooper, John 61
Cooper, Tommy 50
Cope, Cherry 141
Cope, Ivan 141
Copwood, William 171
Corbett 24
Corbett, Sir Richard 25, 175, 177
Cotes, John 167
Coton, Richard 167, 170
Cotton, Beryl 38
Cotton, Enid 111
Cotton, Fred 38
Cotton, Frederick Harold 122
Cotton, Jack 111
Cotton, Richard 171
Cotton, Thomas 171
Court Granville 108
Cowper, Nicholas 116
Coxon, Alice 111
Coxon, Christine 50
Coxon, David 50
Coxon, Thomas 113
Coxon, Tina 55
Coyne, Thomas 27
Cranmer, Archbishop of Canterbury 168,171
Cresswell, Ric 174
Crime and punishment,
    Brunt, hanged 109
Critchlow, George 99
Critchlow, Harriett 99
Critchlow, James 99, 100   83, 84
Critchlow, John 99
Critchlow, Mary 99
Crochle (Crichlow/Crichley), George 55
Croxden Abbey 168, 169
Crychlow, George 55
Curson, John 167
Dale, John 104
Dale, Miss 117
Dallison, Sir Roger 177
Davey, Rev Peter W 31
Davies, Sir John 175
Dawbarn, Stanley 142
Dawson, Annie 40
Dawson, Barbara Eileen 117
Dawson, Emma Jane 117
Dawson, Henry 40
Dawson, John Hanson 117
Dawson, Richard John 117
Day, Rev Frederick 100

Greville, Sconsolate 166
Greville, Sir Fulke 166
Griffin, Michael 144
Grindey family 105
Grindey, Charles 115, 118
Grindey, Elsie 118
Grindey, George 109, 118
Grindey, Mary 103
Grindey, Thomas 103, 109, 118
Grindey, Violet 118
Grindey, William 109, 118
Grindon 150, 157, 161, 165, 171
Gudhall, Robert 27
Guilfoyle, Elizabeth 118, 124
Guilfoyle, William 118
Hall Flats 31, 62
Hall Rev Philip E R 31
Hall, Dr of Waterfall 100, 143
Hall, Frederick 102
Hall, J 115
Hall, Nellie 102
Hambleton, Edith 99
Hambleton, Ellin 99
Hambleton, John 99
Hambleton, Mary 99
Hambleton, Sarah 99
Hambleton, William 99
Hampson, Eden 121
Hampson, Elija 111
Hampson, John 35, 111
Hampson, Mary 121
Hamson, John 63
Hancock, William 27, 156
Hand, Owen 103
Hand, William 124
Hanging Bridge 55, 71
Harding, John 125
Hardy, Mrs Polly 105
Harley, Edward 184
Harley, Lord 146
Harpur 24
Harpur, Sir John 177, 180-181
Harriett, John 124
Harris, Richard 110
Harrison Hill Ltd 25
Harrison, Adam 104
Harrison, Alice 104, 124
Harrison, Ann 39
Harrison, Deborah 124
Harrison, Elizabeth 117
Harrison, Ellen 99
Harrison, Frances 39
Harrison, Frank 101, 147
Harrison, Hannah 104
Harrison, Henry 40, 103, 123
Harrison, Herman 116
Harrison, James 111
Harrison, John 104
Harrison, John, cowkeeper 116
Harrison, Margaret 122
Harrison, Mary 116, 117
Harrison, Sampson 104
Harrison, Samuel 105
Harrison, Sarah 99
Harrison, T 36
Harrison, Tho. 29
Harrison, William 104, 116
Harryson, William 102

Haryson/Rushton, Hanah 104
Haslam, Rev C E 30
Hastings, Lord William 161
Hastings, Sir Walter 164
Hatfield, Ellen 100
Hayes family 142
Hayes, Arthur 37, 128
Hayes, Joan 105
Hayes, Martha Ann 147
Hayes, Mr 126
Hayes, William 117
Haywood, Sarah 73
Healde, John (1621) 21, 26
Healde, Robert 28
Heath, Dorothy 146
Heath, Gilbert 146
Heath, John 67, 146
Heath, Mary 146
Heath, Ralph 146
Heath, Thomas 146
Heath, William 146
Heathcote, John 147
Heathcote, Mary 147
Henry the Abbot 63
Henry, Lord Cobham 175
Herron, Margaret 108
Herthull 23
Hewson, Henry 104
Hewson, Ann 104
Hewson, John 104
Hewson, Maria 104
Hewson, Prisilla 104
Hewson, Thomas 104
Hewson, William 104
Hichecok, Ralph 60
Hickes, Sir Michael 175
Hickton, George 147
Hill, David 110
Hill, Frank 128
Hill, Gordon 110
Hill, Lewis 110
Hill, Mrs 110
Hill, Percy 109
Hillsdale 151
Hilton, Ronnie 50
Hints 165
Hodge, Derek 127
Hodge, Freda 127
Hodge, George 127
Hodge, Sarah 127
Hodgkinson, Thomas 67
Hodgson Estate 73
Hodgson family 106, 110
Hodgson, Brian 60-61, 67, 68, 106, 116, 120, 125
Hodgson, Rev 114
Hodgson, Rev A.O.L. 31
Hodgson, Rev Edward 68, 102
Hodkinson, Joseph 50
Hognaston 161
Holgreve, Henry 27
Hollemans, Jasper 24
Holles, Henrietta Cavendish 184
Holles, John 178, 184
Hollington, 161
Holys, John 158
Honest Miller 56, 99
Hood, Joan 60

Hood, Joane 28
Hood, John 63, 107
Hood, Margery 64
Hood, Richard 35, 58, 63, 97, 164
Hood, Thomas 60
Hopkis, Humfrey 172
Hoskyns, Professor 60
Howard 24
Howard, Catherine 180
Howard, Charles 179
Howard, Elizabeth (Catherine) 24
Howard, Frances 180
Howard, Henry 24, 176-177, 179
Howard, James 24
Howard, Sir Thomas 180
Howell, Miss H 22
Howson, Bill 118
Howson, David 40, 74, 100, 104, 140
Howson, Dorothy 103
Howson, Eileen 109
Howson, Elizabeth 40, 104
Howson, Florence 140
Howson, Gladys 50, 74, 118
Howson, Grandma 50
Howson, Hilda 140
Howson, J W 61, 74, 115
Howson, John 74, 102, 109, 127
Howson, Lucy 140
Howson, Mabel 109
Howson, Mr 126
Howson, Sarah 109
Howson, Thomas 74
Howson, William 74, 104, 110
Hude, John 158
Humphreys, Margaret 143
Hunt, Christopher 165
Hurt, Dorothy 174
Hurt, Nicholas 107
Hychekok, Ralph 27
Ilam 55, 157
Ilam Meadows 56
Industry and Transport,
    Blore Lime Kiln 100
    Bridle path 72
    Cotton mills 66
    Ginny Ring at Blore Hall 67
    Jagger 72
    Lime, kilns & quarry 66, 68
    Mining lead ore and coal 68
    Moat 136
    Pack horses 72
    Turnpike 71, 99
    Windmill 56
Jackson, Mary 114
Jackson, Edward 125
Jackson, Gladys 115
Jackson, Gladys Lily 103
Jackson, Neil 101, 114
Jackson, Sidney 101, 114, 118
Jackson, William 109, 114
Jacobites 75
Jagg Way 72
Jessop, George 29
John, Abbot of Dieulacres 158
John, Clifford 30, 143-145
Joly, Thomas 164
Jukes, R 35
Kebell, Margaret 162